DAN CLAWSON

THE NEXT
UPSURGE

Labor and the New
Social Movements

ILR Press
an imprint of
CORNELL UNIVERSITY PRESS
ITHACA AND LONDON

First published 2003 by Cornell University Press
First printing, Cornell Paperbacks, 2003

Printed in the United States of America

Library of Congress Cataloging-in-Publication Data
Clawson, Dan.
    The next upsurge : labor and the new social movements / Dan Clawson.
        p. cm.
Includes bibliographical references (p.   ) and index.
    ISBN 0-8014-4109-9 (cloth : alk. paper) — ISBN 0-8014-8870-2 (pbk. :
    1. Labor unions—Organizing—United States.   2. Social
movements—United States.   I. Title.
    HD6490.O72U633 2003
    331.88'0973—dc21   2003001232

Cornell University Press strives to use environmentally responsible
suppliers and materials to the fullest extent possible in the publishing
of its books. Such materials include vegetable-based, low-VOC inks
and acid-free papers that are recycled, totally chlorine-free, or partly
composed of nonwood fibers. For further information,
visit our website at www.cornellpress.cornell.edu.

Cloth printing   10   9   8   7   6   5   4   3   2   1
Paperback printing   10   9   8   7   6   5   4   3   2   1

To Mary Ann

Contents

Preface

U nless the United States is transformed—economically, politically, and socially—progressive causes, not only in America but around the world, will continue to suffer more reverses than successes. But a progressive transformation will be difficult or impossible without the active involvement of the working class and its collective voice, the labor movement.

For more than a quarter of a century, conservatives and business have been on the offensive. Today, as for many years past, government power is used to reduce money for the poor and the working class and shift it to the rich. Public services are cut. Control of the poor is tightened through both welfare and crime policy. Environmental degradation is official policy. Politics is driven by campaign contributions. The media distort reality. Money is available for war but not for global warming or Third World hunger.

None of us are very good at predicting seismic shifts in society. When the stock market is booming, analysts and the media tout the miracle of the new economy and assert stocks are a can't-lose investment. When stocks crash, we are told that it was all a speculative bubble and only a fool would have invested at those inflated prices. (Sometimes the same person explaining the speculative bubble was, only months before, leading the hype.)

Right now, conservatives are winning at almost every level; the labor movement and other progressive causes are struggling to survive. Analysts demonstrate that labor's continuing decline is inevitable.

But society can reverse directions as fast as the stock market. Resentment of the rich, concern for the environment, respect for working people, and disgust with money-driven politics are all widespread. As this book shows, it's not just attitudes that show the potential for change. In many places, workers are using innovative strategies and new alliances to win victories that could serve as models for future action. Even unsuccessful struggles create the basis for future action. One recent example is the coordinated worldwide demonstrations to prevent war in Iraq; although they did not stop the war, they created a global culture of solidarity together with specific networks that will make it easier to mobilize not only for peace, but also for other issues.

I'm probably no better than others at predicting whether society will reverse direction. But I'm sure that *if* a new round of social movements explodes on the scene and transforms political realities, suddenly the media and analysts will demonstrate that this was only to be expected. They will point to the kinds of struggles discussed here—antisweatshop activism, innovative labor-community strategies, the global justice movement, living wage campaigns—and explain that these had already shown the potential for transformation. The activists of these movements will suddenly gain public recognition and praise; neglected campaigns will be hailed as precursors. (Of course, if conservatives dominate for the next quarter-century, these campaigns will be regarded as minor curiosities of no great importance.)

This book argues that such a political-social-economic reversal is at least possible—and I believe likely. That process will require, and in turn will reinforce, a transformation of the labor movement. A generation ago, labor and the social movements of the 1960s all too rarely connected. Today's labor movement is, among other things, about healing that rift. A new upsurge, I argue, will fuse the unions of today with the issues and styles of the social movements of the 1960s, producing new forms and taking up new issues. Those are the sorts of struggles that have inspired the greatest energy and commitment; that is likely to be true in the future as it has been in the recent past. Labor advances will come only from a mass movement involving millions, not from a process directed and controlled by a handful of leaders or staff.

If the labor movement were steadily advancing, it would make sense to hold to its present course. Because labor is in trouble, and because it's clear that incremental change at the margin cannot restore unions' strength, analysts and activists need to evaluate and debate new possibilities. The alternatives that matter most are not those that seem logical to academics, but those for which workers have been willing to fight, and they are the focus here. Other struggles could have been selected, and these struggles could be interpreted in very different ways. I think labor needs to learn from these models, but that does not mean accepting them without variation. It means taking seriously the concerns they embody, thinking about why they appeal and succeed, and considering whether these approaches, in whole or in part, can be used in many other circumstances. Saying "that's not the way we do it" is a non-argument; the way labor is currently doing it clearly won't restore workers' power or influence.

One of the best parts of writing the book has been dealing with the (often sharp) responses from those who have read earlier drafts. Their criticisms and disagreements go to the heart of the issues that labor needs to debate. Sometimes I've pushed a point precisely to provoke debate and reexamination; that seems to me more useful than a safe account that troubles no one and is endorsed by everyone. I look forward to many more critical comments and debates; those will be most productive if they are in print (and thus widely shared—reviewers take note), but I'm also happy to continue them one-to-one. (Write me at clawson@sadri. umass.edu or visit the book's web site at www.thenextupsurge.org.)

The people I admire most are those involved in the effort to win the battle of democracy at the workplace as well as in the voting booth. At numerous points in what follows I am critical of the actions (or inactions) of various leaders, unions, or staff; I hope I do so in a way that supports and advances labor. It's been my observation that people are far more willing to be critical of labor than of other movements or institutions; peculiarly, that's often true of people within the labor movement as well as those outside it. Labor needs criticism, but we need to remember that every part of American society has problems with race and gender, every progressive movement has trouble organizing in a probusiness conservative era, and today's labor movement can't (yet?) match the level of militance at the height of the 1930s. We need to judge labor by the same standards we apply to ourselves and to other movements.

In this book, more than any other I've done, it's difficult to know where to draw the line with acknowledgments. I've learned, and incorporated ideas, from workers on picket lines, informal chats at conferences, union leaders and staff in assorted struggles through the years, students, activists in Scholars, Artists, and Writers for Social Change, and a great many books, articles, and papers not directly cited here. The book would not have been possible without fifty formal interviews, most tape recorded; I owe a great debt to those who took the time to speak with me, on or off the record. Some of them are cited by name in what follows; most are not. Hector Delgado helped push me to finally go to Stamford, Connecticut, and shared with me his considerably more extensive research on struggles there. Reference librarians at UMass Amherst, especially Mike Davis, helped me track down facts.

A great many people read part or all of the manuscript. I emphasize that in thanking them I am not saying they agree with what I wrote; many vehemently disagreed with one or another part of the analysis. But their ideas shaped the final product; the time and energy they put in created a better book. Some read all of the manuscript, others one or more chapters. A name listed here seems such small recognition for what, for some of those listed, was many full days of effort. I thank: an anonymous Cornell reviewer, Edna Bonacich, Mark Brenner, Kate Bronfenbrenner, Margaret Cerullo, Laura Clawson, Olivia Debree, Steve Early, Peter Evans, Tess Ewing, Rick Fantasia, Naomi Gerstel, Ray Jones, Tom Juravich, Andy Levin, Stephanie Luce, Joya Misra, Karen Nussbaum, John O'Connor, Jon Perrson, Kris Rondeau, Richard Sanders, John Schall, Ingrid Semaan, Judy Stepan-Norris, Doron Taussig, Eve Weinbaum, Paul Worthman, and Robert Zussman.

A Faculty Research Grant from the University of Massachusetts, Amherst, and support from the Political Economy Research Institute enabled me to conduct and transcribe many of the interviews that form one of the bases for this book.

At the end Karen Mason read and edited the entire manuscript, helped track down missing material, and formatted the manuscript for submission. At a point where I was ready to scream, she made things easy (well, at least bearable). Throughout, Fran Benson at Cornell University Press has been a joy to work with.

The person who has most shaped both my thinking and this manuscript is Mary Ann Clawson. We've shared and talked through a great deal over many years; there's not an idea here that hasn't been formed by that process. Mary Ann was no less central in shaping the manuscript itself. She was my toughest critic; I made drastic changes in response to her comments, although there remain issues on which we disagree. I dedicate this book to her.

THE NEXT UPSURGE

Why Organize?

U nions raise workers' wages and benefits, make it possible to create safer and healthier workplaces, and protect workers from arbitrary management favoritism and reprisals. Union workers earn $718 a week, 24.9 percent more than the $575 earned by nonunion workers, and in percentage terms unions raise wages more for women and minority members than for white men.[1] But at least as important, unions make it possible for workers to win what the AFL-CIO calls a "voice at work," and what I'd rather call "power." (The difference between those two terms is of course significant.) Some employers are willing to pay union wages and benefits in order to keep the union out—that is, to keep workers from having a collective voice and an ongoing way of organizing for better conditions.

Even if workers are unhappy with conditions at work they are often reluctant to connect with a union. They may know their supervisor is a son-of-a-bitch, but they figure he or she is violating company policy, which calls for treating everyone with respect. However, although company policy may call for ideal conditions, the quotas imposed on individual managers may demand speedup. Workers know that a union will call down management ire, and aren't convinced a union can do much for them. Both perceptions are grounded in reality: companies today usually fiercely resist unions, and unions are far weaker than they once were. Unions represent only 13.5 percent of the workforce, and less than 10 percent of the private sector workforce. That makes it difficult to improve conditions significantly and is the reason the labor movement needs innovative ways to organize workers. Workers who want to improve conditions often start out thinking they would do better to go it alone. As the two examples that follow show, there's good reason for workers to connect with the solidarity and experience a union can bring.

The Christmas Massacre

My all-time favorite graduate student, Steve Shraison, worked for many years before he went to college. At the factory where he stayed the longest, worker discontent was high: wages were low, workers froze in the winter and broiled in the summer, machines lacked adequate safeguards, and workers were given no protective equipment when dealing with hazardous substances. As part of his job Steve, for example, periodically had to use his hands or a scoop to load powder from a barrel clearly marked "Has been shown to cause testicular cancer in rats." The barrel's message was a result of "right to know" legislation—passed under pressure from a coalition of unions and environmentalists—mandating that toxic substances be identified as such. The legislation itself was a pro-worker victory; the fact that in practice the substance continued to be used with no protective equipment indicates the limited character of that victory.

Workers at the factory got together in a neighborhood bar to discuss what could be done. Like most workers in such situations, they were unwilling to call a union. Instead they decided—as do most such groups—that someone should go to see the boss, tell him about the problems, and ask that action be taken. Steve, a natural leader both then and in graduate school, was chosen to do so. A union-busting consultant faced with such a visit would counsel an employer to act supportive, say he'd look into the problems, then make some minor changes and perhaps fire a supervisor in order to (cheaply) restore morale (at least for a while). Steve's boss, who himself owned the factory, was less sophisticated: He said no changes would be made and there had better not be any more complaints.

At other workers' urging, Steve called OSHA, the Occupational Safety and Health Administration, to report on conditions at the plant—which clearly violated a host of regulations—and to request an immediate inspection. The inspection did eventually come, but only long after the call. Steve said that in retrospect they should have seen it coming: the company spent three days on a plantwide cleanup and safety check. Workers were delighted because the plant had never been so pleasant; they thought management had turned over a new leaf. The next day, the OSHA inspector arrived; clearly, management was tipped off in advance—again, a familiar pattern. Even with advance notice, violations remained, but OSHA imposed only token fines.

Late one fall discontent increased, and workers began a guerilla campaign, turning up the thermostat every chance they had; supervisors, of course, turned it back down and warned workers they'd be punished if caught tampering. At Steve's urging, workers also began to meet and talk about forming a union, but they still made no contact with any existing union or organizer.

Then, in one act, the owner smashed the burgeoning campaign. He did so not by firing the lead "troublemaker"[2]—the most common employer response in such situations, used by one out of four companies facing a union organizing drive—but rather by simply demonstrating his autocratic power and ability to make life miserable for workers. Christmas that year came on a Tuesday, and many workers needed their Friday paychecks to buy presents for their kids. When the Friday before Christmas came, no one received a paycheck. Asked why, workers were told: "You want a paycheck? Ask Steve to get you a paycheck." The week after Christmas workers were paid for both weeks; workers (eventually) got their money, but kids didn't get their presents. Such an action could have spurred a drive; in this place it crushed one. Workers were demoralized, convinced that people like them could never get their rights; the best thing to do was swallow their anger and keep their heads down.

Would a union have made a difference to workers there? It might have helped Steve, who, a few years later while still in his twenties, developed testicular cancer, brought on, he was convinced, by working without protective equipment with a substance known to cause testicular cancer. He beat the cancer the first time, went to college and then graduate school. While still in his thirties, the cancer recurred and killed him.

"The most exciting night of my life"

I've met few people smarter or tougher or more courageous than Steve Shraison—but even with those personal characteristics, he and his coworkers were left feeling demoralized and defeated, that it was useless to stand up for themselves, or worse than useless because it led to humiliation and grief. At Rhode Island Hospital, in contrast, a good organizer helped nurses find a way to fight back against management, to stand up to abusive conditions, and to make life better not just for themselves but for the patients as well. Nurse Linda MacDonald reports that when the election ballots were counted and it became clear that the union had won, it was "The most exciting night of my life. I would say it was a feeling comparable to having my two children. Absolutely. In fact, *that* was painful; *this* was the most exciting night I could ever remember. The feeling in there when we won—I've never experienced anything like it in my life."

In 1992, Rhode Island Hospital employed more than four thousand workers. Through the years, various unions had tried to organize there, but never with any success; management mounted highly sophisticated anti-union campaigns. Then the hospital raised workers' health insurance rates, for some people by as much as 400 percent, catalyzing the (ultimately successful) organizing drive. Although this was the proverbial last straw, the baseline condition, nurse Barbara Crosby explained to me, was "the total lack of respect for us as professionals" combined with "the inconsistency in the way rules were applied." For nurses, the pay system was also a problem: merit raises depended on a unit's profitability, which meant that highly skilled nurses in units that lost money were getting smaller raises than less skilled nurses in profitable units.

Nurses were agitated and talking about a union. Many choices were available to them; they eventually decided to go with the health care unit of the American Federation of Teachers, mostly because they liked the approach taken by its lead organizer, Richard Sanders.[3] He stressed that "the union" is not the organizers or staff. It's the workers, and from day one that was not just the verbal message but the practice. As Linda Mac-Donald notes, "A lot of what the organizing does is make you realize that the union is you. Meeting after meeting that's the focus. Even when Richard was up there speaking, his whole point was to educate us to know and believe that the union is us, that it's not Richard Sanders and it's not Jack Callaci [another organizer]. This union is going to be whatever we make it when we organize it."

The first step was to identify the leaders in every shift and work area and see if they wanted to be part of the Organizing Committee. Sanders, the lead organizer, says that "anybody else can be on the committee too, but you have to find the leaders, the people who have earned the trust and respect of their co-workers." Once the committee was formed, the second part of the campaign took hold: two or three weeks of training. Part of that was about unions, contracts, the National Labor Relations Board, and the employer's anti-union campaign. More important, Sanders emphasized, people "need to learn how to communicate and learn to be listeners. They never had to be agitators. They need to learn to be organizers. If we are serious about them leading the campaign and the union, we should be committed to training them." Linda MacDonald left her first meeting

> totally exhilarated and it was because the organizers gave you not so much propaganda but information, just simple things about the dues, about strikes. I don't know if you've ever seen Richard work, but there may have been fifty people in a room around the table and he'd go around, have people introduce themselves and their department—and he knows everybody's name. It made me feel very much a part of a group. Even though we had different issues in each department, there was common ground that brought us all together.

Because most anti-union consultants—union busters—are highly predictable, each week organizers told the workers what the hospital would do next, and consistently, Barbara said, "within a week the hospital was saying and doing that. Our credibility rose as people saw that we could not just anticipate what the hospital was going to do, but we could help them be prepared."

Next, the Organizing Committee members tried to get every co-worker to attend a small group meeting. Each member of the Organizing Committee tried to bring together all the workers in her department. Sanders and the committee worked to include anti-union workers, and to provide the space for them to voice their anti-union sentiments. Barbara Crosby, who worked in pediatrics, which is housed in a separate building and was a department where interest in the union was weak, first connected with the union when "a nurse who I worked with on the floor had a meeting at her house. We all told her she was crazy, she was going to get screwed, she was going to get a bad rap, she was going to be working every holiday from now until kingdom come if they find out that you did this. But we went." Barbara checked "no" on the sign-in sheet that asked if she was willing to be on the committee, but she did provide her name, address, and phone number. "I went primarily out of curiosity. I knew that something had to change. My attitude about a union for nurses was that we were already screwed, I was miserable, I wasn't happy going to work, I wasn't happy doing what I was doing and the way people were being treated. So what could be any worse? A union can't hurt." The organizers, sensing her view, ignored the box she checked, and asked if she would set up a meeting at her own house. She did so and went on to become active on the Organizing Committee. Linda MacDonald sees this as typical: people didn't go to the first meeting because of "what a union can really do, what power you have when you're unionized" but rather "for reasons like 'it's about time somebody screwed them [management],' 'it's about time they get what they deserve.'" Richard Sanders adds that people went because someone they knew, trusted, and respected *asked* them to go.

The campaign advanced through these small group meetings, and by committee members talking with people they worked with. Workers were told that when a strong majority of the workers supported the union—but only then—the campaign would go public. Workers were told not to express support if they had any questions, any doubts, any anxieties or fears at all. That was crucial because at the time the campaign went public, all pro-union workers would be asked to sign a public petition.

When more than 60 percent of the workers had committed themselves to supporting the union, the campaign went public. That meant holding a rally—because of the multiple shifts, actually two or three rallies—a kind of coming out for the union. As the lead organizer, Richard Sanders, explained: "The union now is out there, it's dynamic, it's exciting, it's electric. The workers go back into work and they're excited, everybody's talking about it. We do the signing publicly. We do a rally so people can sign and make a commitment publicly as opposed to privately. And they are doing it together—they are really committing to each other and their union." At the union hall a huge poster board was erected, covering every single wall, listing all the units and all the workers in each unit. At the beginning of each meeting, Linda MacDonald reported, "they were yellowing out people who had signed, and again the excitement was there, how many names were yellowed out. I took it personally that I was going to get every yellow."

When the public petitions had been signed by a solid majority of workers, committee members met at the main lobby and marched to the CEO's office to demand recognition of their union. Nearly 150 people showed up, all hospital employees. "We all kind of pushed our way into the CEO's hallway," Linda explained, and Barbara added "It's excitement because nothing like that had ever happened. You don't walk into the CEO's office unannounced, it just doesn't happen." People were "exhilarated. That was the feeling throughout the hospital. We're finally going to take control of the situation."[4]

In order to maintain the momentum of the campaign and prepare people for what was to come, committee members were charged with getting workers to sign a statement asking for fair play. This generated discussion and put the onus on management for running an unfair campaign. The "Campaign Rules for Free and Fair Elections" listed ten points that should define the conduct of the election: No one should be harassed because of union activity; any meeting should be voluntary, not mandatory; no supervisor would take anyone away from work to discuss the union; no supervisor should be punished for refusing to carry out the anti-union campaign; the hospital should not spend money on a union-buster, and if it did hire a consultant, would let workers know who was hired and how much they were being paid; weekly open forums would be held so that workers could come voluntarily to ask questions of either a union or management representative. These rules parallel those used to guarantee fair elections for public officials, but for union elections the government permits managers to engage in a wide variety of practices that are forbidden in most democracies and characteristic only in dictatorships.

The anti-union campaign—run by management at the direction of the union-busting consulting firm—put incredible pressure on people. One of the most powerful techniques, here and in most union organizing drives, was the "one-on-one" meeting. The personnel department and union-busters dug deep into the worker's record looking for any point of vulnerability that could be used to influence or intimidate the worker. The worker would then be called into the supervisor's office; targeted workers were called in repeatedly. The aim of these "one-on-ones" was to isolate the person from all social support and solidarity, leaving the worker alone facing the power of management. Although what a supervisor can do in such a meeting is legally limited, the worker can be disciplined or fired for being insubordinate, in a situation where it is the worker's word against the supervisor's.

At the beginning of the campaign, supervisors played the "friend" card, trying to win the worker over, drawing on their past relationship. They asked what the problems were, expressed dismay at the breakdown in communications, and promised to do better. "You've worked for me for ten years and I always thought we were friends. Ever since this union thing started something has come between us. Remember how I gave you time off a few years ago when your son was arrested for drug possession? I helped you then, but if the union gets in I won't be able to help you [not true, but often said]."[5]

Professional union-busting consultants make their living training managers to use these tactics, and they are often extremely effective. Rhode Island Hospital had hired one of the top union-busters, but because of the strength of the union campaign, and the character of management's past behavior, the tactics didn't work. Linda MacDonald reports that a person's direct clinical supervisor "would call you into the office and say, 'You know I'm your friend, how can you do this, it's not good for you.'" The reaction was not weakening support for the union, but anger at the supervisor and the hospital: "Going back to the fact that we were not trusting our managers, this just led people to say, 'Well why are you coming to me now, you never listened to me in all of these years.'" Barbara Crosby agreed: "Some of it was so blatant. This CEO who nobody had actually laid eyes on, now all of a sudden has you in meetings with him with you calling him by his first name sitting around a little family circle." On one occasion the CEO and the director of patient services "put on uniforms and came up and pretended to work with you for fifteen minutes, like 'I'm listening to you, I understand.' That was the biggest day in the hospital. That spread like wildfire, that the CEO was cleaning the toilet on the ninth floor of the hospital. That was like an insult to what we do. You can't spend a day or an hour with us and understand why we want what we want."

Later in the campaign the aim was more likely to be outright intimidation: "Did you see this leaflet we handed out today? Would you read it please? Read it out loud to me: Read me the part about union corruption. A little bit louder please, I can't hear you. What do you think about that? Doesn't that bother you, the corruption in unions?" But in this case intimidation was also ineffective. One high-level supervisor "was like a madwoman. People didn't have respect for her to begin with and now she had just become so evil and so mean to people that she turned more people towards a yes vote."

Even the CEO of the hospital and the director of nursing were involved; in more than one instance they followed nurses into a room where they were doing procedures on babies, despite the risk that the distraction would cause the nurse to make a mistake that might kill a critically ill baby. "Another time one of these nurses had a needle stick injury because the director of nursing was harassing her while she was taking care of a baby. A needle stick injury in a hospital environment today is a very dangerous thing to happen to you."

In many union organizing drives these tactics crush the pro-union workers. At Rhode Island Hospital, Sanders helped prepare workers for what was coming, and the support of a strong committee, with rank-and-file leaders all over the hospital, gave people the courage to stand up to managers. To deal with one-on-ones, for example, the union trained workers to carry little notebooks. If a person was called in for a meeting, the targeted employee was advised to ask for a witness, or a committee person offered to be a witness. This request was usually denied. A group might then gather to criticize the supervisor for being so disrespectful to them, for being authoritarian and disrupting work by taking someone off the floor. The group might try to stand around and observe. If forced to go in alone, before the supervisor started, the worker was trained to take out her notebook, take a deep breath, and tell the supervisor, "I'm for the union, I want you to know that. I don't want to be here. I have work to do. I don't want to talk with you about the union. I'm not going to answer any questions about the union except to tell you I'm for the union [a worker's legal right]." Then the worker wrote down the date, the name of the supervisor, and told the supervisor: "Would you speak slowly so I can write everything down, because if you say anything illegal we're going to file charges against you with the National Labor Relations Board."[6]

Management was very confident they would win the election; on election day a top manager told others, in the presence of some nurses, where to go for the champagne and celebration. Linda MacDonald thinks this is because "they can't communicate with their employees. They think they're communicating, but they can't do it. My manager thought that her whole floor was voting no, when everybody in the hospital knew that the ICUs were all yes." The final vote came out almost exactly the way the union had called it all along, 60–40 for the union.

What an Organizer Does

Steve Shraison and his co-workers were defeated and humiliated; Rhode Island Hospital nurses were exhilarated and empowered. In the aftermath of Steve's campaign workers concluded that the boss had absolute power; after the Rhode Island Hospital victory nurses met to democratically decide what changes to seek to incorporate in a contract in order to create a better hospital. Other workers in the hospital felt so good about unions that shortly thereafter the maintenance and clerical workers also voted to unionize. All this was due in no small part to the approach taken by Richard Sanders, an approach called "union building." It's worth contrasting this approach with a worst-case scenario of old-time business union organizing.[7]

In worst-case business union organizing, the goal is to increase the number of dues-paying members, not to empower workers. Unions thus try to achieve a minimal union as quickly and cheaply as possible. Typically, organizers stand at the entrance to workplaces passing out a leaflet ("Join the union and get higher wages") and distributing union authorization cards. The employer immediately knows what's happening. Workers who react positively to the union are identifiable to the employer and may well get fired before they receive any training or are protected by solidarity with other workers. The organizing staff is "the union," in their own minds and in the minds of workers. Paid staff make all key decisions, and do things for the workers instead of helping workers to develop their own power. Staff make it as easy as possible for workers to sign union authorization cards and promise that no one will ever know who has signed—that is, workers sign in secret and in fear, without understanding what might be involved, and with very little commitment. Communication from "the union" to workers is via frequent leaflets and occasional meetings where paid staff do almost all the talking. Even if workers are mad enough at management that the union wins, workers may not feel that it is their union, may not feel that they have the capacity—or the right—to democratically make decisions about their priorities. Certainly they don't feel that workers have the power to stand up to management; at best they hope "the union" (meaning paid staff) will do so for them.

In a "union building" approach, by contrast, the aim is to empower workers, to teach them and assist them in building the kind of union they themselves want, giving them the confidence, the solidarity, and the tools needed to stand up for what they believe in and win it. At Rhode Island Hospital, Barbara Crosby reports that "although we had great issues, I really think that it was the expertise of an organizing staff" that made victory possible.

According to Sanders, "More than anything else, a good organizer is a teacher. We are not leaders—though too many organizers fall into the trap and are, indeed, trained to think of themselves and act like the leader of the workers." A good organizer isn't someone who just knows the law and what to expect from the employer's anti-union campaign. More important, he or she brings out the best in workers, helps develop their talents and capacities, and makes it possible to forge a solidarity that is rooted in people's small work groups but reaches beyond to include people the worker has not previously known.

There are many variations of union-building approaches. Sanders's version emphasizes identifying the leaders in each work group, the people that others look up to, that they go to if they have a problem, that they respect and trust. "We don't win without them. And without them we don't build the kind of union that members control and that changes the balance of power at work." If those leaders become the Organizing Committee, if they are publicly visible as pro-union activists, if they are involved in making key decisions about the campaign, if they each work to organize their department, then the union has enormous credibility and power. Supervisors are the anti-union committee in every department and on every shift. If the union Organizing Committee includes the department's most respected worker, the supervisor has little credibility or influence. If the union has no trusted leader in that department on that shift, the supervisor will bully or persuade workers into becoming anti-union.

Timing is important in pulling a committee together. The organizers work to identify the people who will be part of the Organizing Committee, but don't bring the committee together until it is as representative as possible—in departments, shifts, race, gender, age. "People tend to listen to, follow, trust in and respect people who are more like them," Richard notes. As a result, there may be more than one leader in a work group; black (or young) workers may respect and follow one worker, white (or older) workers another. Moreover, "If the group gets together too early, it begins to feel like a club. They act in a way that sometimes is perceived by outsiders, sometimes correctly so, as exclusionary. You don't want it to be that."

The campaign moves step by step; at each step people face a new challenge, but one that is within their capacity. If that challenge is successfully met, the union is stronger, and the workers feel more invested in the union and more able to use the union to exercise collective power. The first challenge for the Organizing Committee member is to bring together the workers in her department; if she can't do that then either she is not a leader or the workers aren't interested in a union. Sanders insists on group meetings because his experience is that people make the kinds of decisions that lead to unions as groups, not as individuals.[8]

> We spend most of the meeting at the front getting people to talk about their issues. You don't want more than eight people there because you want everybody to have the opportunity to talk about their issues, to ask their questions and express their doubts and anxieties. A good organizer can bring everybody into the discussion. We want to understand how people really feel about their work, how deeply they feel about the need for change. We also want to answer people's questions about the union, every doubt, every fear and anxiety they have. If they don't bring up dues and strikes and corruption, we'll bring it up. Because all this stuff is going to come out in the campaign later on.

The meeting also gives the organizer as well as the committee person a chance to assess each worker, and it gives the worker a chance to know the organizer, which might be important later since the employer is sure to attack the organizer's reputation and credibility.

Most organizers use union authorization cards and make it as easy as possible for workers to sign, typically promising that no one will know whether they have signed. Richard Sanders uses a public petition, refuses to let workers sign the petition if they have any doubts or hesitations about the union, and makes it clear that everyone (including the employer) will know who has signed. The campaign does not go forward unless and until a solid majority of workers are prepared to sign a public petition.[9] Workers who sign are pledging their support to each other, not to the organizer, and showing that they now have the collective power to take a stand. For the same reason, the first chance for workers to sign the petition is at a rally, so that hundreds of people will sign within a day of the public launching of the campaign, creating both solidarity and a sense of momentum. The workers, not the union organizer, go to the CEO to demand recognition of the union. Because a large number of workers assemble and go together, the CEO often feels intimidated and sometimes flees—itself an empowering lesson about the effects of solidarity.

A campaign conducted in this way builds workers' self-confidence, skills, feeling that they have a right to democratically decide about work, and sense of collective power. The workers learn the meaning of union long before the election that officially certifies the union. From the beginning workers are acting democratically and developing solidarity. One indicator of this is that even when employers clearly break the law, Richard Sanders does not file Unfair Labor Practice charges with the National Labor Relations Board (NLRB). Partly that is because the NLRB can move slowly, but also, Sanders says, "What could happen is that workers begin to think that the solution to any kind of problem they have lies in the government, in lawyers' hands, in some outsider. We want workers to understand that you can solve problems by getting organized, by getting mobilized."

That is the unique promise of unions: the potential for workers to democratically organize and win a say, not just once every four years in a voting booth, but every day at work. The specifics of what Rhode Island Hospital nurses won—more sick days, overtime pay when they work more than eight hours, a switch from the problem health insurance, putting a stop to a management plan to deskill the workforce—are important, but the ability to have an ongoing say is even more so. Workplace decisions are some of the most important influences both on workers' lives and on society as a whole. This book considers what would be needed to enable workers and the labor movement to gain this influence not just in a few limited cases, but in a widespread movement that reshapes our society.

I

Labor Revival

What Would It Take?

This book examines innovative labor campaigns that show the potential for labor revival. Every chapter is about a movement that has already mobilized people, won victories, and shown the possibility for future transformation. Three arguments are woven throughout the book.

1. *Upsurge, not incremental growth.* Historically, labor has not grown slowly, a little bit each year. Most of the time unions are losing ground; once in a while labor takes off. From the mid-1930s on, in the stretch of little more than a decade, the number of union members increased fourfold. Each period of upsurge redefines what we mean by "the labor movement," changing cultural expectations, the form that unions take, laws, structures, and accepted forms of behavior. The upsurge gives rise to an integrated labor regime, fitted to the economy and society of the time, which constrains some forms of activity and promotes others. In the more than sixty years since the creation of the last labor regime, much has changed. If there is a new upsurge, it too will transform what we mean by "union," how labor relates to other groups in society, laws and regulations, structures and cultural expectations, what sorts of labor action are permitted, encouraged, prohibited.

2. *Fusion with other movements.* In the 1960s, the labor movement was largely missing when a set of new movements arose to fight for racial equality, women's liberation, student empowerment, anti-intervention, environmental protection, gay and lesbian liberation, and much more. The failure of labor and those movements to connect weakened *both* labor *and* those movements. Labor lost a chance to reinvigorate itself and to make advances on issues that are central to workers' lives; as a conse-

quence it tended to become narrow, bureaucratic, and insular. The new social movements, all too often, based themselves primarily on the affluent, neglected the issues of most concern to the working class, and developed organizations that were based primarily on mailing lists and symbolic actions rather than face-to-face meetings in local chapters. If a new upsurge is to come, it will *require* labor and these movements to do far more to connect with each other and to take up each other's causes in ways that transform the movements that now exist. The new AFL-CIO leadership actively seeks to connect labor to other social movements, but a large gulf remains.

3. *The contradictions of organizations.* These days a "union" is among other things a bureaucratic organization, with elected leaders, paid staff, buildings and property, money in the bank. But labor is also, and must be, a *movement*. Established organizations can be a tremendous resource and can also be an obstacle; can bring hope, skills, and resources to workers in need or can discourage and try to clamp down on anything new, risky, or different. Many of the most promising labor developments of recent years have been initiated by the top leadership of national-level unions—Justice for Janitors in Los Angeles, the Stamford Organizing Project, the UPS strike. But unions quickly lose both their purpose and power if the staff (or leadership) take over and do things on behalf of workers rather than developing and mobilizing worker solidarity and power. The situation is worse if the bureaucrats seek cushy jobs for themselves and thus oppose workers' attempts to mobilize. This creates an ongoing contradiction: workers need strong organizations but organizations often stifle workers' self-activity; labor needs bottom-up mobilization, but this is often introduced from the top down.

The remainder of this chapter develops these arguments.

Labor: Decline—and Upsurge?

For more than a quarter-century unions have declined steeply, in numbers, power, public perception, and cultural appeal. In 1954, 39 percent of the private sector workforce was in unions; today only 9 percent are (although the public sector rate is more than 37 percent, creating an overall rate of 13.5 percent). Not only has the number of members fallen, but so too have strikes and other indicators of union power. From 1969 to 1979, an average of 1.5 million workers a year were involved in strikes; from 1987 to 2000, by contrast, despite a larger labor force, in no year did strikes involve even half a million workers. As for public perception, in

1994 *Time* magazine called the labor movement a "toothless dinosaur on the way to becoming fossils."[1]

Within the basic framework of today's politics and society, labor cannot regain the standing and position that it had in 1980, never mind 1960 or 1940. Unions tend to be strongest in those sectors of the economy where employment is declining. As the number of old-line manufacturing workers declines, in order to maintain the same absolute number of members, labor unions need to recruit perhaps 250,000 or even up to 400,000 workers a year, which they are not always able to do. As a result, the total number of AFL-CIO members is smaller today than it was in 1992. In addition, each year the size of the labor force increases by an average of 1.7 million workers (85 percent of them wage and salary workers), so to maintain the same percentage of the workforce, unions would need to organize an additional 189,000 workers per year (a total of 439,000). There are no solid data on the number of new members recruited to unions, but for the sake of argument let's use the self-reported data contained in the AFL-CIO's weekly bulletin, indicating an average of 366,121 new members per year. If the labor movement were able to double that number labor would still not regain the position it had in 1983, when it represented 20.1 percent of the labor force, until 2036.[2]

Despite unions' decline, they remain perhaps the most powerful and diverse progressive force in the United States today. The 16.3 million union members include 6.7 million women, 2.5 million African Americans, and 1.6 million Latinos. Unions have more women members than NOW (National Organization of Women), more black members than the NAACP, more members than the Sierra Club. If we include the families of union members, 40 million Americans are directly affected by union victories and defeats. Moreover, while the members of many organizations are involved only via a national mailing list, unions have more than thirty thousand locals and chapters with regular meetings and elected officers. Many of these are far from vibrant, but others have impressive programs and activities and an active political culture.

Why has labor declined? Workers' preferences certainly can't explain current unionization levels. (Not to mention that preferences are themselves shaped by the media and probusiness culture.) Poll results show that less than 2 million of the 16 million unionized workers would vote to get rid of their union, but more than 40 million non-union workers would vote for a union.[3]

If worker preferences aren't the answer, what is? Three overriding reasons account for labor's decline, all intimately linked to one another, and all explored at much greater length throughout this book. First and foremost is a relentless employer assault, backed by government policies that support employers and attack workers (see chapter 2). Second is a drastic decline in labor's willingness and ability to mobilize: a decline in rank-and-file involvement, an increasing reliance on staff and other substitutes for worker power and solidarity. Third is labor's increased isolation: its separation from other social movements and sources of intellectual-cultural-political dynamism, and the consequent creation of a U.S. culture hostile not only to unions, but to the working class more generally.

The key to labor's revival, and to improved conditions for American workers, is a reversal in these larger trends: for labor to form alliances with other social movements; for those groups, not employers, to have cultural and political momentum; for a mass movement, not staff, to be taking leadership. An incremental strategy of more and more unions adopting "best practices" and recruiting better organizers won't do it. As Nelson Lichtenstein has argued, "For unions to grow again, American political culture has to change. . . . Given the right set of ideological benchmarks, it does not matter all that much what kind of organizing techniques the unions deploy. In the 1930s and in the 1960s, all sorts of maladroit, stodgy unions did quite well."[4]

Anticipating such a change might seem utopian, but it's happened before, and in fact it's the main way that labor has advanced. Historically, unions in the United States have grown in explosive bursts rather than in steady increments. Most notable are the dozen years from 1934 to 1945, but the years from 1898 to 1904 saw a similar spurt; in each period the number of union members more than quadrupled. Each of these growth spurts took place at times of profound changes in the economy, society, and political structure. At the end of the 1899–1904 growth spurt American unions had more members than their British, French, or German counterparts.[5]

The defining burst came during the Great Depression of the 1930s. Politics realigned to create Democratic dominance, the size of government increased dramatically, and a host of progressive reforms were enacted—Social Security, unemployment compensation, new regulatory agencies, and the Wagner Act guaranteeing workers the right to unionize. In 1933 there were 2.9 million union members; that number more than tripled by 1941 (to 10.5 million) and was up more than fivefold by 1945 (to 15.0 million). During this period, workers won what previously appeared impossible, sometimes through pitched battles and ferocious confrontation—as in the Flint General Motors sit-down strike of 1937—and at other times through employers' quick capitulation to avoid what seemed an inevitable union victory. Workers were able to win not simply because of individual heroism, creative ideas, or new organizational forms—although all these played a role—but rather because, in ways no one fully understands, what yesterday had seemed impossible suddenly became commonplace. Cultural understandings shifted, the existing order was challenged in myriad ways, the establishment could no longer be confident that subordinates would know their place or do as they were told, and the world was turned upside down.

During the 1930s labor actions were the leading force, but were joined by a range of other social movements. Radicals, socialists, and Communists were significant players in much of this activity, often shaping and driving labor and other activity. Most of labor's key advances resulted in significant part from an organized Left pushing events forward. Collectively the events of the 1930s threatened social order and indicated a potential for radical change or revolution. That potential made elites willing to accept significant reforms. Joseph Kennedy, for example, declared, "I felt and said I would be willing to part with half of what I had if I could be sure of keeping, under law and order, the other half."[6] In fact, at least a fraction of leading businessmen supported most New Deal reforms, and an argument could be made that it's remarkable how well the New Deal did at containing unrest.

These periods of upsurge are not just "more of the same"; each fundamentally restructures the economy, polity, society, and labor movement, marking a point of rupture when one system, including one labor relations system, is replaced by another.[7] The current labor system was established during the last great upsurge, primarily from about 1935 to 1947. The world has changed drastically since that time. These irrevocable shifts in the economy, social institutions, and cultural-political understandings mean that our current labor relations system no longer corresponds to the world of today.

The economic-political-social system established in the 1930s was based on a large government that was responsible for managing and regulating the economy. An unchecked monopoly capitalism (which arose in the 1890s) was replaced by what might be called Keynesian-stability capitalism, with strong unions as one component of an interlocking system. Oligopolistic corporations continued to dominate the market, mass-produce goods, and concentrate massive numbers of workers in a limited number of locations. But now (in response to strong unions) corporations increasingly ensured stability in employment by providing good wages and benefits, often structured in ways that discouraged employees from changing jobs. Given a relatively closed economy, a mild redistribution of income from the rich to the working class helped guarantee that there would be enough "effective demand" to purchase the society's output, with government prepared to engage in public works or deficit spending to smooth out any dips. The assumption was that a male breadwinner earned a family wage and his wife stayed home to take care of the kids; in 1940 more than two-thirds of all families actually fit that model (chapter 3). The racial minority population was almost exclusively black and was largely confined to the rural South (chapter 4). The vast majority of what was produced in the United States was consumed here, and people bought relatively few imported goods (chapter 5). In 1940 only 10 percent of the population completed even one year of college, but good jobs were available to workers with a high-school education (or less). For many kinds of problems, people saw government regulation as the obvious remedy.

Since the 1970s the era of Keynesian-stability capitalism has been replaced by what could be called either the age of flexible accumulation or the era of neoliberalism.[8] "Flexible accumulation" emphasizes the economic aspect and the lack of stable arrangements; "neoliberalism" emphasizes political and cultural dominance. Unlike 1894–96 and 1929–37, this new era crept in through a period of stagflation, rather than as the result of a cataclysmic depression. Hence its arrival has been less clearly marked. Perhaps the key period of shift was 1978–81, but this can only serve as a marker for a much longer process. Instead of government being seen as the solution, government is seen as the problem (as Ronald Reagan declared). Corporations seek to end secure employment. The stock market moves up when a corporation announces downsizing and layoffs. Whenever possible, work is contracted out; many "manufacturers" no longer manufacture, but instead develop and promote brand names. They make arrangements with subcontractors who compete for the business by offering the cheapest possible prices, achieved by cutting wages and using contingent workers. These employment relations invade even those jobs once known as the most secure; government, for example, seeks to privatize key parts of its operations and universities use contingent faculty. Regulated industries are deregulated. In part to cope with the insecurity of employment, the instability of families, and the squeeze on wages, and in part to gain autonomy and independence, more and more married women are employed (and family arrangements are themselves less stable). The minority population is far more diverse, with the number of Latinos exceeding the number of African Americans and a substantial Asian population as well; this population is far more urban than rural, and is spread throughout the United States. The economy (and culture) is global: the products we purchase come from all over, and the economic competitor of significance may be in Europe,

Central America, or Asia. Since unions have historically succeeded in significant part by restricting competition, the intensification of competition creates major difficulties for labor.

The first and in many ways the primary argument advanced by this book is that the labor movement will not grow slowly and incrementally. It hasn't in the past and it won't in the future. Our challenge, therefore, is to examine how the world has changed since 1935, the problems and the opportunities this creates for any movement by workers, and the ways in which the labor movement has (or has not) been changing and adapting to meet these altered circumstances. Each chapter tries to address such questions as:

1. What are some of the most significant ways in which the world today differs from that of (say) 1935?
2. What strains and problems does that pose for workers and for the old system of labor relations?
3. How is the labor movement addressing, or failing to address, the developing contradictions?
4. What appear to be the most likely future trajectories? What can the labor movement do to maximize its long-run possibilities, helping to make a new upsurge more likely and positioning itself to take advantage should such an opportunity arise?

A new upsurge is by no means inevitable. Perhaps the next generation or more will be dominated by the trends that have been developing: an increase in contingent work (even for many professionals); increasing inequality in jobs and income, including the spread of near-minimum-wage jobs; and an employer-dominated system of "employee involvement." This, combined with employer dominance of politics, the courts, the media, and public culture and understanding, might create a new system that virtually eliminates unions—and greatly weakens all non-business forms of organization—for an extended and indefinite period.[9]

An influential set of scholars, mostly based in business schools but (by the standards of the day) sympathetic to labor, argue that we should not expect (or want?) a social movement unionism. Doing so, Heckscher argues, is "nostalgia for an 'ephemeral era'"; this kind of unionism, he says, "has shown no capacity to sustain itself."[10] Instead these scholars—who include Joel Rogers, Thomas Kochan, Charles Heckscher, and Richard Freeman—argue that labor should adapt to a new labor regime that is emerging within the confines of business dominance. To do so, unions should become less adversarial, more like professional associations and less like unions. Professional associations, they point out, have grown while unions have shrunk, and survey data indicate workers prefer nonantagonistic relations with employers.

Although these scholars address their remarks primarily to labor audiences, the resistance to their proposals comes overwhelmingly from business. It's absolutely true that workers wish management would hassle them less and listen to them more; as Fletcher and Hurd note, "Even those with a more activist bent . . . tire of fighting." But it's weird for the procooperation scholars to write as if unions—especially today's business unions—are the force creating adversarial relations. Ruth Milkman's insightful study of an auto factory shows the most common case. When the (unionized) company announced new, more cooperative relations "workers readily embraced the new managerial rhetoric of participation." Many were thrilled by the training sessions, but as soon as production started up again management actions led workers to resume their belief "suspended briefly during the 80–hour training but soon revived, that management simply could not be trusted." More generally, employers have supported meaningful workplace cooperation only during periods of worker/union power, specifically as a means to co-opt unrest. Addressing "we need more cooperation" arguments to unions but not employers seems misguided or antiworker. As one of the leading advocates of this approach ruefully noted, when President Clinton's Dunlop Commission proposed such policies "the problem was that, aside from some academics, there was no constituency in favor of this!"[11]

The Movements of the 1960s and the Labor of Today

Unless there is a new period of mass social movements, labor is likely to continue to lose ground, and the next labor regime may well involve employer dominance. But even if we have a new wave of mass movements, it is by no means inevitable that it will involve labor.

If an existing movement draws on the energy of new forces and incorporates them then both movements are transformed. Perhaps the single greatest failure of the U.S. Left in the past fifty years is the lack of connection between labor and the movements of the 1960s. This drastically weakened and limited both labor and the black, feminist, environmental, student, public interest, and anti-intervention movements, contributing to the class-biased nature of the 1960s movements and to the ossification and insularity of labor. A significant part of today's union leadership actively works to heal the rifts between labor and new social movements, whether those of the 1960s or those of today. A large gulf remains, but anti-sweatshop struggles and the November 1999 Seattle anti–World Trade Organization protests are dramatic examples of progress.

Following both the 1930s and 1960s upsurges, the issues raised by the movements became incorporated into successor organizations, but the two sorts of organizations differ sharply.[12] In both cases popular consciousness was transformed but the system absorbed and muted the forces of change. The labor upsurge of the 1930s left in its wake established unions, organized in locals that met regularly and elected officers, with growing permanent staffs funded by substantial member dues. The unions signed contracts and established ongoing working relationships with the corporations whose members they represented, relationships that were closely regulated by government agencies and the courts. The relationships were adversarial—the union and management each fought for its side—but confined to certain largely internal processes, operating within legally regulated bounds, and almost always resolved by compromises agreed to by both parties. Occasional tests of strength were a crucial aspect of the system, but these took place within carefully prescribed bounds: workers, unions, management, the public all knew just what to expect from strikes, and the regulatory agencies and courts swiftly intervened if any attempt were made to step outside those bounds (see chapter 2).

What the movements of the 1960s left in place was similar in some ways and sharply different in others. The movements of the 1960s did not create ongoing membership organizations with viable local chapters, although a version of identity politics came to permeate the culture. Most of the more radical organizations, like the Student Nonviolent Coordinating Committee (SNCC) and Students for a Democratic Society (SDS), entirely disappeared. Groups such as the Ralph Nader–inspired Public Interest Research Groups, the National Abortion Rights Action League (NARAL), or Clean Water Action differ from unions in their membership, funding, methods of governance, internal organization, relationship to the state, and characteristic method of achieving their goals. Even the seeming exceptions have relatively few functioning local chapters. Unlike unions, the new wave citizen groups can rarely rely exclusively on member dues: in one comprehensive 1980 survey, only 22 percent of citizen groups received 70 percent or more of their money from ordinary member dues; the rest came from government grants, foundations, or wealthy individuals. Moreover, the groups most likely to grow were those least reliant on member dues.[13]

Typically these "citizen" or "public interest" groups rely on a low-paid, generally young, college-educated staff, a patron of some sort, and a mailing list. The typical member relates to the group exclusively through direct mail or telephone solicitation (in rare cases, door-to-door solicitation) and has never attended any meeting of the group. Unlike unions, members neither hold office in the organization nor vote for leaders. The group's continued existence depends on the ability to tap into high-visibility, hot-button, symbolic issues that either get ordinary people to respond to direct mail appeals or get wealthy sponsors to continue to provide funding.

The organizations that followed the 1960s movements also differ from unions in their characteristic mode of operation. Unions have close, on-going, often intimate relationships with their opponents (management and corporations) and operate through compromise and small victories. Operating in this way, union leaders and staff built something approximating the old-time political machine; the local union leader was like a ward heeler who could help to get your grievance resolved, and these individual-level victories—keeping your job, avoiding discipline, or getting a promotion—built future loyalty to the union and its leadership. In contrast, the post-1960s groups have arm's-length relationships with their opponents, and typically operate either through class-action law suits (say, around environmental impact statements) or media exposure. When the group engages in direct action, it rarely involves the mass participation of a strike—which, to be effective, typically requires 90 percent participation from the affected constituency, all of whom forfeit pay and risk their jobs—and is much more likely to be symbolic. The action has its impact primarily through press and television coverage, not by virtue of its direct ability to affect the functioning of the system. While the structural dynamic of unions pushes them to accommodate and win small victories for members, the structural dynamic of post-1960s groups pushes them to generate publicity and tap into emotional issues that get people to respond to direct mail appeals. The constituency of these groups, together with their reliance on foundations and wealthy donors, gives them a strongly middle-class character, although the groups typically vehemently deny this. Given the class character of the new movements and the nature of the issues, the day-to-day lives of group members rarely depend on material victories. Such groups may be less inclined to compromise, because the symbolic statement is more important than the incremental advance. Workers may be more inclined to compromise because a slight improvement in health benefits or two extra personal days has a direct and significant influence on daily life.

For many years the distinction was sharp and clear between the style and character of unions and citizens'/public interest groups. But in recent years unions have adopted many of the tactics of the post-1960s groups—the symbolic protest, background research seeking opponent vulnerabilities, strategic use of lawsuits, finding ways to take battles to a wider public. If unions substitute lawsuits and press conferences for their greatest source of power—the participation and solidarity of millions of members able to disrupt the economic functioning of the system—it will further undercut the unique promise of the labor movement. But if unions are able to combine the new style and tactics with the mass mobilization characteristic of unions at their best, this would create an awesome political force whose potential is only now being explored.

A Top-Down Revival?

In 1995, in the AFL-CIO's first contested election, the "New Voice" team of John Sweeney, president, Richard Trumka, secretary-treasurer, and Linda Chavez Thompson, executive vice president, won a narrow but decisive victory on a platform that called for reviving the labor movement and emphasizing new organizing. For many years the labor movement's leadership had lacked vision, ambition, and energy. Their aim was to hold on to what they had. In 1972 George Meany, president of the AFL-CIO for much of the postwar period, presented the old-line labor position on organizing: "Why should we worry about organizing groups of people who do not want to be organized?" Important members of the labor movement were often racist and sexist—as were many other members of society—and looked with suspicion on movements for social change. Many union leaders were more concerned about the size of their treasuries—or their own salaries—than about the union's ability to organize or increase worker power.[14]

The 1995 New Voice team, and the changes they introduced, once seemed the most promising labor initiative since the 1940s. The new leadership brought an energy and openness that encouraged the activities reported on in this book, and created a sense of hope and momentum. They self-consciously thought about the long-run future of the labor movement. But several years later the early wave of optimism has given way to caution or pessimism. The John Sweeney change has been limited and deeply problematic for at least two reasons. First and by far the most important, John Sweeney and the New Voice team are not the product of a social movement; they came to office in something that more nearly approximates a palace coup. They want to restore labor's power, expand its membership, and improve conditions for millions of workers, but I know of no historical precedent for a mass movement being created from the top down.[15] It's not clear whether the New Voice team really wants a movement, and it seems highly unlikely they are willing to take the kind of chances a full-scale movement would necessitate. They do, however, provide the space that makes such a movement possible, and they legitimate and facilitate many movement activities. (See chapter 2 and the book as a whole.)

Second, the labor movement is broader and more complex than many accounts recognize. The "union" is a precisely circumscribed institution, a legally constituted collective bargaining agent that has elected officers, signs contracts, owns property, and represents workers in complex relations with employers and government. The "labor movement" is a more fluid formation whose very existence depends on high-risk activism, mass solidarity, and collective experiences with transformational possibilities. The union's long-term survival depends on an ability to deliver wages, benefits, and a systematic defense of workers' everyday workplace rights. As at least two decades of employer assault have made clear, in the (not so) long run the "union" by itself can't succeed even within the narrow confines of contracts and business unionism, unless the "union" is embedded within a labor movement. Unions' legitimacy and very existence depend on an ability to constitute and reconstitute themselves as social movements. The labor movement is broader than the legally defined union, including both individuals and institutions that are not part of unions—occupational health and safety groups, university labor extension programs, the NAACP or ACLU labor section, women's groups, Jobs with Justice.

Even within the boundaries of unions narrowly understood, President John Sweeney has only limited control over the AFL-CIO. The AFL-CIO is a federation of sixty-six independent and largely autonomous unions, ranging in size from the 1.3 million–member International Brotherhood of Teamsters to the 500–member International Union of Journeymen Horseshoers of the United States and Canada. The central AFL-CIO controls only about 1 percent of the total labor budget; the national and international unions control 21 percent; and local, district, or regional bodies control about 78 percent of the budget. The AFL-CIO officers can lead by example, can call for, verbally encourage, and offer limited material support to the kind of initiatives they would like to see—but for the most part they can't order constituent unions what to do.

To further complicate matters, the affiliated unions no longer have clear jurisdictional lines. On the one hand, each union contains many different kinds of worker. The United Auto Workers, for example, includes graduate students, child care and social service workers, clerical and municipal employees, graphic artists and writers. On the other hand, each occupational group may be spread across many different unions, and this makes it difficult to gain leverage. Eighteen different unions (or quasi-union professional associations) organize nurses. If one of those unions begins a campaign to end mandatory overtime, a second focuses on needle-stick injuries, and a third on wage increases, how much leverage can any one of them exercise?[16]

The consequence that must always be kept in mind is that there is enormous variation within the labor movement. A focus on the "best practice" to be found somewhere among the thirty-thousand-plus union locals does not necessarily provide a sense of what is average today, or how rapidly—if at all—today's best practice will spread. This radically decentralized federated structure is both a strength and a limitation, making it harder to achieve solidarity but providing room for experimentation.

Interregnum or Fading Days?

Looking at this chaotic structure, both of bureaucratic organizations and of social movement initiatives, many different stories could be told. This book does not focus on day-to-day activities in ordinary unions. Such a book might tell about local heroes and small campaigns, but for the most part it would be much more discouraging: boring meetings, individual grievances, routine contracts, constant battles to stop new employer depredations, union leaders/staff/activists not having the time or energy to make many advances, and rank-and-file members often too discouraged to act or frustrated when they try to mobilize.

Instead, this book focuses on innovative campaigns in areas of major social change. Each chapter centers around labor activities closely related to one of the most important social movements of our time: the women's movement (chapter 3), civil rights and immigration (chapter 4), global justice (chapter 5), and living wage and antisweatshop (chapter 6). Much of my analysis is based on existing studies of recent innovative campaigns, but almost every chapter also contains significant original research, and many of the campaigns discussed here are little known even within the labor movement. The data used here include personal experience, field work, close to fifty in-depth interviews with a range of figures both unknown and well-known, and conversations with a wide range of labor movement participants. I draw on many more people than are explicitly cited.

Movements arise because many people are so gripped by an issue that they break with their routines and take risks to make changes. Therefore, the focus here is not on issues that one or another expert says should concern labor, but rather on those issues that have already driven large numbers of people to act. The task of an analyst is not to invent a utopia, to tell people what they should want and fight for, but rather to observe people's struggles, to try to clarify them, to help a movement become self-conscious about its goals, tactics, and strategy. To the extent that a theorist is able to do so, the theory in turn helps to advance future praxis.

Predicting the future is inherently problematic, and that is even more true of attempts to predict moments of discontinuity. Imagine a knowledgeable and analytic observer in December 1959 asked to assess the possibilities for a new round of social movements, both their probability and their likely character. The Montgomery bus boycott was three years in the past; even an avid news reader might think it an anomaly. The most recent large-scale mass movements were the labor struggles of the 1930s and 1940s, and the largest strike in U.S. history was in 1959. But strikes largely fit within an established pattern and labor seemed to be incorporated into the system, although wildcat strikes were spreading. All in all, an observer might have concluded—as did Daniel Bell and Seymour Martin Lipset—that the era of social movements and radical activity was at an end. Two months later, four black students sat at a lunch counter and asked for a cup of coffee. Within a few months, more than fifty thousand people participated in sit-ins, and for more than a decade transformative movements spread from one issue, and one location, to another.

If the vise (and vice) of business dominance continues to tighten, then the campaigns described here may be forgotten and treated as minor curiosities. But my hope is that these campaigns show that the groundwork is being laid for a possible explosion of labor action. As Eve Weinbaum has argued, most successful social movements are preceded by a long string of "failures." Only in retrospect do we see that these "failures" were testing the limits and vulnerabilities of existing structures, seeking new sources of strength and connection, and by doing so making possible a paradigm shift from one system to another.[17] If current trends continue, twenty years from now the campaigns described in this book may seem insignificant historical oddities; if my hopes come true they will be seen as the prehistory of the upsurge.

2

The New Deal System

Employer Offensive, Labor Response

The labor system created in the New Deal, which with important modifications reigns today, was intended to provide significant benefits to workers and their unions. The National Labor Relations Act (NLRA), or Wagner Act, of 1935 set rules and created enforcement mechanisms to guarantee fair play between employers and unions and to actively promote unionization. In doing so it established a regulatory regime enabling some kinds of activities and constraining others. This regime helped establish labor by maintaining a system that provided employers a stable labor supply along with significant benefits to workers and unions providing they acted within established channels; by doing so it became one of the cornerstones of the postwar economic boom.

One account of labor's decline is that it happened "naturally"; manufacturing declined, the new workforce had less need of unions, and as a consequence they withered away. But today's workers need unions as much as ever; unions are quite capable of adapting to new circumstances and new needs. This chapter argues that unions didn't just fade away; they were ground down under an employer offensive.

In the 1940s through (perhaps) the 1960s, when labor was powerful, corporate leaders basically accepted the New Deal labor system; unions and employers lived together in what many scholars have called "the accord." Employers, however, continued to challenge labor and to chip away at its strength. Established unions received real rewards for playing within the rules of the game, and were reluctant to put these benefits at risk by mobilizing action that challenged the existing legal framework. But labor gains its power only through the reality or (credible) threat of a movement that can go beyond the existing rules; the system itself is dominated by employers and gives them multiple ways to exercise leverage. The longer unions operated within the legal-regulatory limits the more the rules came to favor employers.

Over time union power weakened, and it became increasingly clear that most unions had neither the inclination nor the capacity to mobilize as a movement. At roughly the same time, around 1970, the economic and political system as a whole faced a crisis, albeit not one marked by a major depression. Competition with Europe and Japan, a wage-price squeeze caused in part by the very successes of unions operating within the system, the U.S. defeat in Vietnam, and the rise of social movements combined to challenge the existing regulatory regime. Employers responded not only by squeezing harder on a company-by-company basis, but also by mobilizing their own movement to substantially restructure the system. While corporate leaders engaged in future-oriented strategizing, the labor movement was largely caught napping and did little either to rethink its own approach or to counter the employer offensive.

The success of the 1970s–80s employer offensive dramatically shifted the balance of power. As a result of a cumulative series of "minor" changes, it is far more difficult for workers and unions to win within the normal framework. A successful regulatory regime must channel activity within accepted limits; to do so it must provide rewards for accepting the regime. Because the altered system provides workers and unions much less hope of winning within the rules, labor is in effect coerced to try new and innovative approaches. If the regulatory regime provides few benefits or protections, what reason is there to operate within that framework?

Many unions have thus begun to experiment with a range of innovative strategies, concluding that the only way to win is to act more like a movement. The post-1995 AFL-CIO New Voice leadership has encouraged these innovative approaches; union leaders and staff have often been the driving force in attempting to create more movement within the ranks of labor. Simultaneously, however, existing leaders and staff (including the New Voice itself) benefit from the existing system and are reluctant to break with it. This creates the contradictory situation facing current progressive union leaders: Stay within the system or break out of it? Run a better bureaucracy or take the risk of trying to mobilize a movement? At the present time established leaders are often a major force pushing for change and simultaneously insist on a top-down approach, opposing any activity that might threaten their control and afraid of real democracy or debate.

The New Deal Labor Regime

Most of this book is about the "labor movement"; it is important to understand, however, at least some of the ways in which the current system defines and circumscribes the "union." Perhaps the fundamental characteristic of the New Deal labor system is that the state regulatory apparatus effectively determines what constitutes a union and what unions may (and may not) do. A union is a legally certified entity that represents employees and bargains with employers within boundaries established by the state. The National Labor Relations Board (NLRB) and the courts not only set the overall framework; they determine the details of union-employer relations.

The existence of the New Deal labor relations system constrains and channels all actions. All parties operate within the basic framework while contesting it at the margins. This system is built into the internal structures of each of the major actors (unions, employers, the state); into the history and character of their relations and interactions; and into the cultural understandings governing what is and is not possible. A new upsurge, a paradigm shift, would necessarily and inevitably change these limits and definitions, but the likelihood is that any new U.S. system would borrow heavily from the existing system, transforming some elements but leaving many in place.

The initial basic framework, the Wagner Act (or National Labor Relations Act [NLRA]) of 1935, was simple and intended to protect workers. If workers sought to form a union, they could show the National Labor Relations Board (NLRB, or "the Board") that a significant fraction of the workforce (30 percent or more) wanted a union. The Board would schedule an election for a few weeks later, and would supervise the election to be sure it was free and fair. If a majority of workers voted for the union, the Board would certify it as the sole bargaining agent and the employer would have to negotiate with the union. Unions and employers had to live up to any agreements that they made, and the Board could penalize them if they failed to do so.

The system has evolved since then. The most significant change in the law was the 1947 Taft-Hartley Act, which employers promoted to restore "balance" to labor law. Also important are a host of rulings by the NLRB and the courts, as well as the accretion of "past practice" and custom.

Over time the system became increasingly legalistic and arcane. Today it regulates every detail of worker-union-employer relations. For example, if workers want to be in a union, the Board (not the workers or union) decides who will and will not be included in the bargaining unit, based on its determination of which workers have a "common interest." At Rhode Island Hospital the union and employer argued over who should be included in the unit: Per diem nurses? Various small groups of technical employees? Management's primary aim was to delay the process; its secondary goal to include workers who would be likely to vote against the union. At the NLRB hearing Richard Sanders, representing the union and wanting to avoid delay, said to the hospital's lawyer, "You decide; you want them in, we'll include them; you want them out, okay." Even with that the employer asked the NLRB that the matter be litigated, in hopes of additional delay so that the hospital's anti-union campaign could gain force. The NLRB not only determines what workers are in the bargaining unit, but also when the election will be held, what rules will govern the election, what happens if the rules are broken, what subjects the union can and can't bargain about once they have won, under what circumstances workers can go on strike, what sorts of strike activities are acceptable, and dozens of other matters. Every aspect of this can be, and often is, litigated, first before the Board and then (sometimes) in the courts.

In many ways this system worked well for workers, employers, and unions. By law, employers must agree to bargain about wages and hours and working conditions. These are so-called mandatory subjects of bargaining; employers can refuse to bargain about many other subjects, for example, whether the company will continue to dump pollutants in the river or whether it will hire more black workers.[1] Employers benefited from a stable, loyal, committed, and productive workforce. Routine problems were handled through a grievance system, some version of which was incorporated in almost every union contract, and (official) strikes occurred only at the time a union contract expired. Because that was predictable, management could minimize disruptions.

Workers used their unions to win impressive wage gains, tying worker pay to industry productivity. From 1949 to 1973 the average family's income more than doubled. Wage increases weren't a result of corporate benevolence: a large proportion of the workforce was unionized, and "from the late 1940s through the early 1970s [exactly the period of rapid income increases], strike levels in the United States stood higher than at any time, before or since." Workers knew that prosperity didn't just happen, that it came from the union. As Jack Metzgar notes in his autobiographical account of growing up in a steelworker family, "Take 1946, for example. The union wanted twenty-five cents . . . but the company allowed it could afford only a dime"; the final settlement was eighteen and a half cents. The material things the union made possible, "Aunt Bettie's curtains, Stan's hunting vacation in Potter County, Frommy's first car, and always 'that full collection plate' that allowed us to keep up and improve our church . . . were more than just themselves. Each was a token of freedom." The union was equally vital in winning benefits like health insurance and supplemental unemployment compensation. Metzgar argues that "if what we lived through in the 1950s was not liberation, then liberation never happens in real human lives."[2] Seniority provisions meant that promotions and desirable jobs were not dependent on the supervisor's whim, and workers did not have to be subservient to move up. Union contracts also regulated a host of on-the-job conditions. If employers violated the conditions of the contract, workers could seek restitution through the grievance system. Companies repeatedly tested the limits of union power. They accepted wage and benefit increases in order to gain labor peace and because the structure of the political-economic system enabled oligopolistic corporations to pass on their wage increases by raising prices if necessary.

Unions didn't just win wage gains; the grievance system gave workers a measure of protection and sometimes even significant control over work. If a worker feels the union contract has been violated, he or she may file a grievance. The grievance is processed through multiple steps; at each stage the union and management square off. If an agreement is reached, that resolves it; if not, it goes to the next higher level, and ultimately to the decision of an arbitrator. Ruth Milkman's *Farewell to the Factory* presents examples of auto worker grievances in a New Jersey General Motors factory around 1980. Many grievances focused on Paragraph 78 of the National Agreement which addressed production standards and appropriate workloads. "A representative overwork grievance reads, 'I charge management with violation of Paragraph 78 of the National Agreement whereas my job is overworked. I demand that this extra work be removed from my job so that I may work in a safe and normal manner.'" Other grievances addressed a wide range of the "minor" annoyances of work life which create hazardous conditions, make the job more difficult, or violate workers' dignity: dirty restrooms, missing equipment, unsafe machinery. For example: "I charge management with violation of LD [Local Demand] #4 in as much as I was kept waiting 4 hours to be released fr. work for an emergency. I demand an explanation of this delay as well as a commitment by mngt that the newly negotiated provisions re: emergency calls will be lived up to as well as the provisions previously negotiated."[3] At the plant Milkman studied, and elsewhere, workers won a large number of these grievances.

A Postwar Accord?

The standard left-wing interpretation of postwar labor relations is that these rules and this system were part of an "accord" that developed between unions and employers, with employers accepting the existence of unions, learning to work with them, and in some circumstances even welcoming unions as a way to discipline and control the labor force by letting off steam in carefully controlled ways. Unions, in their turn, became bureaucratic staff-driven entities, working within (and perhaps welcoming) this legal framework, unwilling to challenge employer control or to raise larger issues, concerned at their best to win wage increases for workers and to function as lawyers/social workers who effectively handled grievances, and at their worst run for the benefit of a highly paid staff and leadership. Michael Burawoy, for example, argued that "the trade union must be sufficiently strong and responsive to labor in order to command the allegiance of its members and yet not sufficiently strong to present a challenge to management prerogatives in the organization and control of the labor process."[4]

That perspective captures one important facet of postwar labor relations. Employers did usually accept the union and work with it, settling grievances and negotiating contracts. When workers went out on strike, for example, companies made no serious effort to break the union by hiring replacement workers. In some circumstances, companies actually assisted unions. During a 1970 strike, with the UAW's strike fund dwindling rapidly, General Motors agreed to lend the union the money needed to pay for worker health benefits; "After the strike was over, the UAW repaid the $46 million–due bill at 5 percent interest."[5]

Unions for their part did help to discipline and regulate the workforce, preventing unpredictable explosions and channeling discontent and militance into predictable forms at rare and predictable times (that is, when contracts expired). Unions were legally required to prevent spontaneous worker self-activity such as wildcat strikes, and often did so with relish, experiencing wildcats as direct personal challenges to the union staff and leadership (as, indeed, they often were). The grievance system provided workers a way to express their discontent, but to do so through a lengthy and complex legal process which individualized grievances and led workers to rely on the staff instead of their own solidarity and direct action. In Michael Burawoy's study of a machine shop, he found that at union meetings the most intense interaction occurred around the discussion of grievances. "Each time a *collective* grievance or an issue of principle outside the contract, affecting the entire membership or even a section of the membership, is raised, Jim [the union president] insists, 'Have you got a grievance? If you have, let's hear it. If you haven't, give the floor to someone else.'"[6] A resolution achieved by mobilizing collective solidarity was foreclosed.

Union leaders and staff often spent much of their time resolving grievances and cutting deals with management, adopting a "servicing model" instead of a "union building" model. They focused primarily on relatively routinized day-to-day enforcement of the contract. In the process they became a combination of informal social workers, employment lawyers, and old-time machine politicians, developing an organization based on their ability to resolve grievances and cut deals in exchange for loyalty. Staff also negotiated contracts. As Nelson Lichtenstein emphasizes, the late 1940s defeat of national health care, and the general failure to enact social democratic reforms, meant that union contracts became enormously complex, because they had to address health insurance, pension, and supplemental benefits issues that in Europe are covered by government programs.[7]

As these activities increased in importance, the number of union staff positions expanded exponentially. The UAW's staff, for example, grew from 407 in 1949 to 1,335 in 1970 without an increase in union membership.[8] It's easy to defend such an expansion: if small changes can have multimillion-dollar consequences, then qualified, experienced staff are needed to determine the best pension and benefits packages, to cost them out, to write the legal language that covers contingencies. This may be one reason why U.S. unions have "the largest and best-paid stratum of full-time salaried officers in the labor-movement world." U.S. unions at the end of the 1950s had one full-time staff person for every three hundred union members, "while the European average was about one full-time officeholder per two thousand unionists."[9] A legalistic grievance system provided another push toward permanent and professional staff.

The concept of an accord accurately captures the fact that for many years the regulatory regime operated successfully for both labor and employers. A successful labor regime requires that both business and labor receive benefits from cooperating with the system, that both business and labor pay a cost for not doing so, that there be legitimate but bounded ways for business and labor to contend with each other, and that there be some means of enforcing decisions. A successful labor regime need not be based on equality between the parties; in fact, there is no outside objective means of determining what constitutes equality. But to operate as a regime the balance of power must be such that each side prefers to conduct the contest within the accepted rules rather than to break those rules and engage in open unbounded warfare. In the quarter-century after World War II, this was usually the case.

Any such system is unstable, however, because of a fundamental imbalance between business and labor. Business gains its greatest power by operating within the accepted system; in normal circumstances business, after all, dominates the economy and politics. Labor gains its greatest power precisely through its ability to disrupt the normal functioning of the system, and to do so in unpredictable, uncontrollable ways. In a successful labor regime, unions had a stake in playing by the rules, maintaining relations with management and outside political forces, acting responsibly, protecting the union's buildings and investments, and avoiding risks.

The labor movement's power, however, depends on the ability to involve and give voice to the concerns, hopes, and fears of millions of ordinary workers. In many unions, rank-and-file movements arose to challenge the established leadership, though few succeeded in taking power.[10] If staff individualize problems and address them through bureaucratic processes involving long delays, this undercuts workers' sense of empowerment and responsibility. Moreover, worker power depends on its unpredictability and at least occasional willingness to risk all.

Therefore, the longer unions stayed within the system, the more they increased staff, and the more staff were hired for their expertise as negotiators and quasi-lawyers, the less capable labor was of mobilizing as a social movement and the more the balance of power shifted towards business. As a consequence, over time labor received fewer and fewer rewards for cooperating with the existing labor regime. Especially after the 1970s, the "accord" became one-sided; labor acted like it had an accord, business was on the attack. In many cases, if unions today hope to win they must operate outside the bounds of the established labor regime, a point I will develop in chapters 4 and 6.

The most important single event weakening worker-union power was the Taft-Hartley Act, passed in 1947. It contained dozens of provisions that made it more difficult for workers to form unions or to exercise leverage through the unions they formed. The general principle, for the Taft-Hartley Act in particular and for labor law in general, is that any tactic that gives workers power is illegal. To that end, supervisors are forbidden to form or join unions, a rule that has become increasingly important as employers argue that nurses are supervisors and fast-food restaurants create "assistant shift supervisors" earning twenty-five cents an hour more than other workers. Radicals and Communists were ordered expelled from unions, a provision that was found unconstitutional, but only years after it created havoc in unions and helped consolidate the hold of business unionism. Secondary boycotts were outlawed: cannery workers may picket the cannery (which does not sell to individual consumers) but not the grocery store that carries the canned goods. This limit applies only to unions; any other American, or group of Americans, has a free speech right to picket the grocer. Taft-Hartley not only rules that secondary boycotts are illegal; it also requires the NLRB to give priority to secondary boycott charges over all other charges and to seek court injunctions. If there is a long backlog of cases, with fired workers waiting for their cases to be heard, secondary boycott cases do not wait their turn, but are taken up immediately. These cases, the ones of most concern to employers, are thus given priority by statute over even the most outrageous violations of worker rights. If Congress underfunds the NLRB, workers may wait years for a resolution, but the cases that matter to employers will be decided forthwith.[11]

But the Taft-Hartley Act does not stand alone; it has been reinforced, and conditions for workers made worse, by a host of subsequent decisions by the NLRB and the courts. Workers suffer not from one big blow, administered more than fifty years ago, but through a thousand cuts, opened each year. Consider two of these.

As the workers at the Rhode Island Hospital found, one of the most intimidating employer tactics is the "one-on-one" meeting in which a worker is questioned by a supervisor about his or her views on the union. For many years, the NLRB held that "any systematic employer interrogation of employees about their protected union activities was per se an unfair labor practice." To reverse this policy, the Board chose an almost perfect example of why the rule should have been kept. Every single worker at the Blue Flash Company signed a union authorization card. Five days later the employer interrogated the employees individually in his office, ostensibly so he could know whether the union really represented the workers. Every single employee, concerned about being targeted for reprisal, denied having signed a union card. The NLRB decided that such an interrogation was totally reasonable, that the employer should be permitted the "free speech" ability to engage in such interrogations, and that doing so did not coerce or intimidate workers or interfere with their free speech.[12] This policy remains in effect today; although generically these are referred to as "one-on-one" meetings, in fact employers often involve more than one supervisor in grilling the hapless worker.

The "captive audience" meeting—with workers rounded up and forced to hear why they should oppose the union—is another standard part of today's organizing campaigns. From 1935 to 1947, under the Wagner Act, the NLRB held that any such meeting was an unfair labor practice which by itself invalidated the representation election and entitled the union to a new election. Taft-Hartley reversed this by stating that an employer had a "free speech" right to hold captive audience meetings. But in the late 1940s, the NLRB held that if employers held such meetings, they were required in fairness to also permit the union to hold a similar meeting, during work hours, again with mandatory employee attendance. Under Eisenhower, during the supposed high point of the postwar accord, the Board reversed this ruling to allow virtually unlimited employer use of captive audience meetings; unions, on the other hand, are not entitled to any equivalent access to workers during work hours.[13]

The system contains inequitable penalties for unions as opposed to employers. Most of the actions that unions can take to increase their power are subject to harsh penalties. If a union goes out on strike during the term covered by a contract, or if it engages in militant picketing, or if it launches a secondary boycott of an employer, the employer may sue the union for damages and the courts can issue an injunction (among other penalties). Penalties begin almost immediately and can involve enormous sums.

In contrast, an employer who violates the law in the most outrageous and devastating fashion—firing a worker simply because he or she supports the union—can delay any penalty for years, cannot be penalized more than a token amount, and has absolute legal protection if it libels the worker during the process. If a worker is fired for pro-union activity, the courts cannot issue an injunction to immediately rectify the situation. The worker and union must file a charge with the National Labor Relations Board (NLRB), but the worker does not get his or her job back until the process has gone through every possible employer appeal—even if every ruling is against the employer and for the union. If an employer chooses to do so, it can drag out the process for three years. It's not only that the process involves such long delays, but also that during it the employer attempts to prove that the worker was fired for some reason—any reason—other than union activity. As Thomas Geoghegan, a labor lawyer, explains about his defense of a nurse fired for pro-union activity during an organizing drive:

I don't even tell her the truth, which is that for three years she'll see her name dragged through the mud, with doctors, administrators, even parking-lot attendants coming in to say:

"She didn't change the patient's bedpan."

"I saw her yelling at a patient."

"I saw her flirting with a patient."

"I saw her having *sex* with a patient."

And finally: "She's on drugs."

And the hospital can swing away, since in a hearing it has absolute protection from libel.[14]

If the worker manages (three years later) to win, what happens? The employer does not pay a fine, much less serve jail time. The employer must rehire the worker and pay him or her the wages missed since the worker was fired—minus anything the worker earned during this period. If the union drive failed, the worker is left with no protection. One study found that "of employees who did go back, nearly 80 percent were gone within a year or two, and most blamed their departure on vindictive treatment by the employer." As a final insult, firing a worker is not, in the view of the media, a newsworthy event, and rarely is covered in newspapers or on television.[15]

Given all this, faced by a union organizing drive that could raise wages and benefits by 10 or 20 percent, by the logic of economic rationality an employer should ignore morality and fire a few of the leading union activists. And that's exactly what employers do. Kate Bronfenbrenner's research shows that in one out of four union organizing drives the employer fires one or more workers for their pro-union activity.[16]

Business Mobilization

If the law were all that mattered, business could have launched an all-out assault on unions much earlier than it did, since even during the height of the accord much had been done to weaken worker and union rights. Employers did not begin such an assault until the 1970s, primarily because of labor's strength, but in part because they themselves were reasonably content with the status quo. In the 1970s, however, business developed a sense of crisis, mobilized to change conditions, and by the early 1980s had fundamentally shifted the balance of power not just at the workplace, but also in politics, the economy, and the culture more broadly.

My account implies that throughout this period business was dominant and the already circumscribed power of labor was gradually being eroded. But in the early 1970s business did not see its own power as secure. Despite the incremental changes favoring business, unions remained powerful in key sectors of the economy; workers were winning substantial increases in wages and benefits. It was clear that unions would fiercely resist any attempt to change that, and as a result profits were squeezed and the competitiveness of U.S. corporations threatened. Employers' initial concern was kept at a high heat for many years by the economic stagflation of 1974 to 1982.[17] More important, however, containing U.S. labor was not enough to secure business power.

Events of the 1960s shook the foundations of the U.S. (and world) capitalist class. The rise of Europe and Japan as economic competitors, an emerging monetary crisis, the Vietnamese ability to defeat the U.S. military in all-out war, and above all the movements of the 1960s, called into question the security of the regime. As David Rockefeller, scion of the most powerful capitalist family in U.S. history and chairman of the Chase Manhattan Bank, wrote in the bank's 1971 annual report: "It is clear to me that the entire structure of our society is being challenged." This was by no means an isolated observation. At closed 1973 meetings, business executives said to each other: "We are fighting for our lives"; "We are fighting a delaying action"; "If we don't take action now, we will see our own demise. We will evolve into another social democracy."[18]

In part because the movements of the 1960s and the labor movement remained separate from each other, the 1960s movements demonstrated no immediate potential to take over the country, either through electoral means or by mass action, yet they were genuine *movements* with increasing popular appeal and power. Each of their victories was profound and in some meaningful sense irreversible. Although these movements were very far from achieving the ultimate goals of their most militant elements, they transformed popular culture and taken-for-granted wisdom, and were incorporated into the institutions of economic, political, and social life. Today, leading corporate polluters take out ads supporting Earth Day[19] and arch-conservatives at least claim to stand for equal rights for all races and both sexes. This is a direct result of these movements, not a product of "modernization" or a moral awakening by those with power.

But at least the radical elements in these movements hoped to do much more. Part of the reason that did not happen is that the power brokers in the system immediately began to respond with a combination of concessions and countermobilization. Richard Nixon, famous as an anti-Communist, withdrew U.S. troops from Vietnam, recognized "Red

China," and initiated détente with the Soviet Union. He also proposed and signed into law several important pieces of environmental legislation, a tax reform, increased funding for the arts, and affirmative action regulations; business supported and extended many of these changes.

Although people sometimes think that only out-groups participate in social movements, as business and its allies countermobilized they also took on many of the characteristics of a movement. As one corporate executive told me about the late 1970s: "There was a genuine movement, the closest thing I've ever seen on the part of business in this country. . . . It was a genuine virtual fervor. Let's go out there, and we can do it, we can change the system."[20] Consider just a few elements of that business mobilization.

Point of production. Employers increased direct pressures on workers and unions in a variety of ways. Three of the most important were by refusing to resolve grievances, resisting new organizing, and relocating operations to avoid unions. At General Motors, for example, the number of grievances increased tenfold between 1947 and 1980 (compared to a 30 percent increase in UAW membership). For organizing one measure of an "accord" is an employer's willingness to accept an election to determine whether workers want a union; if the employer simply agrees, rather than insisting on hearings and filing appeals, it is called a consent election. In 1962, 46.1 percent of all NLRB elections were conducted as consent elections; by 1977 only 8.6 percent were. A 1983 study, using systematic quantitative data, concluded that increased employer resistance "is the salient factor in the recent decline in union organizing success."[21]

More important than these visible battles, however, is a more fundamental and far-reaching management strategy. As Thomas Kochan and his collaborators argue, management operates within the collective bargaining agreement at unionized worksites, but channels expansion into new nonunion plants. They argue that the informal rule of thumb is that "no plant which is unionized will be expanded onsite." Nonunion plants get modernized and expanded; unionized plants become gradually obsolescent and the company opens a new operation elsewhere, hoping to keep the union out. One study found that employers have been systematically using this anti-union tactic since long before the 1970s political assault. Klein and Wanger conclude that "most of the union plants were built before the mid-1950s, while those plants built since have remained predominantly nonunion."[22] Corporate power over investment decisions is more important, in this account, than case-by-case resistance.

Policy groups and think tanks. Business had long used think tanks and policy groups to magnify its influence. During the 1970s existing "moderate" groups became more conservative. The Committee for Economic Development, for example, the quintessential "corporate liberal" policy group, began the 1970s as quite liberal, focusing on the social responsibility of corporations and coming close to advocating wage-price controls. By the end of the 1970s, as a result of a series of self-conscious initiatives and interventions by its business members, the group was emphasizing the need for government to operate within the constraints of a market system.[23]

At the same time, new groups were created. Consider, for example, the Trilateral Commission, a policy group formed in 1973 at the behest of David Rockefeller. It brought together business and "public" leaders from Europe, Japan, and the United States to promote the principle that true leadership demanded support for policies that promoted an open world economy—even when those policies hurt the population in the leader's own country.[24]

Conservatives also created or reinvigorated think tanks (Heritage, Hoover, the American Enterprise Institute, and numerous lesser, more specialized groups) to provide a refuge for prominent conservative scholars and politicians, and to promote their work. At the beginning of the 1970s, moderate (by the standards of corporate politics) think tanks and policy groups were funded at three times the level of conservative groups; by 1980 the conservative organizations had substantially more than the moderates.[25]

War of ideas. Corporations and wealthy individuals began to use conservative politics as an explicit factor in targeting charitable contributions. They funded right-wing student newspapers such as the *Dartmouth Review*. Corporations also used their money to create an essentially new form of advertising—what has been called "advocacy advertising" promoting a corporation's public policy positions rather than its products.

Electoral politics. Nor were electoral politics neglected. In 1974, labor Political Action Committees (PACs) outspent business PACs (including both corporate and trade association) by almost a third; in 1980, business gave well over twice as much as labor, and today gives fifteen times as much.[26] Multiplying the importance of this, business changed its strategy to much more aggressively support conservatives, especially conservatives who could displace powerful liberals.

Not only did business forces try to change election outcomes; they also mobilized campaigns around key bills in Congress. The best example of this is what happened in 1978, when labor was perhaps the single most important element in the Democratic coalition and the country had a Democratic president and overwhelming Democratic majorities in Congress. The Labor Law Reform Bill of 1978 was intended by labor not to introduce significant new measures, but simply to provide a means of implementing and enforcing the labor laws already on the books. It would have accomplished this by streamlining some procedures (in order to avoid lengthy delays caused by frivolous employer appeals); slightly increasing some penalties (for example, for firing workers for pro-union activity); and imposing substantially stronger (though still mild) penalties for repeat (but not first-time) labor law violators. Unions believed that most corporations would support the law, or at least not oppose it, since most corporations largely complied with existing law and the new legislation's only significant consequences were for serious labor law violators. Labor was totally surprised when business conducted an all-out mobilization and defeated the bill.[27]

Anti-NLRB campaign. A corporate campaign specifically targeted at labor can serve as an example of the sorts of resources business can and does mobilize. This little-known campaign was one of the first shots in the corporate mobilization, beginning in the mid-1960s when a group of corporate executives were concerned about the "prolabor" character of NLRB decisions. These executives decided that their anti-NLRB protests needed to be more closely coordinated and concluded that a unified long-range effort was needed to change the "climate of public understanding." The business groups had multiple layers: what they called a "Troika" of three key executives, "Twelve Apostles" from "very big blue chip" companies, and a "Blue Ribbon Commission" (BRC) of "more than one hundred management lawyers representing the country's most powerful corporations as well as other employer interests." They commissioned attitude surveys and launched a public relations campaign, but regretted the fact that they had very little substance to work with. Therefore, they decided, "If this Labor Law Study Project is to be launched successfully we will have to create our own climate."[28]

The BRC hired Hill & Knowlton, the world's largest public relations firm, to develop a campaign; member corporations contributed a million dollars to fund the effort. The public relations firm advised that the very existence of the Blue Ribbon Commission and all associated groups be kept secret, and that all efforts appear to be innocent, independent, and spontaneous. Hill & Knowlton collected and doctored for public consumption individual "horror stories" that personalized what could be presented as unfair and irrational NLRB decisions. The agency pledged "that it would meet privately with 'leading liberals' such as John Kenneth Galbraith, David Reisman, Seymour Harris, Robert Heilbroner, and

C. Wright Mills" to see if they expressed sympathy with any elements of the employer attack on the NLRB. If liberals could be found who would express anti-union sentiments, the agency would then arrange media interviews with those who were the "most flexible and amenable."

Simultaneously the agency worked on the media directly.

> Hill & Knowlton said that it would work with television drama writers to get them to put illustrations of unfair labor laws into their continuing series. Television comedy series were also to be used "to focus gentle derision" on the NLRB and organized labor. . . . The agency also planned to get union abuse worked into the story line of nationally syndicated comic strips, such as "Gasoline Alley," "Blondie," "Pogo," or "Peanuts."[29]

The agency did not neglect the long-range payoff that could be had from "influencing junior high and high school textbooks and courses." Efforts were also made to feed "story outlines and data to authors who were regular contributors to 'Think' publications such as *Harper's*, *The Atlantic*, *Commonweal*, *Commentary*, and *Atlas*, because these journals had 'influence entirely disproportionate to their circulation.'" One of the two Hill & Knowlton vice presidents in charge of the campaign was Malcolm Johnson, whose book had formed the basis for the Marlon Brando movie *On the Waterfront*. Johnson—without revealing that he was being paid to create anti-NLRB sentiment—used the "horror stories" the agency had generated as the basis for speeches he gave around the country, explaining "his transformation from a 'starry-eyed' and 'militantly pro-labor' reporter, to a 'disillusioned' member of the Newspaper Guild, to an investigator of union corruption."[30]

This campaign culminated in a set of hearings before a committee chaired by Senator Sam Ervin (of Watergate fame). Theoretically the committee was to examine the role of administrative agencies in governance, but the NLRB was the only agency examined. Virtually everyone who testified before the committee was a member of the (still secret) Blue Ribbon Commission and its so-called Labor Law Reform Project. A conservative columnist, either not in on the secret or possessed of enormous chutzpah, wrote that "if it were merely a matter of professional right-wingers and chronic labor baiters" making these attacks, then "the Ervin hearings would be quickly forgotten." But that, he assured readers, was not the case: testimony came from a wide and impressive range of figures. The only one to attempt to blow the whistle on the effort was Senator Wayne Morse—also the most vigorous elected opponent of the Vietnam war—who gave a speech noting the huge number of almost identical editorials, and arguing that "where there is smoke there is often a speech machine," and "Hill & Knowlton seems to be one of the main smoke machines in this effort to becloud public understanding."[31] This business campaign paid no immediate dividends, but was part of a long-range policy of altering the climate of public opinion and mobilizing the business community to promote aggressively conservative policies.

Labor Mobilization?

In the 1970s, as business's mobilization reached full steam, the labor movement was largely caught by surprise. For the most part both leaders and workers reacted with disbelief, sometimes even with a sense of betrayal. By the 1980s labor fully understood that it was under assault; some unions and locals did their best to accommodate business, and others began to fight back. But in order to fight back unions needed to develop new approaches, and—as is true of most experimentation—there were many more failures than successes. By the 1990s labor had a new set of techniques and some understanding of how thoroughgoing mobilization needed to be in order to win; labor began to win more of the key struggles. The 1995 victory of the Sweeney New Voice AFL-CIO leadership was the central step in that process, and marks a turning point of some kind—though how significant a turning point is yet to be determined. A handful of AFL-CIO affiliates—CWA, SEIU, HERE, UNITE[32]—lead the change process.

The steps that have been taken are arguably bolder and more visionary than any AFL-CIO actions for at least a quarter-century, but they are timid by the standards of what would be needed to transform American politics and reverse labor's decline. Sweeney and other labor leaders deserve high marks for their efforts to change the culture, labor's image, and the terms of debate, as well as for their efforts to form alliances with other movements. There's plenty of room for further improvement, but the change has been dramatic. Consider a couple of examples.

Union Summer, as much as any other single initiative, made clear that the New Voice brought a profoundly different vision. In the late 1960s, when Students for a Democratic Society (SDS), the leading group of radical students, at least among whites, announced a plan to send students to work in factories for the summer, the AFL-CIO denounced the effort. It sent out an advisory warning unions to be on the lookout for infiltrators.[33] In sharp contrast, almost immediately after his election, John Sweeney committed the labor movement to recruiting a thousand young people, mostly college students, to spend three weeks in the summer intensively working with and for the labor movement. Recruits were paid $210 a week, lived together in housing provided by the labor movement, and spent about eighty hours a week learning about the labor movement and working intensively in ongoing campaigns. They marched on picket lines, leafleted the public, met with workers to hear their personal experiences during organizing drives, assisted ongoing drives by accompanying workers in visits to the homes of undecided workers (in union language, "making house calls"), and participated in a wide range of other creative activities. Most of the participants with whom I have spoken found it a transformative experience; some had not previously had contact with workers of any kind and few had had direct experience with the energy and commitment of workers in struggle.

Union Summer, explicitly patterned on the 1964 Freedom Summer, was not intended to give an immediate boost to organizing campaigns, though in some cases it did so. Rather, the goals were twofold: first, to change public perceptions of labor, and second, to create a new generation of student activists who would be focused on (or at least sympathetic to) labor-related issues. The publicity and media accounts were overwhelmingly favorable, and in the process a spotlight was focused on employer practices that normally remain hidden. The image of dedicated college students choosing to fight for workers instead of seeking big bucks for themselves became one of the available tropes for labor, alongside of, and sometimes replacing, that of the cigar-chomping union "boss." The AFL-CIO hoped that Union Summer graduates would follow through and create groupings of student labor activists on campuses around the country. Within two years the antisweatshop movement emerged full-blown on a wide range of college campuses. In a break with the previous quarter-century, student activism was now centered on labor issues. As such, Union Summer must be judged a resounding success.

That same eagerness to change the culture was shown in a "teach-in with the labor movement" at Columbia University attended by two thousand people (many times more than originally expected) and following that three dozen other teach-ins around the country. At the founding of an organization formed to further develop these connections John Sweeney made it clear that he expected the group to disagree with the labor movement on various issues, and encouraged it to do so—a major change from unions' previous attitude.

The new generation of labor leaders has also been eager to work with a range of other groups. Labor leaders have eagerly sought out churches and faith-based activist groups. They've joined living wage campaigns. They've supported the global justice movement. Sweeney created a Working Women's Department to advocate for working women.[34] Jobs with Justice is an organization started by the left wing of the labor movement and long regarded with suspicion by much of labor as a kind of dual unionism that might be opposed to "real" unions. "Some AFL-CIO headquarters officials initially questioned whether Jobs With Justice was still needed in light of the Sweeney Administration's own plans to revitalize labor," but the federation subsequently gave a hundred-thousand-dollar contribution and a letter of support.[35] The money wasn't much, but enough to demonstrate commitment. Jobs with Justice builds ties with community groups, and asks members to support each other's struggles, and to pledge to "be there" at least five times a year for one of the group's officially endorsed actions. When I interviewed Marilyn Schneiderman, the new head of AFL-CIO Field Mobilization, I noted her program sounded like it was borrowed from Jobs with Justice, and she replied, "There's nothing wrong with that."

These changes are extremely positive—and many more such could be enumerated—but labor's record is more mixed in other areas and sorely lacking in a couple of key dimensions. The record is mixed, I would say, in the commitment of resources, in the willingness to rethink the very concept of what a union is and does, and in creating a sense of crisis. Unions talk about committing 30 percent of their resources to organizing—and with a total of five billion dollars a year in revenue that would provide the resources for a major push—but almost no unions in fact do so. Labor has embraced graduate student (and other unconventional) unions as well as living wage campaigns, but most thinking about what a union is and does is still bound within the limits of "this is what unions always [in the speaker's experience] have been." Labor often says that labor law is in crisis and that workers have lost the right to organize, and it issues press releases and holds mild-mannered demonstrations to make the point. But most of the public is completely unaware of the barriers workers face if they try to form a union, the vicious employer actions that are routine in organizing drives, and the extent to which outrageous violations of worker rights are legal under existing law and court interpretations. Certainly there is no sense that this is a crisis, or that restoring worker rights is a moral imperative.

Labor's record is weakest in fostering internal debate, encouraging internal democracy, and empowering rank-and-file workers. The revitalized AFL-CIO news sources—which are dramatically more appealing than those they replaced—include snippets of letters to the editor, but have yet to include a single serious debate on any question of significance. Democracy is messy, and has its problems. But without vibrant internal democracy, unions inevitably turn bureaucratic. Look at all the good that resulted from one contested election; imagine what would happen if this were a regular feature not only in the central AFL-CIO, but also in the sixty-six federated unions.

The most serious limitation of the "new" labor movement, a limitation closely related to the problems with debate and democracy, is the failure to empower or activate the rank and file. The model is still staff-driven. At the staff level, there has been a clear paradigm shift in terms of the kinds of people hired and the language they speak. A substantial proportion of the new staff are past participants in, or at least are comfortable with the culture of, the new social movements. For those who are based in such middle-class movements, and for those in and around college and university towns, communication with the new union staff is easy and comfortable because they often share a common language and past experiences. The New Voice leadership is willing to be arrested at demonstrations, but has made little or no effort to empower rank-and-file movements. Substantial resources have gone into recruiting college students (as organizers, for Union Summer), but no equivalent efforts have been made to design innovative programs for rank-and-file members. Steve Early's powerful critique notes a host of problems with "parachuting in" college students as opposed to relying on member organizers. AFL-CIO leaders and staff publicly favor activating the rank and file, but do not necessarily support it in practice—and may not know what would be needed to do so.[36]

This should not be surprising; in some sense it is a restatement of the (obvious) fact that we are not now in a period of upsurge. The new generation of progressive labor leaders—people like John Sweeney at the AFL-CIO, John Wilhelm at HERE, and Bruce Raynor at UNITE—did not win their positions as leaders of social movements from below, but rather by working their way up through the bureaucracy. They and other progressive leaders were able to win power because key players recognized the labor movement was in crisis and needed talented individuals with fresh ideas. Although there have always been left and rank-and-file movements inside the labor movement, their influence has not increased in the last couple of decades, and with the important exception of Teamsters for a Democratic Union they have not been a major factor. The talents that brought progressive labor leaders to power are not the same as the talents that would be needed to foster and lead a rank-and-file movement from below.

Today's most progressive union leaders are operating from the top down. They are incredibly smart people, with a long-run vision, fostering active efforts to change the culture, seeking to help create a new political-economic-social alignment of forces. But any top-down effort, and any effort that relies primarily on staff, will necessarily be thin, particularly given the decentralized and fragmented character of the labor movement. The arrival of these new leaders generated a sense of excitement. Now, several years later, excitement is gone, or at least is rarer and harder to muster. A new leadership has not been able to increase labor's membership, and hopes of a quick fix have ended. It's clear that top-down changes won't be able to reverse the slide. What might it take to do so?

Labor can't simply replicate what corporations did, because labor is positioned very differently from business in both its strengths and its weaknesses. However, labor can and should learn a great deal from the corporate mobilization. First, such a campaign requires fighting on all fronts. This means changing the culture; shifting underlying common sense about what is and is not reasonable; creating an institutional infrastructure to facilitate and undergird this transformation (and doing so through both new institutions and the transformation of existing arrangements); breaking with conventional political wisdom; forming alliances with other groups; and taking nothing for granted. Second, quick results are not to be expected, or even sought. Business began a full-scale mobilization by the early 1970s, and was surprised to achieve victory as early as 1980–81, a victory embodied not just in election results but in sweeping policy changes. Third, business's political mobilization was controversial inside the business community; only a minority of corporations were full participants and some harsh words were exchanged, but the mobilization leaders were ultimately backed (or at least not opposed) by the more passive corporations. Fourth, business was not afraid to push hard, to be aggressive, to politicize what had previously been considered beyond the appropriate bounds of politics (such as charitable contributions or relations with universities), and to take risks (as it did in 1980 in opposing powerful Democratic incumbents who chaired key committees). Labor can't expect to win unless it does at least as much.

The business unionism that dominated labor for at least a quarter-century, and which still has a major presence, focused overwhelmingly on playing it safe, winning improvements for those already in unions, sticking to limited workplace concerns (above all wages and benefits), using insider political strategies such as campaign contributions and lobbying, defending the union's treasury, and avoiding entanglements with larger movements or issues that might involve controversy. If labor wanted to reverse our nation's political direction, create a more just and equitable world, and help workers win at least a voice at work, and if the labor movement were prepared to take some risks, its strategy—as opposed to business's—would need to rely not on material resources but on people. Solidarity by large numbers of people—not just leaders, not just staff—is the most powerful force labor has available. If workers, family members, and community allies develop solidarity and are prepared to take risks and make commitments, there is no limit to what they can accomplish.

Some possibilities:

1. Unions would bring workers together to talk about their problems, to share stories and frustrations, and building from that would intensively educate and mobilize their own members. Rather than beginning the discussion within the framework of "this is what is politically feasible," people would talk about what they want and need, and would move from that to thinking about what would be necessary to achieve it. A lot of anger and frustration would come out; people would identify problems that could not be immediately solved, and that process would involve risks. Labor would help mobilize people's sense of inequity, create a sense of moral righteousness about an alternative program, and push it hard.

2. Labor would need to be willing to fundamentally rethink the very concept of what a union is and how it operates. Just as business pushed to deregulate industries, just as corporations underwent mergers and downsizing, unions would need to be ready for fundamental restructuring. This would begin with democratic transformation but also include a realignment so that all health care workers, or all teachers, were in one organization, with the added leverage that would provide. Unions would ignore the definitions in existing labor law, insisting that new groups (managers, students, maids) are entitled to unions. Unions would take up new issues—even if these issues were not envisaged in 1935 when the Wagner Act was passed.

3. Unions would form alliances with other movements and groups, and be prepared to push hard for those issues. The underlying rationale would be that labor is prepared to take up any problem that workers and their families face. New forms would blend union and community or see work-family issues as fundamental to the problems today's workers face.

4. There would be a larger push to change the culture and the terms of

debate—in the media, in colleges and universities, in churches and city councils. People would stop accepting corporate and media formulations such as "antiglobalization movement" or "replacement workers" and would call things what they really are (global justice movement, scabs).

5. Labor would be willing to put major resources into this push. Doing so would require that some other tasks go unfunded, or that dues be raised. And of course workers couldn't be asked to sacrifice unless union leaders and staff led the way; any mobilization would be doomed if workers were asked to support expanded staff for business-as-usual approaches.

6. Last but by no means least, labor would need to create a sense of crisis. Business can do so through its dominance of the media and the economy; labor would need to undertake dramatic actions. Labor might pick a highly visible target and lead mass civil disobedience. Or unions might decide that, since the National Labor Relations Board election process does not protect worker rights, unions would henceforth refuse to use it, that they would organize unions only through non-Board campaigns of various sorts. Whatever action is taken, unions need to be willing to break the rules. Inevitably, a few militant unions will take the biggest risks and will drive the process; a larger group needs to support these actions and speak up in their favor.

Taken together, these sorts of actions, together with similar activities by other social movements and community groups, would change people's sense of what's possible and increase the chances for a new round of social movements. Actions and consciousness would develop together, each reinforcing the other. If such a transformation comes, John Sweeney may or may not support it, but will have helped to make it possible.

How likely is an upsurge leading to a revival of labor? No one knows, and if it happens it may be triggered by some yet unanticipated event(s). Perhaps it will be a corporate scandal, like Enron; perhaps an economic crisis; perhaps a group of workers whose militance and issues catch the public imagination. I'm an incurable optimist, so despite the widespread (and totally justified) sense of pessimism, this book focuses on some of the good reasons to be optimistic: the global justice movement, antisweatshop struggles, living wage campaigns, the emergence of a set of labor leaders with a long-run vision who eagerly pursue alliances with other movements. For at least two decades political-economic actions have given great benefits to the rich while squeezing workers and the middle class. Business, working with sympathetic politicians in both parties and a range of media and "intellectuals," has largely succeeded in a task that in 1974 *Business Week* saw as posing an incredible challenge: "It will be a hard pill for many Americans to swallow—the idea of doing with less so that big business can have more. . . . Nothing that this nation, or any other nation, has done in modern economic history compares in difficulty with the selling job that must now be done to make people accept the new reality."[37] The task for labor and the progressive left is far easier. It "only" has to find ways to assist people in fighting for and winning what they already want: a sense of community, the power to have some meaningful level of control over the decisions that shape their own lives, and the dignity and respect to be accepted as full and equal participants in our society.

3

Gender Styles and Union Issues

The 1930s upsurge created the New Deal labor regime. It was subsequently modified not simply by the employer assault, not only by labor's struggles, but also by changes in society and the political economy. The world today differs from 1935, and even if the labor regime were unchanged (an impossibility), it would look and feel very different given the new shape of society.

Asked to name the social-economic changes since the 1930s with the greatest implications for the labor movement, the first response by most of my friends is "globalization." Clearly that's important (see chapter 5). Much less frequently mentioned is another profound shift: the dramatic increase in the number of women, especially women with children, who work for pay outside the home, a change that is so ubiquitous, and so thoroughly pervades almost all our lives, that it sometimes goes unremarked. In 1900 only 4 percent of married women were in the labor force, by 1940 this had increased only to 17 percent. In sharp contrast, in 1999, 71 percent of married women were in the labor force, as were 58 percent of married mothers with children under one year old.[1]

Gender is a system of power that privileges men and disadvantages women. It is built into the structure of major institutions—the family and employment as well as unions—and into cultural expectations. Like any system of power, it can only be maintained by constant effort by some and acquiescence by others. Historically, unions sometimes contested male power, but more frequently helped to reproduce it. Unions (and male workers) often worked to exclude women from the best jobs, and rarely fought for meaningful gender equality.

This chapter considers a variety of efforts to reshape unions so that they do more to address women's concerns. After some brief background information on changes in women's work and family lives, and on the gender composition of unions and jobs, the chapter examines the relationship between the labor movement and the early women's movement. Had these movements been able to fully connect, it might have transformed both labor and the women's movement. In regretting the failure of these movements to connect, I do not intend to imply that if only this or that leader had taken a different stance, history might have taken a different course. There are good historical reasons why labor and the feminist movement so rarely connected. Unions were male-dominated, insular, and conservative. Many of the women who were the leading edge of Second Wave feminism were radicals opposed to the conservative white establishment, which in their view included union leaders. These radicals were usually college-educated, from professional-managerial class backgrounds, and not in the long term holding working-class jobs. McCarthyism and the Taft-Hartley Act's requirement that radicals/Communists be expelled from unions eliminated the groups most likely to help connect labor to other social movements.[2] Many labor-feminist struggles of course did take place—this chapter looks at some of them—and the people who were working to build that sort of movement are those whom I most admire and with whom I identify. But, for a variety of reasons, there were too few such people and too much resistance to their efforts. They've created a base on which to build, but an upsurge would require a much more thoroughgoing transformation than has so far been achieved.

Much of this chapter looks at union campaigns and activities around two issues of central concern to many women workers, pay equity and work-family issues. Emphasizing different issues is one part of creating unions that will solve women's most pressing concerns (and of course work-family issues are also of concern to many men). But another reason that unions sometimes fail to appeal to women is the macho style prevalent in many unions. Some male union leaders judge toughness and commitment by whether someone—male or female—swears like a truck driver, uses vulgar sexual allusions, and works sixteen hours a day with no interruption (ever) for family. Although that style has some strengths, it also involves significant weaknesses, especially for women, but also for many men. A drive to unionize Harvard University's clerical and technical workers developed a distinctive style for both the organizing campaign and the subsequent union contract, a style emphasizing connection, support, and a reduction of tension. Kris Rondeau, the lead organizer, says that in doing so "we created our own culture." It's a style that is probably especially appropriate to white-collar jobs, but that I believe offers important lessons for the labor movement as a whole. Many in the labor movement, however, strongly object to the Rondeau-Harvard approach—and this is true of women at least as much as men. The sharpest criticism I received on the manuscript focused on my inclusion of, and admiration for, this approach, which many see as in conflict with the rest of the book's message. The chapter's conclusion tackles these issues; I would argue that the sharp disagreement indicates something important is at stake.[3]

Although women have pioneered most of the changes discussed in this chapter, these innovations are not "for women only" and many women prefer more traditional approaches and issues. (As one woman who read an earlier draft noted to me: "Some of us like conflict and militance, and join unions for that.") The campaigns, issues, and union style discussed here are not typical of most current organizing among women workers; all the campaigns discussed here focus on clerical workers, and two out of three qualify as private sector. A study asking California labor leaders to identify recent labor successes found that less than 10 percent of the campaigns mentioned concerned pink- or white-collar workers even though they constitute more than 60 percent of the California work force.[4] Most current campaigns to unionize women address the same issues, in roughly the same ways, as campaigns to unionize men. From 1975 to 1985 pay equity and comparable worth seemed the wave of the future, and the issues continue to top the charts in the AFL-CIO's "Ask a Working Woman" survey, but neither pay equity nor child care feature in very many of today's organizing campaigns. If the issue is where the labor movement is currently succeeding at incremental change—which is important—this chapter is looking in all the wrong places. But the kind of major transformation involved in an upsurge will require profound changes in who gets included in unions, their internal style-culture, and the issues they see as appropriate and central.

Women, Work, and Unions

A typical woman who came of age during the Great Depression, when the New Deal labor regime was forged, could expect to live in her father's house until she married and moved into her husband's house. She would have been unlikely to go to college—in 1940, fewer than 10 percent of women had completed even one year of college.[5] She might well have worked for pay for a few years before marrying, probably giving part of her pay to her parents but also gaining some independence through her earnings. If white, at marriage or soon thereafter she almost certainly quit paid work outside the home to do housework and child care. She also stayed married to the same man—even if unhappy in the marriage—quite possibly never again working for pay, or not doing so until in her fifties, when her children were grown and out of the house. (Black women were much more likely to work for pay even if married.) Women had little opportunity to develop economic independence and, at least until widowed, rarely lived on their own. Given these conditions, the focus—by women as well as men—was on the need for men to earn a "family wage," enough to support a family at a decent level.

A typical woman coming of age fifty years later, in the 1980s or 1990s, had almost a fifty-fifty chance of attending college, worked full time after completing her schooling, lived on her own for some years, was much more likely to use birth control and legal abortion, married at a later age, and had roughly a one-in-two chance of experiencing divorce or separation. Like her Depression counterpart, she did a large majority of the housework and child care, but also kept right on working for pay, frequently with brief interruptions for childbirth and infancy but in many cases working even when her children were infants. These structural changes—college, later marriage, divorce, and her own income— made it more possible, and more necessary, for a woman to develop some independence, to be less tightly and directly tied to a man. In 1940, more than two-thirds of all families had employed husbands and stay-at-home wives, but today less than one in five families fit that pattern while more than 40 percent have dual earners and more than 10 percent are headed by an employed single mother. In families where both the mother and father work full time year-round, "wives contribute over 40 percent of the total household income" and 21 percent of such women earn more than their husbands.[6]

Profound as have been the changes in jobs and in women's employment, there have been equally significant shifts in what it means to be men and women and how they relate to each other. As recently as the 1960s, the idea of equality between men and women was a subject of ridicule in the House of Representatives.[7] Laws, college rules, and job ads openly discriminated against women. At work as well as at home, men expected women to do personal services such as preparing and serving coffee. Today even conservative men declare support for equal treatment at work and in law, although inequality in family and in caring tasks is often regarded as acceptable.

Another major change in the labor force has developed at the same time as, and in interaction with, the increase in women's employment: a shift from the manufacturing to the service sector. In 1940, the number of manual workers exceeded the number of white-collar workers by more than 25 percent; in 1998 there were more than twice as many white-collar workers as manual workers. Women are much more likely than men to be white-collar workers. Among men today, there are almost as many blue-collar as white-collar workers; among women, there are fully seven times as many white-collar as blue-collar workers.[8]

Related to this, women are less likely than men to be represented by unions: in 2000, 15.2 percent of male workers, but only 11.5 percent of women workers, were union members. That means, however, that four out of ten union members are women, a dramatic change from 1940, when only one in ten were.[9] Women are still underrepresented in unions, but a majority (55 percent) of new union members are women, and almost a third of all organizing campaigns are in units composed of at least 75 percent women.[10] Leadership has not changed as much. The first woman did not become a member of the AFL-CIO Executive Council until 1980; even today only 13 percent of the council are women and 20 percent are people of color (which is nonetheless a substantially higher percentage than is found among corporate executives). Women are now about a quarter of all lead organizers; in campaigns where the unit is 75 percent or more women, women are 42 percent of the lead organizers.

No future union upsurge will be possible without a gender breakthrough, because in the future, as in the past few decades, most of the fastest-growing occupations will be "women's jobs." Over the next decade, the dozen fastest-growing occupations are projected to be (in order): cashiers, systems analysts, general managers and top executives, registered nurses, retail salespersons, truck drivers, home health aides, teacher aides and educational assistants, nursing aides (including orderlies and attendants), receptionists, secondary-school teachers, and child care workers.[11] Nine out of twelve of these (all but systems analysts, general managers and top executives, and truck drivers) are predominantly female jobs, and seven of the twelve are more than 75 percent female. Unions must incorporate areas of the economy that predominantly employ women, both from self-interest—that's the only way they can grow—and because it's the only way to represent and address the concerns of a large fraction of the workforce.

An Opportunity Lost

Dorothy Sue Cobble persuasively argues that "Our understanding of the cycles of feminism in the twentieth century has been class biased, based primarily on the activities of elite women." Her work shows the existence of a labor feminism that might have formed the basis for connections between labor and Second Wave (1965–75) feminism. In the 1950s and 1960s, in several unions women constituted either a majority or a substantial minority of members; top national leaders were overwhelmingly men, but women activists operated at the local level. These women organized to advance their interests not only as workers and union members, but specifically as women workers. Equal pay demands, for example, underwent a transformation. Once made by male unionists as a way to ensure that employers would exclude women, by the 1940s "equal pay became a demand supported largely by women" and specifically by women in unions where women constituted a large fraction of the membership. The International Union of Electrical Workers (IUE), 35 percent of whose members were women, held its first National Women's Conference in 1957, bringing together 175 women from around the country. They not only called on GE and Westinghouse to grant "equal pay," but also explained that "by this we mean not only equal pay for identical work but equal pay for work of equal value no matter where it is done," a clear statement of the comparable worth concept. By the end of the 1950s, for example, every single culinary contract in California included equal pay.[12]

The positions taken by union women were not always the same as those dominant in the women's movement that developed in the late 1960s and thereafter. Most unionized women favored protective legislation; most in the Second Wave [1960s–70s] women's movement condemned it. These differences are probably explained in significant part by structural location; the professionals of Second Wave feminism were actively competing for men's jobs. Even among unionized women in the 1940s and 1950s, "Women competing directly with men often favored repeal because the laws put them at a disadvantage in securing employment; women who were more insulated from direct competition (usually as the result of strong sex typing of jobs) saw protective laws as beneficial." Protective legislation was no threat to waitresses and hotel maids, and its benefits were important to them:

> Former hotel maid Bertha Metro, representing the primarily black Hotel and Club Service Workers, declared that many working women with children in day care would be forced to quit their jobs if required to work overtime. "Who's going to pick up the kids, cook their dinner?" asked Elizabeth Kelley of the San Francisco Waitresses' Union. "We're happy that we have a little legislation, and we'll fight to keep it. We're not a bunch of college women, we're waitresses."

When the women's movement revived, and the Equal Rights Amendment (ERA) came to the fore, there was never a question of extending protection to male workers. Instead, as IUE officers noted in a 1971 statement to the House, the amendment was "a force eliminating benefits rather than creating any." Waitress vice president Myra Wolfgang saw the ERA as a proposal promoted "by 'middle class, professional woman, college girl oriented' activists who did not act in the best interest of working-class women." In the Hotel Employees and Restaurant Employees (HERE) union, many waitress locals were sex-segregated, open only to women. "A 1974 court ruling banning sex-segregated HERE locals weakened waitresses' decades-old practices of single-sex exclusivity and confirmed their worst fears"—ironically at about the time that many in the women's movement were insisting on separatism. Initially many unions opposed the ERA, but this changed in the early 1970s, and by 1973 the AFL-CIO and most major unions had endorsed it.[13]

Few connections developed between late 1960s Second Wave feminism and the union women's movement. As Cobble notes: "By the late 1960s the postwar generation of working-class feminists felt the sting of rejection by the younger equal rights feminists who came to dominate the movement."[14] Although there was of course enormous variation within the Second Wave women's movement, most younger college-educated feminists had little consciousness of, much less interaction or political alliance with, older trade union feminists.

This is ironic because Betty Friedan, whose book *The Feminine Mystique* was crucial in launching Second Wave feminism, herself came out of the labor movement feminism of the 1940s and 1950s—a fact she took great pains to conceal. Friedan had written pamphlets attacking sexism when she worked for the electrical workers' union, UE (United Electrical Workers), a union with a high proportion of women and a strong left presence. Although she later presented herself as a political naif, she had been intimately involved in a union and milieu where feminist issues were much discussed. In addition, one of the driving forces behind the formation of the National Organization of Women (NOW) was the flood of sexual discrimination charges filed as soon as the Equal Employment Opportunities Commission (EEOC) opened in the summer of 1965. More than twenty-five hundred were filed in the first year alone; the complainants were "overwhelmingly working-class and often trade union members."[15]

Second Wave feminism generated a huge outburst of spontaneous activity in the late 1960s and early 1970s, primarily but by no means exclusively among young college-educated women. Probably the most famous element of this was consciousness-raising groups focused on personal life and intimate relationships, but another significant form of activity was the workplace-based women's caucus. An article in the second issue of *Ms.* magazine, in August 1972, explained:

> It usually happens at lunch. Several women co-workers are sitting at a table, and a very angry colleague joins them. She has suffered one of the routine slights all women are subjected to on the job, but for some reason, this one was the last straw, and she's ready to say so. There is a pause after she speaks, and then the floodgates open. . . . Before that historic lunch ends, plans have been made for an employees' meeting to discuss job discrimination. And out of that meeting, another women's caucus will be born, to go forth and do battle with management.[16]

These caucuses, the article stated, were known to exist at more than a hundred companies, including many of the largest and best known of the Fortune 500.

The labor movement—and the women's movement—lost a huge opportunity when unions failed to connect to, and assist, this spontaneous self-organization around labor-related issues. Wage-earning women in the 1960s "could expect to have to provide personal services to the men in their work places, to clean up after them, and to endure demeaning familiarities from them as a condition of employment." The response was predictable: *Ms.* stressed that *"Without exception, a principal demand of the women's caucuses is for respect,"*[17] exactly the same issue that is central to most union organizing drives. The caucuses often debated whether or not to unionize, but few chose to do so, partly because "many women office workers believe that unions have not represented women's interests" and partly because "women are aware that employers react violently to the idea of unionization." Instead of unionizing, the caucuses typically "secured a lawyer and filed charges with the EEOC" (Equal Employment Opportunity Commission). The women who initiated these actions were often professionals who found that to strengthen their charges they had to broaden their ranks and include lower-level women; making these connections was sometimes a struggle.[18]

Innovative organizing in response to caucuses came not from the labor movement, but rather from feminist-based groups like "9 to 5," organized and operating not like traditional unions, but more in the style characteristic of the "public interest" movement (see chapter 1). "Neither professional associations nor unions, office worker organizations constituted a new model, one that used research, creative publicity, and media-savvy direct action." The approach adopted by these groups had much to offer the labor movement. Today many unions have fully incorporated these tactics, but in the 1970s they were almost unheard-of (in labor circles). Karen Nussbaum was one of the founders of "9 to 5," which eventually turned itself into a union, and later she became director of the AFL-CIO Working Women's Department. According to Nussbaum, in 1976, "When we started . . . the union people scorned women. They didn't care to take the time with us women, who didn't know anything about unions."[19]

The missed connection between the far too weak labor feminism, and the far too professional-managerially oriented Second Wave feminism, hampered the development of both labor and feminism and undercut the ability to win advances for working-class women. If the two movements had more fully connected, unions today would have an entirely different character, as would the women's movement, and together they would have pushed the transformation of American society much further down the road. Instead of labor declining in the 1970s and thereafter, it might have been rejuvenated, not only in the number of members but in its sense of purpose. The women's movement might have reached far deeper into the working class. Together those changes would have benefited many women. Wages are by no means the most important part of this, but they are one indicator. Since the 1970s higher-paid women have benefited far more than working-class women. For the bottom third of women, wages declined; for the top third, wages increased by double-digit percentages.[20] The low pay many women receive is one of the factors demonstrating both the need and the potential for a strengthened labor feminism.

Pay Equity

Equal pay for women (and people of color!) is likely to be a priority issue for a revitalized labor movement. The other issues discussed in this chapter—organizing style and work-family concerns—clearly benefit men as well as women. Pay equity has the potential to pit women against men; it is remarkable that, at least in the Yale case, men strongly supported women's demands.

In 1965 and in 1975 women earned less than sixty cents for every dollar men earned; by 1999 the figure was up to 76.9 percent.[21] Both sides of the coin need to be emphasized: substantial progress in achieving pay equity, with large remaining inequities. Moreover, the "progress" comes primarily from a reduction in men's earnings rather than from an increase in women's wages.

Little of the current pay inequity is a result of women being paid less than men doing exactly the same job. Most of the problem comes from gender-segregated employment in which men and women are assigned to different jobs, and any job performed primarily by women is paid less, even if the skills it demands are almost identical to those of a similar "men's" job. In response, comparable worth says that jobs should be compared and assessed, then pay rates set to reflect the actual level of skill and responsibility required. For a time, comparable worth seemed a cutting-edge issue; for the past fifteen years it has largely disappeared from the agenda, but that's not because pay equity has been achieved. Although both labor and academics now focus much more on work-family issues (discussed in the next section) than on pay equity, in 1997, when the AFL-CIO Working Women's department did its "Ask a Working Woman" survey, pay equity was respondents' number one issue.

San Jose

In the city of San Jose workers put the issue of comparable worth on the agenda, at first operating outside their union, and then through it. San Jose had a woman mayor, women were a majority of the members of the city council, the state representative and deputy city manager were women, and the city proclaimed itself "the feminist capital of the nation."[22] But a feminist employer is still an employer, and the city government opposed the workers at every step. Victory came only as the result of a strike.

What eventually became an important union drive began in a women's caucus not connected to a union. Clerical workers, upset at their low pay and blocked career mobility, in 1973 formed City Women for Advancement, meeting monthly for lunch and thereby forming new networks. At the same time, library professionals—80 percent of them women—also began to mobilize to gain more reward and recognition, forming Concerned Library Active Workers (CLAW). Although neither group used the term "comparable worth," they began to make charts comparing specific men's and women's jobs in terms of skill levels, training requirements, and degrees of responsibility and authority.

Initially, neither CLAW nor City Women for Advancement saw a union as a means of seeking redress, but soon they reached out to the union, and at the next election librarians swept most of the key positions. The union, Local 101 of the American Federation of State, County, and Municipal Employees (AFSCME), had a new business agent "with a background in both feminist and union activity and a commitment to integrating the two"[23] who introduced them to the formal notion of comparable worth.

The women reluctantly decided that in order to get more recognition and a substantial pay raise they would need to support a formal job classification study, conducted by supposedly neutral outside experts. Such studies are a problematic union weapon: the experts who conduct them are hired by management and depend on its approval for future business.

Both San Jose's city manager and Hay Associates, the company doing the study, had assumed the union would withdraw once a study began, but instead, through mass mobilization and relentless pressure, the union took effective control of the process. "The city had originally planned to include only one employee representative on the ten-member evaluation committee, and had not intended even to provide the union with a copy of the completed report."[24]

Instead, under union pressure, the city council decided to deemphasize market factors, those appointed to the committee were primarily workers (with the union careful to be sure they were not all from the union, so the committee could not be dismissed as a union front), and workers became actively engaged in evaluating their own jobs. Although Hay Associates tried to keep their job-rating methodology secret, city workers used their research skills to find published articles that included details on Hay's charts and techniques. "Union clerical and library activists organized lunch-hour workshops on the questionnaires" and trained each other on how to make the most effective case for the importance and difficulty of their jobs. They then fought hard to have all relevant aspects of their jobs included in the job descriptions. One librarian reported that "we protested some descriptions three or four times because we wanted all of the important things we do included." Workers' active engagement in the process helped develop their awareness of the skills their work involved and built interest in the results. "Expert" studies typically mystify and depoliticize an issue. In this case the study became a vehicle for union mobilization and worker empowerment. By the end of the study process, (women) workers were more than ever convinced that pay inequities existed and needed to be addressed.[25]

As a result of this union pressure, "the study found that female-dominated jobs paid 15–25 percent less than the comparable male-dominated jobs" and presented five specific and dramatic comparisons. The city tried to keep the results confidential, but copies were widely circulated, and many workers knew exactly where they fell. In contrast to an earlier study of management jobs, after which raises had been promptly implemented, the city resisted responding to the study of workers' jobs. When it became clear that the city would not provide the raises called for by the study, a one-day sick-out was held, called "Hay Fever Day." After additional months of agitation, workers went out on strike for nine days. When the (woman-majority) city council refused to accept the initial agreement reached by city negotiators and the union, union members were outraged, storming the council chambers and picketing the mayor's house until a deal was reached.

This was a dramatic mobilization and in some sense a union victory, but with numerous qualifications. The publicity for the strike was impressive, with a front-page story in the *New York Times* as well as coverage in the *Washington Post, Wall Street Journal, Los Angeles Times, Time,* and *Newsweek,* and on television. But participation in the strike, even though it was relatively brief, did not reach the level that would normally be needed to gain a victory; the union business agent estimated that only five hundred of the two thousand workers went on strike. Union membership increased somewhat in the aftermath of the strike, but not dramatically. On the one hand, this is troubling; on the other, most major advances by both unions and social movements have depended on the mobilization of a relatively small minority willing to take substantial risks and backed by the passive support of a larger number. And it's worth noting that today San Jose's labor council, headed by Amy Dean, is one of the best and most innovative in the nation.

Organizing and Comparable Worth at Yale

Workers at Yale mobilized what was in many ways an even more impressive campaign, against a much more hostile employer, and in the process solidified an alliance between the mostly women clerical workers and the mostly men maintenance workers. The two groups were represented by two separate locals of the Hotel Employees and Restaurant Employees (HERE) union. Although the union never used the term "comparable worth," the organizing and strike were centrally about pay equity.

Despite its high ideals and lofty reputation, for many years Yale treated its workers shabbily. Yale's 1971 graduation was disrupted by club-wielding New Haven police attacking striking blue-collar workers. After two failed drives by other unions, in 1980 HERE Local 35, Yale's maintenance and custodial workers, began a campaign to organize clerical and technical workers.[26]

Members of Local 35 had concluded they would always be vulnerable, and have a tough time winning improved conditions, as long as only a small minority of Yale workers were unionized. The largely male workforce of Local 35, a substantial proportion of them people of color, therefore decided to provide staff and resources to assist a clerical organizing drive to create a largely female Local 34 (which is about 20 percent people of color). The lead organizer for the HERE drive was John Wilhelm, a Yale graduate, who has since gone on to help direct impressive organizing campaigns in Las Vegas, and now serves as national president of HERE. The campaign was tactically brilliant, consistently catching Yale off guard.

The Yale and Harvard clerical worker organizing drives provide interesting comparisons and contrasts. (Harvard's drive is discussed in this chapter's final section.) The basic situations were similar in several ways. Both were spectacular union successes in the 1980s. They took place at our nation's two leading private universities. Yale's unit, similar to Harvard's, was 82 percent women, with 2,600 workers scattered in 220 buildings. The drives were led by two outstanding organizers and built vibrant locals with high levels of worker participation. At both Harvard and Yale, the union won by only the slimmest of margins, at Harvard by 44 votes and at Yale by 39 votes out of 2,500. The two campaigns were similar in many ways, because good organizers use many of the same tactics. At Yale as at Harvard, "During the first year and a half of the union drive, they used no leaflets, buttons, or membership cards, just talk."[27] At both Harvard and Yale the strategy emphasized not issues but personal contact.

The two campaigns differed in two notable and presumably related ways. First, at Harvard, the lead organizer (Kris Rondeau) and most of the organizing team were women; at Yale, the lead organizer (John Wilhelm) and most of the organizing team were men. Second, the campaigns differed in their ways of dealing with worker fear and tension. As this chapter's final section emphasizes, Harvard's union campaign stressed reducing the fear and tension through humor, one-to-one contact to lower the stress level, and reducing the level of confrontation ("It's not anti-Harvard to be pro-union"). Yale's union campaign dealt with fear and tension through mass solidarity and public confrontation. Like the Rhode Island Hospital drive discussed in the beginning of this book, the campaign was officially and publicly launched in what the union called "standing together": a statement signed by four hundred people publicly identifying themselves as union supporters. The aim of the statement was to use mass solidarity to break down

a lot of the fear that people have about what it means to be in a union. . . . Many of our organizing committee members started out by saying, "Well, all right, I'm for the union. I'm crazy. I will do anything for the union. I will sign my name publicly; the boss can fire me; I don't care. I'm proud of being from the union, but you're not going to ask me to get my co-worker to stick her neck out." And we said, "Wrong! We *are* going to ask you to get your co-worker, not to stick her neck out, but sign and go public, because that saves all of our necks."[28]

Instead of the Harvard strategy of reducing tension in order to maintain friendly relations with everyone, Yale involved a more traditional strategy of workers pushing not only the university, but also each other. As one worker explained, although their actions "brought with them a lot of controversy," they "rested on the basic belief that, if we push each other and struggle with each other and respect each other, ultimately what we do is push Yale. When members say to me, 'I don't like being pushed,' I reply, 'It beats being crushed.'"[29]

Yale's workers won the election on May 18, 1983, and immediately focused on developing contract proposals, with over four hundred organizing committee members distributing questionnaires to both union and non-union workers. The Yale administration, demonstrating the bizarre and laughable strategies often used by employers, stalled by claiming there was nowhere on the Yale campus to meet. Since clerical workers routinely scheduled rooms and had no trouble finding space, it took chutzpah to make such a claim. After almost a year of this, workers voted to authorize a strike for the end of the month, put off the strike three times, then accepted a partial contract and kept negotiating.

In wage increase negotiations the union's campaign emphasized comparable worth issues, including explicit comparisons between the qualifications and salaries of clerical workers and those of others on campus, but without ever using the term "comparable worth." Numerous factors led the union to avoid the term. First, "comparable worth" had become virtually synonymous with "must be determined through a neutral study by experts" and in any such contest Yale, with its enormous prestige and stable of world-renowned authorities, would have a huge advantage in debates over credibility—even were it promoting a position as silly as its claim that no rooms were available on campus for negotiations. Second, the clerical and technical workers, newly organized in Local 34 of HERE, had been strongly supported at every stage by the overwhelmingly male blue-collar workforce of Local 35. Comparable worth comparisons could potentially take the form "the women of Local 34 are underpaid, the men of Local 35 are overpaid." Local 34's strategy "has not been to say, 'I'm a secretary and I should make as much as a truck driver,' but rather, 'I do important work and it is not valued.'"[30] Third, the union was committed to making a special effort to raise the wages of the lowest-paid workers, many of them black, and many of them also possessing the fewest certifiable skills. "Although black C&Ts [clerical and technical workers] had the most seniority of any group working at Yale, they earned the least pay."[31]

Although the term may not have been explicitly used, the mobilization campaign and the strike that began September 26, 1984 focused on the importance of clerical and technical work, Yale's failure to value it, and the impact on women's lives. The strike began with strong support from clerical and technical workers, but support weakened as the strike dragged on. Many students and faculty supported the strike, and some mass arrests took place, but few faculty, for example, continued to participate in activities. The strongest support for the strike, surprisingly, came from the overwhelmingly male blue-collar workers in Local 35, who honored the picket lines of Local 34's clerical and technical workers. This may be the most remarkable aspect of the Yale story.

To understand how remarkable, it's necessary to detour to consider Ruth Milkman's research on gender and union organizing. Using data collected by Kate Bronfenbrenner on a sample of the organizing campaigns conducted in 1986–87, Milkman found that (controlling for other factors) when the workforce was all male, the probability of the union winning was 60 percent. In bargaining units that included somewhat more women, the union's victory rate dropped substantially: when 25 percent of the workers were women, the probability of winning dropped to 33 percent, and when 50 percent of the workers were women, win rates dropped almost to 25 percent. Viewing only that much of the data, observers might reach the conclusion that women were less committed than men to unions, and this explained the decreasing union win rates. But the rest of the picture totally changes that analysis: Milkman found that in campaigns to organize predominantly female workforces, union win rates went back up, with the highest win rates in all-women bargaining units.[32]

What makes organizing difficult, these results indicate, is not women (or men) workers, but rather a gender-mixed workforce. Organizing predominantly women succeeds better than organizing predominantly male workforces, but the most difficult challenge is organizing when the bargaining unit includes substantial numbers of both women and men. Racial differences almost certainly create the same dynamic.

Why should union election win rates be lower in gender-integrated bargaining units? Unions at their best create a culture of solidarity, a sense of support and belonging that transcends narrow material considerations and businesslike relations. That solidarity is often *necessary* for a union to win in the face of a determined employer assault. Unless solidarity goes beyond rationality and invokes an emotional identification with other workers, the union is unlikely to win. That culture of solidarity, however, has often implicitly depended on bonding based on race and gender.

How then can we explain why the men of Local 34, perhaps half of them men of color, so strongly supported (predominantly white) women strikers in a battle over a women's issue? First and perhaps most important, they did so because of their own past bitter confrontations with Yale, long history of militance, and similar structural situation. Local 35 members hated the Yale administration, knew that if it crushed Local 34 they would be next, and themselves had a contract due to expire four months later. Their logic was that a solidarity strike, with all Yale workers out together, would be more effective than permitting the Yale administration to pick the locals off one at a time. Second, both sets of workers were organized by the same union, operated with many of the same staff members, and had worked hard throughout to build solidarity, understanding that each would be strengthened by the success (and weakened by the failure) of the other group. It took education and organizing to build this support, especially since many of the "35 men" had hated the "secretaries from the suburbs" who, in past strikes, had crossed Local 35's picket lines. Third, because in more than a few cases, the clerical and technical workers were the wives, sisters, daughters, friends, or neighbors of the maintenance workers.

The strike lasted for nine weeks, by which time it was substantially weakened. In an internally controversial move, bitterly opposed by some but supported by a four-to-one vote, the clerical workers' local decided to go back to work without a contract for the Christmas break. Workers voted to go "Home for the Holidays" in part because an administration-initiated arbitration seemed likely to compel the blue-collar workers of Local 35 back to work on the basis that they were violating a no-strike provision in their contract. Equally important, it's demoralizing to picket a deserted campus in the middle of winter, and not likely to be effective.

Yale historian David Montgomery reports that after the union proposed this strategy for consideration, and before the vote was taken, "the whole bloody university had turned into one big debating society. It was clear that more intellectual activity took place at Yale last week than all the rest of its history combined: in every street and every bar, and every restaurant, all up and down that area." After the vote was taken, "Yale was completely baffled by this decision of the strikers to go back to the job. The administration went bananas."[33] Although strikers returning to work would ordinarily be understood as a sign of weakness, Yale increased its money offer for the first time.

Shortly before the new strike deadline, with the possibility of a renewed strike by both Locals 34 and 35, an agreement was reached in January 1985, providing for wage increases averaging 35 percent over three years, with especially strong provisions for the lowest-wage workers, some of whose salaries increased by as much as 80 percent. The contract also improved pensions, protected flextime, created a committee to study child care, and created a "bridge" permitting women to interrupt their Yale service (for example, to have children or take care of relatives) for extended periods while still protecting their seniority.[34] The contract for maintenance workers was settled a week later, also on terms favorable to workers. Yale's unions have remained vibrant and participatory. Just as Local 35 supported organizing the (mostly) women of Local 34, more recently Locals 34 and 35 together have aided efforts to organize Yale's graduate students, and all three groups have supported organizing at Yale's hospital.

Work and Family

The child care, flextime, and family leave issues Yale's contract addressed almost twenty years ago have become increasingly important to workers and unions. The rapid increase in the number of women working for pay outside the home not only transforms workplaces, union style and culture, and pay issues, it also transforms the relationship between work and families. If unions are to address the issues of most concern to the working class, they must be concerned with more than just what happens on the job.

The phrase "working families" has become almost a mantra among unions. The implicit message is that labor isn't concerned only with its own members, or only with union-specific issues, but rather with entire families, including not only the families of union members but also those workers and families who don't (yet) have the benefit of a union contract. In 1989 the Bureau of National Affairs, a for-profit group that reports on unions, projected that "work and family concerns may become the dominant issue of the 1990s for the American labor movement." Although that didn't happen in the 1990s, it might well emerge as part of a future upsurge. To explore union approaches to work and family issues, Naomi Gerstel and I conducted interviews with key people in all but one of the unions that have 300,000 or more members.[35]

What, however, are "work and family" issues? Most public discussion sees the issues in terms of such matters as family leave, flextime, and child care. But union leaders don't accept that definition, arguing that it is far too narrow. "When you look at a union contract," noted one union informant, "there's lots in there that's a work-family issue, for instance, your pay, your insurance, your hospitalization, your pension, your days off." Much of what professionals take for granted "you don't realize are work and family issues until workers no longer have them—for example sick leave or vacation or disability pay—all of which are things that for the most part were originally union-negotiated benefits." One union survey found that "one-third of low-wage women don't even have paid sick leave, much less have it for their children." In that context, some unions are justifiably proud of the benefits they have won and conscious of the ways they improve family life:

> One of the most striking differences between unionized workers and non-union workers is in the area of benefits. Our typical member with thirteen years of seniority has four weeks paid vacation, and that's for men and women. Thirteen paid holidays is the average for our typical member. So you're talking about six to seven weeks of paid time off, which is significantly higher than comparable non-union workers. That's a big family issue, having that kind of time off.

Middle-class professional and managerial employees often assume that health care benefits, for example, will be extended to all family members, but unions frequently have to fight for this:

> There have been times in the history of our union when employers have proposed that we negotiate benefits simply for the individual worker, and that if anyone's concerned about dependent coverage he or she can pay for their own dependent coverage, and we have always insisted that we negotiate for the full family, and that has been a potential division for our membership, because not everyone in our membership has dependents. But we have insisted that all of us fight for all members of families.

Increasingly unions also contest the meaning of "family," insisting that benefits be extended to the domestic partners of gay and lesbian workers, or that bereavement leaves cover stepparents as well as biological parents.[36]

Some of the union people we spoke with ranged even more widely, including as work-family issues "contaminants coming out of the mill into the community," the learning disabilities of the children of lead workers, the eight-hour day, voter registration, and food banks. Remembering this broader perspective, it remains important to examine child care and flextime, two of the issues conventionally understood as work-family issues.

Child Care

For unions, child care is a double issue: helping working parents get access to quality child care, and helping the workers who provide such care win better wages and benefits. Building an alliance of working parents and child care providers would strengthen both groups; a similar alliance was crucial in SEIU's Los Angeles home care workers campaign, labor's biggest organizing victory of the past fifty years. According to statistics compiled by the Center for the Childcare Workforce, in 1998 half of all child care workers made less than $6.61 an hour, half of all pre-school teachers earned less than $8.32 an hour, and benefits were as minimal as pay. Not surprisingly, 96 percent of these workers are women and one-third are women of color. Just as predictably, the low wages lead to high turnover (about one-third of workers each year), which is hard on children. Less than 5 percent of child care workers have the benefit of a union contract, unlike grade-school and high-school teachers, the vast majority of whom are covered by unions, and who receive much better pay and benefits.[37]

Why don't child care workers unionize? Because child care (unlike kindergarten through high school, or even higher education) is, for the most part, located in the private sector and paid for by parent fees. Across all families, parents pay 60 percent of the cost of child care and early education; in contrast, for public higher education tuition and fees cover only 23 percent of the cost. Parents struggle to pay for child care even with the miserably low wages child care workers now receive; in 1993 a median-income family with young children spent 11 percent of its income on child care, and a family with half the median income spent 24 percent.[38] As long as funding comes from parent fees, there's no realistic way the centers used by working parents can pay higher wages. The only general and long-term solution to this is universal (voluntary) publicly funded programs for children, beginning by age two or three and continuing to (full-day) kindergarten. Such programs are standard—and noncontroversial—in European countries, with facilities designed for young children, well-trained personnel, very low staff turnover, and a stimulating and developmentally appropriate set of activities, all at little or no cost.[39] If universal publicly funded programs were instituted in the United States, hundreds of thousands of child care workers might unionize, raising their wages and benefits, reducing the turnover in personnel which is harmful to children, and creating a mobilized constituency to promote and defend quality care.

Union leaders are clear: the goal is to win publicly funded programs for all children, whether or not they are in unions, and whether or not their parents work for pay. This involves political mobilization, and unions are central to many state-level efforts to promote improved programs. But union members also need immediate help, so unions attempt to negotiate child care benefits that their members can use. Professionals assume that parents want the best possible child care; but for many workers the best is beyond their reach. "A lot of times, work site centers are real model programs—they are higher-quality, they might be accredited, they might have a lot of the bells and whistles because the corporation or, in some cases, the state, wants it to be a showcase. People know it's not going to be affordable, so what good is it to them?" One union that has negotiated funds that helped set up over fifty centers has found that "one of the ongoing struggles has been that it's difficult for our members to afford them. So what we've wound up with is a wonderful management center for high-level professionals, but we don't represent the professional group, so this is a problem." Another of the people we interviewed told us that the referral service that the union negotiated was used by only 0.1 percent of the members because it provides "advice on how to get child care you can't afford."

Most members, even those with young children, don't expect their unions to address the issue. As one person noted: "People still believe that things like child care are their own burden. They are not society's burden, they are not their employer's burden, it is not the union's job. It's just something they have to do. They chose to have these kids, and they just have to deal with it." As a result, in union surveys, when members are asked about their priorities "child care might rank at best third, maybe fifth." Union leaders who are committed to these issues compellingly argue that member survey responses are misleading, dramatically understating the issue's potential. There is a need for child care despite the lack of what an economist would call "member effective demand." But if members aren't asking for it, why should unions make it a priority? And if staff or leaders wish it to be a priority, will members support them?

One response to this situation might be to blame the members, or to sit back and wait for a general cultural shift. Those feelings de facto shape the responses of some union leaders, who would like to move on the issue but feel their hands are tied. Others, however, argue that the demand is there if workers and the union could break through the sense that they have no right to expect good work-family policies. Once a policy is in place, they argue, it will develop a powerful constituency, so the problem is "only" how to insert that entering wedge.

The union that won one of the most impressive child care programs did so primarily because of the efforts of one leader.

> I felt very strongly that this was an issue that we all needed to address through using our collective power, and all of us were looking at it as a personal problem and workers were looking at it as a personal problem because there weren't widespread policies. People would think, what can the union do? They [wanted] more wage increases, more holidays, and they wouldn't think about child care because there weren't a lot of models out there.

Rather than simply accepting this, she pushed hard to make this a union priority, even without evidence that members viewed this as one of the most important issues. Because of her position as one of the leaders of the bargaining team, she was in a position to say to the employers:

> "No settlement without [child care]." Basically, that's what I had to say. [The other side] said, "This is not going to be a strike issue if we don't give it, and it's not going to be a deal breaker." And I said, "How do you know? You could put this either way: I could say, 'This is not that great, it's not going to be a deal buster for your side either. Your employers are not going to not approve this whole package if you added [a small amount] for child care.' And no, I'm not recommending to the negotiating committee that they approve this unless you say yes."

With the threat of a strike over the issue, with child care as a potential issue that would prevent an agreement from being reached, employers accepted a fund, with payments equal to a small percentage of payroll. The fund provides varying levels of subsidy: higher amounts for formal licensed care, but significant funding for informal care (even if the care is provided by a relative—anyone other than a parent).[40] Once the fund was won, it created a constituency and a sense that workers had a right to expect this, such that now there is no going back (at least not without a major fight). As one person noted about one of the largest existing programs:

> Last year we served eight thousand children with some type of child care benefits, but we had benefits requested on behalf of twenty-nine thousand children. So we could use 1 percent or 1.5 percent of payroll [instead of the current 0.3 percent]. The fact that this large amount of people are requesting child care or some type of benefit—whether it's after-school care or weekend care, summer camp, whatever—[means that] if the employers try to take this away right now there would be an absolute uproar.

Our interview with another union that has won a similar benefit indicates that they had a strikingly similar experience. Although members wanted the benefit, demand for it was not especially pressing. Once it was won, however, the union was surprised at the enthusiasm of the response: "We set up an application week in which we intended to open the first day at 7:00 A.M., first come first served, and there were people standing outside the office at 3:00 A.M. in the dark in [a dangerous downtown area] with their children, waiting to apply. We realized how insensitive that was of us. The next year we had an in-person application week run by lottery."

These examples demonstrate that existing attitudes can't be taken as fixed or definitive. As workers' circumstances change, their views also change: workers *without* benefits feel child care is their own responsibility, and workers *with* benefits feel that families and children deserve support from employers and unions. The new circumstances don't just appear; they are a result of human effort, in this case through unions.[41]

It's wonderful that these unions were able to win child care benefits for their members; it would have been even better if it had not happened through a top-down strategy. A campaign that helped change workers' consciousness and mobilized them would be more likely to create the basis for large-scale advance. When one or two leaders win something for the membership, this can create worker passivity rather than vibrant democratic organizations.[42]

Why have so few unions won child care benefits? Many feminists see this question as equivalent to asking "Why haven't unions made child care a priority?" But that's not the only way to understand the issue. When we asked someone at a union with one of the two best policies why they had been able to win the benefits, the response was "We are an active union. The members are extremely active and participate." Our follow-up query asked why members were active on these issues and not others, and the leader rejected that formulation:

> I don't think that's the particular way to look at it; our members are active, period. . . . When you've successfully, continually, and aggressively

organized nonunion [establishments], you're able to maintain an increased standard of living for the members, and so that's our top priority. We're able to continue to grow so the standards have been able to include things like child/elder care. Does that make sense? If you do not continually organize, you become less and less powerful where you are. If your power diminishes you're unlikely to be able to negotiate new programs like child/elder care. We're a fighting union. We have one of the highest quality-of-life experiences for [industry] workers in the country, and it's because we are constantly organizing our members to stand up and be involved in constantly organizing non-union properties—that's the core of our existence, and that's why we're able to do breakthrough things like this.

That is, union commitment to particular issues is at best half the equation. Just as important is the strength of the union, itself determined in large part by organizing. The two unions with the best child care benefits both represent a high proportion of workers in their jurisdictions. One person reported that at her international, the local with the best policy has "got a good part of their market up there organized. You can't do this if you've got 20 percent of the stores organized, because you have no clout." This is not to say that union strength alone is the answer, but neither can a solution come from simply changing the priorities of existing unions. Workers won't win work and family benefits unless and until an existing movement—call it feminist labor or working-class feminism—becomes far more powerful. Union leaders and feminists each have a tendency to look for changes by the other; victories aren't likely until the two join forces in creative ways.

Flextime and Overtime

Work time issues provide another potential area to broaden and deepen labor movement attention to work-family issues. Kris Rondeau reports that at Harvard, half of all problem-solving cases (what HUCTW has in place of a grievance system), or about five hundred cases a year, involve issues of scheduling. Both workers and employers talk about flexibility, but with opposite meanings. Increasingly, employers use "flexibility" to mean that workers will be assigned nonstandard hours. As a consequence, workers and unions have a range of contradictory reactions to discussions of flexibility and alternative schedules.

One leader noted that the key to the differing positions workers and unions take "is actually control over work hours as opposed to flextime. . . . The real issue is whether you make those decisions yourself or whether those are all management decisions." For an informant at a union that represents many public sector clerical workers flextime was an unequivocal benefit: "The need and the desire for [flextime] is huge, and I think people feel that if they get some of that flexibility it makes them feel so much less stressed, and it makes them feel that their employer understands that they're trying to work and do a good job at work and do a good job at home, and when they don't get that from their employer, they're very angry." In contrast, a representative at a predominantly male union representing factory workers reported that one of their most important recent campaigns had focused on resisting flextime:

> In 1999 [a major employer] had put a stake in the sand saying giving flexible work hours was their chief goal in the negotiation, to get 24/7 coverage so that they could run their factories around the clock, compete by using all of the productive capacities all the time. Our members just said . . . the slogan was "Seven Day–No Way." It really became a work and family issue. How can you have a family life if you're working five shifts and seven days a week? It just doesn't compute. And we were able to resist the company's demands for that. We organized a very aggressive campaign to educate our members about what the company's proposal really was and to let people know what the effect of that would be, that there was going to be some more money on the table, but it would really disrupt their family life. At the end of the day the company didn't even propose it. When we got to negotiations, they had got the message; they knew if they put that on the table it was going to cause a huge problem.

Another argued that in practice flextime came to mean that workers had impossible schedules, but never received any overtime. As a consequence, "Our standard position, every time I go into a local I always ask what do you think about alternative work schedules and they go, 'uh-uh, no, no, no—we'll do anything but that.' That, I would say, is the majority. There's always a few people who say 'I would love to have an alternative schedule. "

Even when flextime means workers gain some control over their time, it may be a very limited control within oppressive constraints:

> When I talk to working women and ask them, do you have flexibility, and they say, oh, yeah, I've got a flexible work schedule; I work nights and my husband works days. So the fact is people have a painfully contracted view of what flexibility means; it means I don't have to pay a baby-sitter because somehow we can always manage to have someone at home, but I haven't seen my husband in four years.

If flextime is (at least, is supposed to be) about controlling work schedules, mandatory unscheduled overtime is the opposite. Many employees come to work each day not knowing whether work will end as scheduled at 4:00 P.M., or whether at that time the employer will tell them they are required to stay until six or seven or eight. At Wal-Mart, a 2002 lawsuit charged, workers were sometimes locked in and forced to work overtime off-the-clock with no compensation. Workers and unions are hamstrung in their ability to fight mandatory overtime: the NLRB has ruled that workers may not engage in a "partial" strike, such as working an eight-hour day and then refusing to work overtime; if workers do so they may be fired. Recognizing this, a union local with an all-women workforce coordinated a wonderfully creative action that does not qualify as a strike:

> A group of women had mandatory overtime, meaning that at the end of your shift your supervisor could come up to you and say you have to stay two more hours. So the women who had children called their baby-sitter who said "I'm sorry; I can't stay." So what the women were doing as a group, they made a decision as a group—I'm talking five hundred or seven hundred employees—they started having the baby-sitters drop the children off at the plant. The security guards were, "what are we supposed to do with these kids?" When the women were confronted by the managers they would say, "I would be put in prison and my children would be taken away from me if I leave them at home alone—I cannot do that. You told me I had to stay, so they're going to come here." It was basically a showdown.

Historically, the labor movement was the primary force pushing for shorter work hours; as the bumper sticker notes, "The Labor Movement: The Folks Who Brought You the Weekend." At one time employers posted notices reading "If you don't come to work on Sunday, don't come to work on Monday." These days unions are battling not to reduce the length of the official working day, but rather to reduce the amount of overtime that workers are required to work. This was one of two central issues in a three-week strike by Verizon phone company workers in August 2000; the workers won a reduction in mandatory overtime. Before the strike they could be required to work fifteen hours a week of overtime; as a result of their victory workers cannot be required to put in more than eight hours of overtime in a week.[43]

Perhaps the most crucial battles, however, have been by nurses who are concerned not only about their own lives and families, but also about the health and safety of their patients. To improve their bottom line, many hospitals intentionally employ too few full-time nurses and require them to work overtime. Often nurses are required to work double shifts; towards the end of their first eight hours they may be told, "You don't get to go home, you have to stay and work another eight hours." Ignore for a moment the effects on the nurses themselves (including on their own health) and on their children, their children's caregivers, and on the nurses' spouses and families. Imagine being the patient whom the nurse cares for after fifteen straight hours on the job, all of that time under the stress of making potentially life and death decisions. Will the nurse remember all the things that need to be checked, be able to pick up on subtle indicators, perform procedures accurately and expertly, remain cheerful and friendly? Amazingly, most of the time the answer is yes. But to the nurses (and patients!), "most of the time" is nowhere near good enough. If performance drops only slightly, that could cost someone's life. Nurses at St. Vincent's Hospital in Worcester, Massachusetts, negotiating their first union contract, made mandatory overtime their most important issue. To win, they needed a forty-nine-day strike and strong community support. The contract they ratified in May 2000 limits overtime to no more than four hours per shift and no more than eight times per year. It's easy to imagine that other such struggles could help create, or be part of, a new labor upsurge.[44]

Lessons from Harvard

In order to create a resurgence, unions will need to address new issues. But they'll also need to reconsider some of the attitudes and approaches that are built into many organizing campaigns, and into the rules and structure of union operations. An exemplar of what that might involve is the 1988 victory, following a vote by more than three thousand workers, of the Harvard Union of Clerical and Technical Workers (HUCTW), the culmination of a struggle that had been in progress, in one form or another, for fifteen years. This section first considers the troubled history of the organizing effort's relation with unions. That history exemplifies unions' resistance to innovative methods and independent-minded organizers; in this case, that resistance can't easily be separated from gender issues. The chapter then considers the ways that both the style of organizing, and the character of the contract that resulted, owe much to the women's movement.

Troubled Relation to Unions

Efforts to unionize Harvard clerical workers date back to 1973, when, as a direct consequence of the women's movement, then just out of its infancy, a women's caucus was mobilized in the medical school area. The women demanded better treatment and managed to get the dean of the medical school to establish a Committee on the Status of Women.

Some of the activists behind the creation of the Committee on the Status of Women affiliated with District 65, at the time an independent (and left-wing) union. Kris Rondeau began working at Harvard in 1976, after some initial reluctance quickly became involved with the union, and was a leader as it fought and lost a close certification election. In 1979 Rondeau was hired by District 65 and it affiliated with the UAW (United Auto Workers). While most of Rondeau's organizing focused on small offices and retail stores, she kept working on Harvard, and in April 1981 lost another close election in the medical school.

After the 1981 defeat, Rondeau was assigned to work on organizing Yale clerical workers. She recommended that the UAW pull out and leave Yale to HERE, which Rondeau felt had the support of the workers. In response the UAW fired Rondeau, but literally that same day the NLRB ordered a new election at Harvard, based on a finding that Harvard supervisors had illegally influenced the 1981 vote. A half-hour after firing Rondeau, the UAW rehired her.

A new Harvard drive did not take off immediately, and in 1984 Harvard won an NLRB ruling that henceforth any union organizing campaign would have to include all university employees, not just—as had been the case to that point—those in the medical school area.[45] As the drive gained steam, UAW staff began to intervene more actively, pushing the Harvard organizing team to adopt the methods that the UAW had found effective elsewhere, including leafleting, attacking the boss, and emphasizing a handful of key issues. The UAW wanted to conduct a poll, and thought it could get women to participate by giving them free pantyhose if they did so; the Harvard organizing team was horrified by this suggestion and ignored it.

In August 1985, the head of the UAW region ordered Rondeau and Marie Manna, another key organizer, to go to Detroit to work on another campaign; they refused to do so, and were fired. Other staff were locked out of the office. They responded by quitting and working on an unpaid basis, constituting themselves as an independent group, the Harvard Union of Clerical and Technical Workers. The resignation of the entire staff, and their willingness to work without pay, were virtually unprecedented—a clear indication that something significant was at stake, that the Harvard team had an alternative vision of what a union should be and how to build it. HUCTW organized around standard union issues—wages, improvements in health benefits, dental care—but a central focus was always the wish to participate and gain a voice in workplace decisions.[46]

The Harvard organizing staff worked on their own, as independents, for sixteen months, supporting themselves by raising donations, for example by holding employee talent nights to raise the rent for staff members. (Rondeau and Manna both had employed spouses; others did not.) "We found our own voice at that time," Rondeau reports. "It was a wonderful liberating experience among people who had no idea they needed to be liberated. . . . When we were independent we became better in every way at what we did."[47] This is not because they had been in "a cultural straight jacket. . . . The UAW had treated us respectfully more or less until the end." The group had been "part of the mainstream labor movement for a long time but we weren't really treated that way. We were women, we were isolated within it. We created our own culture and our own words." The break from the established labor movement and the group's ability to sustain itself for sixteen months as an independent organization were undoubtedly crucial to the team's ability to develop its own distinctive approach.

In January 1987, however, HUCTW, recognizing that on its own it did not have the resources to take on Harvard, affiliated with AFSCME and received a three-hundred-thousand-dollar no-strings organizing grant. Gerald McEntee, president of AFSCME, explained that "they impressed us as knowing what the hell they were doing, and we wanted them to have their own identity so the boss would have difficulty painting them as this big union from Washington." The union was also aware that organizing Harvard would be "an outstanding coup . . . a symbol of success like almost no other."[48]

In large part because of HUCTW's unusual style of campaign, based on personal contact, "We used so little literature that we filed a petition and caught Harvard completely off guard." Anne Taylor, in charge of orchestrating Harvard's anti-union campaign, agrees: "By the time we were aware that something was going on, they were unbeatable." In May 1988, at Harvard's third election for clerical and technical workers, this time including the entire campus, the union won by a margin of forty-four votes out of just over three thousand cast, a turnout of 90 percent. This turnout is typical for hotly contested union elections and contrasts sharply with the low turnout in political contests. In thinking about this case, we need to consider both that it ended in victory and that it did so by the narrowest of margins.

Had the margin been an equally small defeat, that is, if twenty-three people had changed their minds, the postcampaign retrospectives would have portrayed this approach as a failure. As impressive and as promising as the Harvard style of organizing is, winning union elections is exceptionally difficult: even with an experienced team of top organizers, even in liberal Massachusetts, even going up against a wealthy nonprofit organization that prides itself on its public image—even with all that, HUCTW barely pulled out a victory.

Gender and Organizing Style

Many unions are dominated by a macho style; that was even more true in the past. From the nineteenth century to today, for many machinists, auto workers, and truckers, being a union stalwart meant being a *man*. Demanding dignity and respect, standing up for others, were seen as specifically manly qualities. In 1958, Nick DiGaetano, a UAW militant, committeeman, and chief steward, and a radical who had been a Wobbly (a member of the IWW, Industrial Workers of the World), looked back at the changes from the 1920s through the 1950s: "I tell you this: the workers of my generation from the early days up to now had what you might call a labor insurrection in changing from a plain, humble, submissive creature into a man. The union made a man out of him. . . . Before they were submissive. Today they are men."[49]

In this view, one that is common in the labor movement and elsewhere, union militance was defined in part around a masculine style. Solidarity often developed in significant part around race and gender. The railroad unions are "brotherhoods"; many unions began as fraternal orders using secret rituals to bind members as (fictive) brothers.[50] Construction unions use drinking rituals and sexual joking along with the apprenticeship process as ways of creating bonds of solidarity, a solidarity that is also based on whiteness.

Today every union would condemn open racism or sexism, but a tough-guy macho style is widespread: vulgar language, eagerness for conflict, testosterone challenge as proof of militance and commitment. Also widespread is the view that union organizing is so demanding that it is incompatible with active parenting. These views came up repeatedly in Daisy Rooks's 2001 interviews with new organizers. One of them, Kathryn, reported that unions require that organizers "not have a life and put everything else aside, and make [organizing] absolutely the center of your life. . . . There's this theory out there that in organizing you [must] devote your entire life, and if you can't do that, you don't belong here." Another, June, said, "I would love to stay in the labor movement . . . but I can't be an organizer [because] I want to have a family and a life." She reached that conclusion in part because her boss "puts in at least 16 hours a day. . . . He has 3 kids and he sees them every three or four months. That's it for them. He has not made them his priority." Erin, who worked six years as an organizer, wants to return to it some day but "my vision of how I want to do the job is not compatible [with being a parent]."[51]

Roslyn Feldberg argues that "women's absence or limited place [in unions] results in large part from the exclusion of 'women's culture' from the unions."[52] The "women's culture" recommended by Feldberg, and developed by Rondeau, owes much to Carol Gilligan, a psychologist who emphasizes the differences between men and women, an approach that is sharply criticized by many other feminists. "Women's culture" explanations are fraught with peril; the implication is that these differences are biological, not social, and that they apply to all women but to no men. I reject every one of those implications, but nonetheless find elements of this approach useful for thinking about unions.

Karen Brodkin Sacks's insightful analysis of a 1970s clerical workers union organizing drive at Duke University's hospital develops Feldberg's point, and aims at "examining leadership in a grassroots movement through working-class Black women's eyes and actions."[53] Although most of the workers were women, most of the visible spokesmen for the union were just that, men. When a walkout took place, "although those involved in that walkout were overwhelmingly Black women, they chose the walkout's 'lone Black male' to present their petition to hospital management (though they were right behind him)."

Sacks reports that this situation "did not sit well with me as a feminist activist, and I did my best to promote women's leadership," specifically by arranging a major public event at which all the speakers were women: "The women did beautifully, and I felt I had furthered women's leadership role until the women themselves called me into a meeting where they expressed fairly sharp criticism. After talking among themselves, they had discovered that they were all quite angry at being manipulated and pressured into doing something they did not want to do, even though they too thought they had done well."[54] As one of the women on the organizing committee put it, "Women are organizers; men are leaders." Sacks concluded that the organizing drive—by worker choice—contained two different kinds of leaders. Although one kind, visible spokes*men* were more prominent, the other kind, what she called "center*women*," were more vital to the success of the movement. At meetings, for example, the male leaders could talk all they wanted, but nothing happened, Sacks concluded, unless one or more centerwomen weighed in with a remark endorsing the proposal, at which point others would join in and carry it forward.

From the standpoint of gender equity and women's empowerment, acceptance of a gendered division of leadership in which men speak for a movement and hold the visible positions seems deeply problematic. Sacks emphasizes that these two forms of leadership are not necessarily sex-linked. But the central insight is both feminist and fundamental: organizing drives and movement building depend on (typically low-visibility) people who do much of the routine work, talk to other people and make them feel part of the drive, and are respected by other workers who look to them for direction. Without their support it's difficult to win an election and impossible to build a strong union.

Kris Rondeau, lead organizer for the Harvard drive,[55] has developed numerous gender-related insights from her reflections about what characterizes the Harvard group's organizing. An interview with her contrasted sharply with interviews I conducted with (successful) male organizers, some of whom also organized predominantly women workers. Rondeau's insights echo and extend what Sacks learned from the Duke hospital drive.

All the organizers I interviewed emphasized that they sought out natural leaders, but male organizers typically followed with the addition that they wanted someone who was a fighter, someone with fire in their belly. In contrast, Kris Rondeau's first criterion is someone who is not angry. "A long time ago," she said, "I was told to look for the angry ones. You look for the angry ones and you spend a life in hell I think. The angry ones first of all are people who are not handling stress well."[56] Her ideal is "a healthy cheerful person who can listen." In her approach, "once you're organizing somewhere you're there forever" so she looks for people "who can get better and better at it, people who can develop others, people that the boss will have to respect."

Early in her organizing Rondeau noticed that workplace events can be devastating, "as important as anything that can happen to you in your family." Some people handled calamities and were able to land on their feet while others were crushed. The difference, Rondeau concluded, was that some were part of a community; they had networks and social supports. "Community really works. The ability to go forward and even fight your enemies when you had to came from just being supported. All our grandmothers could have told us this. So we decided to build our union like that; unions had to be a place where people got a sense of safety and community."

Rondeau says that "you can't be a regular worker in this country and experience an anti-union campaign and ever feel the same about work ever again." Harvard supervisors told workers that the union would go on strike and force pregnant women to walk the picket line even if that led to a miscarriage, that black and Puerto Rican workers would be bused up (by the union!) to take workers' jobs, that workers would be laid off if they voted for the union. For the 1981 election, Harvard hired police with guns to walk back and forth in front of the polling booths.

Rondeau recounted her first experience with a captive audience meeting, when she worked at Harvard before she took a paid position with the union. By law, employers can require all workers to attend such meetings; anyone who refused to do so could be fired. "They rounded us up to go; there were animal care labs that don't close in the worst blizzard and I think if you'd taken a searchlight out into those labs you would find nobody." The event was carefully orchestrated by Harvard to show that (some) workers opposed the union and that management had its eye on workers. Several anti-union workers had been given cards with questions for them to read out. When Kris Rondeau spoke up for the union, Harvard's general counsel, the speaker for the event, called on her by name—even though they had never met. The orchestration of power and anti-unionism was so effective, Rondeau reports, that "when [the meeting] was over I was at the elevator with people that I had organized and they were crying and they wouldn't talk to me."

The kind of person who goes on to become an organizer is typically someone who can handle pressure and confrontation. Rondeau herself is a formidable figure. Over the years she has developed a soft and supportive gender style, but it's no surprise that in 1976 she was the worker willing and able to stand up in an auditorium to take on Harvard's general counsel. She could handle the pressure, but for many workers it was devastating and disabling. "We [the organizers] can describe it but [emotionally experiencing] the actual fear is something different." Harvard's campaign raised the tension-fear level, which is the self-conscious aim of employer anti-union drives. In a tactic typical of many employers fighting unions, at Harvard, Rondeau recalled, a group of anti-union workers (called ICE, Independent Concerned Employees) "had free rein to just go around and organize against the union and they would scream at people just to raise the tension level." The result was that on the day of the vote seventy pro-union workers (the margin of defeat that year) stayed home; they "were so scared that they couldn't come to work to vote for the union."

The employer anti-union campaign, with the fear and stress it generates, is the central problem faced by any U.S. labor organizer. (Such employer campaigns are not allowed in most of the world's democracies.) The most common response by good organizers is to sustain a high degree of worker militancy, to hold numerous worker-initiated events that demonstrate workers have solidarity and are able to challenge the boss.

Kris Rondeau and her team of organizers (most of them women) take a different approach. They view it as their responsibility to lower the tension level and use a variety of means to do so, including preparing workers in advance for what will happen, walking with workers to captive audience meetings, "just being relaxed ourselves," and above all using humor to cut the tension. Lowering the tension level refers not simply to union-management relations, but above all to *worker-worker* relations. "A huge amount of the pain of the anti-union campaign is generated worker to worker. It's one thing to have the employer creating tension and screaming and hollering like the Wizard of Oz and it's another thing to have your co-workers screaming at you." The organizing strategy Rondeau had been taught—the standard strategy for old-time organizers everywhere—is to figure out who is pro-union and who is anti-union, then organize the middle. In Rondeau's view, "This kind of strategy maybe works in war but it didn't work in building an organization. The idea of workers fighting each other just played into management's strategy. Partly our interest in not polarizing had to do with what we wanted to be later on."

The key problem for workers in an organizing drive—and therefore for the union—is tension and fear. "People would say it to us very openly, 'I'm just scared, there's nothing else, there's no other reason.'" The way to overcome that is to reduce the tension, provide support and reassurance, and end people's isolation—all long-run union goals in any case. "You'd be nuts to vote Yes if you are isolated. If isolated, Che Guevara would vote No." Ending worker isolation is a goal shared by most organizers, but Rondeau's team did something I had not heard of before: "To some degree I think in order to preserve the atmosphere that we wanted we actually let people vote No. Certainly we walked a lot of No votes to the polls but more than that we clearly decided to do everything we could to not polarize the campus."

The union's slogan for the drive, which came from a speech by Barney Frank, Democratic member of Congress for the Boston area, embodied this approach: "It's not anti-Harvard to be pro-union." One dramatic instance of the campaign's style was the (successful) vote. In contrast to the 1981 election with its gun-toting off-duty police officers creating an atmosphere of fear and intimidation, in 1988 the union worked with students who got up at four o'clock in the morning and put balloons everywhere: "all of Harvard Square was pretty and all around everywhere was beautiful." The union also set up a worker-partner for every person eligible to vote, and walked the person to the polls. Perhaps balloons and a festive air provided the narrow margin of victory.

In many ways even more interesting than the organizing victory itself is the type of union that Harvard workers established in the wake of the victory. Because the campaign had made every effort to avoid polarizing the workforce, "When the union got recognized the union membership went practically to 80 percent within a two-week span." Rondeau believes it would have been "a disaster" if the union had won at the earlier 1981 election, because at that time "there was an atmosphere of fear and tension and even those who voted yes were petrified." Harvard continued to fight the union even after the election victory (as most employers do), with President Derek Bok indicating the university would petition the NLRB to rerun the election. (As a law professor, Bok had written a book urging employers to accept unions.) For five months Harvard continued to refuse to accept the union, but then finally changed tactics. The union deserves at least partial credit for Harvard's willingness to accept the outcome, rather than fighting bitterly to the end: the union's campaign, because it worked so hard not to polarize the campus, made it easier to establish a working relation.[57]

The contract promoted by the Harvard union, and with numerous modifications accepted by Harvard, is virtually unique. As John Hoerr reports, "In a formal sense, there are no rules at all. . . . The agreement was most significant for what it did not contain. There were no union work rules involving seniority, job classifications, and such matters. . . . For its part, Harvard did not insist on the usual broad 'management rights' clause listing all the areas of decision making that workers are forbidden to enter."[58] Since there are no rules, there is also no formal grievance procedure. Instead, the preamble to the contract notes that in governing Harvard, workers—like administrators, faculty, students, and alumni—are "a valued and essential participant in this process."

In place of formal rules the union sought and won a process of joint problem solving. When an issue comes up, the worker is encouraged to meet directly with her supervisor to try to work things out. The union representative provides support but encourages the worker to handle the problem by herself. If they don't resolve the issue, "it goes to one of 30 'local problem solving teams,' consisting of one management and one union representative" and if that fails to solve it, it goes to higher levels, and ultimately to mediation or arbitration. In fourteen years, only sixteen cases have done so. Hundreds of workers also participate, with administrators, on various joint councils that meet to address workplace issues.[59]

Although programs that appear similar have been introduced by management at many enterprises under the term "employee involvement," at Harvard these were introduced at the union's initiative and against the opposition of a skeptical management. On the one hand, there is a less adversarial relationship; on the other, the union claims the right to address virtually any issue, rather than being restricted to specified grievable items. (This is discussed further in the chapter conclusion.) After winning a contract the union maintained the same style as during the organizing drive, with an emphasis on direct personal connection, building relationships, creating community, and, to the extent possible, avoiding actions or policies that might lead to polarization.

Objections and Responses

Periods of upsurge construct new labor regimes, redefining what we mean by "union": who is included, how people get organized, the structures and mechanisms to be used, what issues are addressed, and the culture that regulates activity. The next upsurge *requires* a feminist transformation: How can it be an upsurge if it does not address the concerns of half the workforce?

Key moments of struggle provide unique opportunities to fuse movements and create something new. Although there were more than a few successes, we largely lost the feminist labor opportunity of 1965–75, to the detriment of both the feminist and labor movements. Second Wave feminism and union women's caucuses of the 1940s to 1970s rarely connected. In lulls between periods of mass movement, such as the current period, it's much harder to build a new force, yet some elements of future transformation are being painstakingly developed. The change in the gender of the workforce needs to change the issues that unions address and the priorities they assign. Increased attention to pay equity and work-family concerns might mobilize previously neglected constituencies.

Women's increased participation in the labor force must change not only the issues, but also labor's style. To some old-style union leaders, the only available approach is fighting, machismo, and slugging it out toe-to-toe. A feminist approach doesn't mean backing down, giving in, or setting modest goals, but it might mean a different way of proceeding. In victory, Harvard workers negotiated not a legalistic confrontational grievance system, with elaborate rules about what could and could not be grieved. Rather they sought a joint problem-solving process, a right to discuss virtually any workplace problem, and a recognition that a clerical worker is "a valued and essential participant" in governance. One (non-Harvard) study indicated that "women's workplace problems and disputes are different from men's and are less likely to be covered by the provisions of union contracts"[60] and that women were much more willing to approach the union when they realized that most problems were handled through mediation. This is exactly the kind of approach that Harvard's union developed; a new upsurge might lead to a major expansion in this (or other) alternative form(s).

This feminist style emerged among women working with predominantly female workforces, and may be especially useful in white-collar settings where workers and their supervisors have close personal contact. But it holds vital lessons for all workforces. In addition to outright fear and intimidation, most employers' strategy is to raise the level of conflict, attempting to persuade workers that there will be "a state of perpetual conflict if the organizing campaign succeeds." A survey of workers in one white-collar campaign found that the swing voters "are more likely to be affected by the conflict generated during the campaign than they are to be intimidated by perceived management threats." In commenting on the paper reporting these results, the Director of Organizing for the Teamsters pointed out that most organizers respond to conflict by mobilizing the workers to demonstrate their militance and willingness to stand up to the boss. He then raised the question: In doing so, are we making the boss's argument for him? Are we establishing just what the boss said, that with a union the level of stress will be high? In the paper reporting the survey results, the authors plaintively note, "It is almost as if the union is being pressured to assume responsibility for ensuring that worker organization will proceed without continual struggle."[61] They seem to regard this as an impossibility, but of course this was precisely the strategy of the Harvard clerical workers drive.

The advantage of a women-driven approach was dramatically illustrated to me at two strikes a few months apart at towns a few miles apart. At the first strike, an all-male workforce was extremely militant and never broke its solidarity: the strike lasted for a year and only a handful of the original workers ever crossed the picket line. When the employer started bringing in strikebreakers, workers called them ugly names and physically confronted them; more than a few scab cars and homes were damaged. The tough male approach led to testosterone challenge; scabs had to cross the line or self-identify as cowards too scared to keep going. The scabs stayed on the job and the strike was eventually lost. At the second strike, a 75-percent female workforce— told by their union "business agent" that they were just girls and couldn't bring off a strike—adopted very different tactics. They too had a militant picket line, but when scabs came to apply for jobs, the women workers stood in their way and said, "Can I talk to you for a minute and tell you why I hope you'll honor our picket line?" The picket line and nonthreatening physical obstruction were important elements of the package, but the plea, the question, the initiation of human contact, were vastly more effective than the first plant's "I'll beat the shit out of you if you go in there" approach. A large majority of those who came to apply for a job left without going in. Most job applicants had no idea that a strike was in progress, wanted a job but sympathized with the workers' struggle, and in an astounding number of cases had no idea what a picket line was or what it meant.[62]

Yale's strike tactics illustrate the same contrast. By far the most common union approach has been confrontation to the death. Yale's clerical workers didn't buy into that culture. A macho style would have insisted that to back down an inch would be to show weakness. The mostly male organizing team, backed by the mostly female workforce, decided that returning to work would both reduce workers' vulnerability and increase their ability to spread the message. Yale's panicked reaction and the quick settlement demonstrate the promise of the approach; by breaking with established patterns the workers threw Yale off stride.

This chapter, and especially its praise of the Rondeau-Harvard approach, has provoked two very different sorts of sharp response, both of which raise good points, and neither of which I'm prepared to (fully) accept. First, it is argued that there is very little new in Rondeau's approach: good organizers—men as well as women—have always worked to create a sense of community and support, used humor to reduce tension, avoided creating hostility among "no" voters, minimized the use of literature, and maximized personal contact. These are important in organizing men as well as women. Nor should it be implied that all men want confrontation and all women wish to avoid it; many campaigns in all-women units involve conflict and militant confrontation. (See the next chapter's discussion of Stamford for an example of that.) Absolutely. I agree, and this approach and these insights should *not* be seen as "for women only"—nor should they be seen as "for white-collar workers only" (which might be as sensible a characterization). At the same time: the difference in emphasis and style is marked, and there's every reason to see that difference as linked both to gender and to the character of many white-collar jobs (which involve close contact, and personal relations, with supervisors).

Second, critics object that the Rondeau approach, and the Harvard contract, involve accommodation with management and create a company union; as such they contradict the social movement unionism promoted in the rest of this book. Management wants employee involvement, argues everyone is on the same team, opposes restrictive rules, and says conflict is unnecessary. Unions that go along with that are duped and lose their power. Unions, I am told, must mobilize and confront. A number of people—not all of them men—have expressed hostility to Rondeau or HUCTW. One angry Massachusetts labor leftist told me that HUCTW wasn't really a union, that they don't have a real contract. The union's problem-solving approach, he said, might be good "for getting the desks rearranged" but it couldn't take on "the real issues."

But in some office situations rearranging the desks might be the issue—might do more than anything else to improve the quality of work. It is by no means clear that eight-hundred-page union contracts, and thousands of worker grievances, are necessarily the best way to exercise worker power. It's always valuable to mobilize workers and increase their participation in decision making (both in the union and in day-to-day work life). But the best way to do so will vary from one situation to the next. Union contracts and grievance systems aren't ends in themselves; they are (supposed to be) ways to exercise power. In order to gain contracts and grievances, unions and workers usually must accept legalistic, bureaucratic, and limited rules, with a clause providing "management rights" to decide anything not clearly spelled out in the contract. Ultimately we'd like a world in which workers have a say in every decision. The Harvard approach has that as its aim. Could it be co-opted by management? Of course, but that's also true of every other approach.

Nor should it be concluded that the Rondeau style promotes quiescence. Just as in the picket line incidents just described, a less confrontational approach is sometimes more effective, and in practice may require more commitment. (Figuring out how to talk to a potential enemy can be harder than yelling names at him or her.) When the Harvard contract came up for renewal, and the administration was intransigent, HUCTW didn't give up. But neither did they yell and scream. Their seventy-three public events included one with Jesse Jackson speaking to three thousand people in Harvard Yard. But HUCTW also met the Harvard president with a kazoo band, and it organized a "how the other one-percent lives" bus tour of deans' houses, complete with cucumber sandwiches.

I think the labor movement could learn a great deal from taking Rondeau's approach more seriously. Labor needs new models, even if they involve complications and risks. Traditional union approaches are not succeeding at organizing private sector clerical workers, so new models can't be dismissed. Labor needs to think about, and experiment with variations of, alternative approaches. Key elements of the Harvard approach just might be crucial to a new upsurge, to changing the rules of the game and establishing labor action in places where it is now weak or nonexistent.

An alternative reservation of a very different sort is to say that Harvard, Yale, and "the feminist capital of the nation" (San Jose) are hardly representative examples. The fact that an approach worked there by no means shows it can be applied elsewhere; Harvard and Yale were paper-thin victories, and San Jose strike participation levels were below the average for other strikes. These are vulnerable institutions, it could be said, dependent on public good will, subject to moral pressure, with ample resources to make concessions. Workers had high levels of contact with students and faculty and workplaces were open to the public. It would be much harder to win in the typical private sector clerical workforce.

Absolutely true. But the entering wedge victory for a new strategy or category of worker often comes in such circumstances. There are hundreds of such colleges and universities, and many of the same circumstances apply to numerous nonprofit (and some for-profit) institutions. Lots of women's employment has these characteristics, and that's precisely the point: different kinds of jobs require altered strategies and create new kinds of unions. Each similar victory will make the next one easier; a couple of dozen in a year might create the momentum that would transform the culture and make even the most recalcitrant employer vulnerable. A new upsurge would be underway.

4

New Tactics, Community, and Color

magine two labor-friendly people in 1929 talking about the state of the labor movement and its potential for growth. They'd be likely to conclude that forty years of history conclusively demonstrated that:

- unions succeeded primarily by focusing on workers with a difficult-to-replace skill
- unions worked best if they included a small fraction of the total number of workers at a site
- a worksite should include several different unions (one for each skill)
- (perhaps unarticulated, but understood) unions should concentrate on white men
- the most effective way to exert leverage was to withdraw labor, which usually did not mean a militant confrontation

The 1930s and the CIO changed all that. Similarly today, although we think we know what a union is, what's happening on the ground is already beginning to change that. If an upsurge comes, twenty years from now people may look back on our current understandings as quaint, wondering why people thought that unions should be organized on an industrial rather than a community basis, why unions once upon a time dealt only with workplace issues, why twentieth-century unions insisted on grouping workers by worksite/employer, and why anyone ever bothered to get unions certified through the National Labor Relations Board.

The potential for such a shift has been created by the neoliberal assault of the 1970s.[1] Because that assault made labor law largely ineffective, and because the age of flexible accumulation introduced a host of political-economic changes, it is often almost impossible for unions to win within the rules of the game as currently defined. Two responses are possible. Probably most workers and unions are discouraged, seek to avoid risks, feel that any bold initiative is almost certain to be defeated, and accept concessions or modest contracts in order (they hope) to protect what they have. But more and more workers and unions are trying innovative new approaches that go outside the law, either entirely ignoring it or using it as one weapon in a larger mobilization.

The emerging paradigm has two elements—increased militance and a community orientation—and so far is based largely in communities of color. Increased militance and different tactics lead to a changed relation to the state. For an NLRB certification election, victory depends on getting the (possibly passive) support of 50.001 percent of the voters; in order to get that last marginal voter, the union may believe it needs to be as moderate as possible. One new approach, self-consciously patterned on the civil rights movement, is willing to use civil disobedience and often wins without going through the NLRB election process.[2]

Sometimes self-consciously, sometimes by unplanned force of circumstance, these campaigns do not rely on the state and its legal processes to win workers' rights. Although the state may be used as one of many means of gaining publicity and mobilizing community support, there is no expectation that normal state processes can or will guarantee the rights theoretically contained in labor law. The workers and union operate on the premise that in order to win they will have to act like a social movement. Recent research has confirmed what unions are learning on the ground: although employer opposition makes it much harder to win, what unions do also matters. A statistical analysis of a large sample of union organizing campaigns has confirmed that the more the union involves rank-and-file workers in activities and demonstrations, the more likely it is that the workers and union will win.[3] This research has significantly influenced union thinking and become one of many factors pushing the labor movement to adopt a social movement orientation, if not through conviction then simply because it has been shown to be the most effective way to win.

In order to develop this movement and power, workers and unions are adopting the second element of the new paradigm, a community-based labor movement that breaks down the barriers between "union" and "community," mobilizes and connects a range of individuals and organizations (not just those defined by an existing employment relationship), and builds a social movement that transcends what we now mean by "union." In many ways this is a new/old form that re-creates forms of struggle that would have been familiar to activists of 50, 100, or 150 years ago. The approach is, however, a significant break with the paradigmatic labor forms of the past forty years.[4] In some cases the demands and goals differ radically from those of traditional unions, in others the goal is familiar (employer recognition of a union) but the campaign and forms of mobilization mark a break with the past.

Robin Kelley argues that "the new multiracial, urban working classes . . . hold the key to transforming the city and the nation." Certainly they have pioneered the new approaches discussed in this chapter. Partly this is because their life conditions make it evident that the problems people face "do not respect the boundaries between work and community . . . The battle for livable wages and fulfilling jobs is inseparable from the fight for decent housing and safe neighborhoods."[5] Partly it is because the ghettoization of American life often creates dense and overlapping social ties within some communities of color.

Today, class consciousness is attenuated. Workers (as workers) often expect—and accept—discrimination and abusive treatment. But if most of the workers are black or Latino or Asian, and most of the supervisors are white, workers are much more likely to mark and resent the conditions, and community members are more likely to offer support. A feeling of solidarity is more likely to develop when class coincides with color such that people can draw on a preexisting racial-ethnic consciousness. Although one basis of solidarity has been an underlying awareness of racial-ethnic identity, these campaigns typically involve what Bill Fletcher and Rick Hurd have called "organizing for inclusion." The campaigns do not "explicitly organize workers around issues of race or gender" but rather mobilize people as workers or community members and seek to create class solidarity.[6] Even when almost all the participants are people of color there have often been significant ethnic-nationality differences among the participants (African Americans, West Indians, Mexicans, Mexican Americans, Salvadorans, etc.); to succeed the campaigns have needed to confront and transcend these differences.

The chapter begins with a historical retrospective and an examination of some of the factors underlying this new unionism. Most of the chapter then focuses on some revealing recent struggles.

Community Roots of Labor Power

A hundred years ago, labor-community connections were more central than they have been in the past quarter-century. From 1886 to 1955, union locals were able to affiliate directly with the AFL. Many of them, instead of being defined by craft or industry, "were chartered as geographic unions, corresponding to the geographic territory of either a town, community, or region" sometimes with an added twist, as in "The Working Girls of Toledo." For the past hundred years the labor movement has also had Central Labor Councils (CLCs) which bring together representatives of all the union locals in a geographic area. In the 1930s and 1940s often these were actively involved in progressive politics and built strong relationships with community groups; for many years, however, most CLCs were largely moribund, dominated by the building trades, and concerned primarily with preserving union labor in public works projects.[7]

One hundred years ago, in many areas community pressure was as important a source of strength as was workplace action. In the 1880s a South Norwalk, Connecticut, factory owner complained:

> Our situation is becoming intolerable and the whole community is influenced against us. We tried to board our men that we brought here [scabs], and not a boarding house would receive them. Even the restaurant keeper at the depot refused to supply them with food. We brought them down to this factory, and Mrs. Goodwin, the wife of our watchman, consented to supply them with food. . . . Today, she was waited on by a committee and told that if she continued to supply them with food, she should not purchase anything more in South Norwalk. . . .[8]

Frederick W. Taylor, the creator of "scientific management" and "time and motion" study, and one of labor's most implacable foes, came from an elite Philadelphia family but (in the 1890s) when young worked in a factory, where he tried to show that workers could speed up and produce more. He explained: "If the writer had been one of the workmen, and had lived where they lived, they would have brought such social pressure to bear on him that it would have been impossible to have stood out against them. He would have been called 'scab' and other foul names every time he appeared on the street, his wife would have been abused, and his children would have been stoned."[9]

Attempts to build on community solidarity, however, often encounter a major obstacle: racial-ethnic differences make the "community" a source of division, not solidarity, unless the labor movement explicitly challenges this divide. Through American history most unions have accepted racial division; white workers and unions have often fought to maintain their racial advantage.[10] In those all too rare instances when unions do challenge racial-ethnic divides, both labor and the community

can benefit. For example, in Alabama, around 1900 the racial climate de-
teriorated: segregation was extended, the black population was disen-
franchised, discrimination and racial violence increased. The labor
movement was by no means exempt: a variety of white workers "engaged in strikes against the employment of Negroes between 1899 and
1901." But in the country as a whole this was a period of labor mobilization—the AFL's membership quadrupled from 1898 to 1904—and as in
the 1930s upsurge, this (sometimes) involved transformations in the labor movement. In Alabama, many white workers and union leaders became convinced that in order to build strong unions, black workers
would need to be organized. Some, like the editor of the *Railroad Train-
men's Journal*, did so reluctantly: "It is humiliating, no one will take
kindly to it, . . . but unless the Negro is raised, the white man will have to
come down." Others, like the editor of *The Carpenter*, did so with considerably more enthusiasm: "We are banded together in our grand Brotherhood for the purpose of elevating the condition of our entire craft, regardless of color, nationality, race or creed."[11]

Black workers joined in droves because the unions stood against
racism. "In every U.M.W. local in Alabama with black members,
whether all-black or integrated . . . black miners served as officers." A
formula was worked out that guaranteed certain positions to black miners, "including the vice-presidency of the district organization and of integrated locals, three of the eight positions on the district executive
board, and places on every union committee, whether functional or cer-
emonial." That arrangement reflected the underlying reality that, even in
the most difficult of circumstances, black and white members were together in the union. Some mining camps with almost completely segre-
gated living conditions nonetheless "met at integrated union halls,
heard reports from black officers, and elected black men as local com-
mitteemen and as convention delegates." Black delegates chaired meetings and spoke in integrated meetings to oppose positions articulated by
white miners. When the national president of the UMW attended a district convention and supported a resolution urging miners to patronize
only unionized enterprises, the black vice president of the district spoke
strongly against it because many local unions discriminated against
blacks. The convention tabled the resolution.[12] The Alabama State Federation of Labor, under the influence of the UMW, followed similar policies, with black vice presidents and black representation on committees.
Despite the fact that the state excluded black voters, even the political
arm of the State Federation had black members as vice presidents and as
members of a committee to get out the vote for prolabor candidates.

Because black workers were delegates to the 1902 state labor convention in Selma, city officials refused to supply a hall. "'Rather than see one accredited delegate, black or white, thrown out of this convention,' a member of Birmingham's typographical union asserted, 'I would go to the woods and hold this meeting.'" This wasn't necessary: with the union taking a strong stand, the city's United Confederate Veterans (!!) offered the use of their hall. At the next year's convention in Bessemer, "the Federation's black vice-president joined the mayor and the white president of the Federation on the platform to address the guests" at a smoker given by "Bessemer citizens." Alabama's interracial union did not permanently survive the increasingly hostile racial climate and a series of employer assaults, but it stood against them for some years.[13]

Community mobilizations were also crucial to labor's 1930s successes. In 1934, prior to the Wagner Act which created the National Labor Relations Board and union certification elections, unions won three key struggles—in Toledo, Minneapolis, and San Francisco—only because thousands of community members went to the streets in a general strike. Similarly, the Flint sit-down strike of 1936–37, which brought unions to the automobile industry, was won not only because of the heroism of the strikers themselves, but also because of a community mobilization, including a militant women's brigade, that placed thousands of people around the factory, bringing food and supplies to the strikers and preventing a police or National Guard assault. It is difficult to exaggerate the importance of these contests, both as victories in themselves and as a message to the political establishment that workers and communities would take matters into their own hands unless the system provided recognized legal means to create unions.[14]

Underlying Factors

Labor regimes typically correspond to the material conditions and balance of class power in the society—although there are numerous strains and contradictions, and every system is under stress. What material conditions help explain the decline of a community orientation from the 1940s through the 1980s and its revival in recent years? Two 1950s changes—contract unionism and suburbanization—reduced union-community connections.[15] More recently, three other factors—the change in communities of color, the rise of the service sector, and the proliferation of contracting out—have led unions to strengthen community ties.

The Wagner Act, NLRB certification elections, and long-term signed contracts all brought major benefits to both workers and unions—but the NLRA was probably also the greatest force limiting community unionism. The state structure channeled worker militance and union activity, encouraging some sorts of behaviors and penalizing or prohibiting others. Under the NLRA, an employer must bargain about wages, hours, and working conditions. But what happens if the union demands that the company raise the quality of its products, support the community battered women's shelter, increase hiring of black and immigrant workers, or stop dumping waste products in the river that supplies the town's drinking water? Legally, the employer does not have to discuss these issues (though it may if it chooses to do so), and legally the workers may not go on strike over them. It's not surprising that unions moved away from community connections and towards contract business unionism; that was one purpose of the law.

Suburbanization was a second important factor reducing community unionism. It meant that workers were less likely to live close to their workplace and less likely to ride public transportation, where they could meet workers from other worksites. If workers are scattered over a wide area, the union has less information, and less reason to be concerned, about pollution, housing, or community needs.

If contract unionism and suburbanization eroded community unionism, three material factors are creating the basis for its revival, and are in fact pushing unions to adopt such an approach. The first and perhaps the most important of these is changes in the color line. In 1940, the great bulk of the minority population were blacks in the (rural) South, who constituted almost three-quarters (73.3 percent) of the total U.S. nonwhite population. Outside the South, nonwhites were only 3.9 percent of the population.[16]

By the 1990s, racial and ethnic minorities were a slightly smaller proportion of the southern population than they had been in 1940; in the rest of the United States, they were a much larger proportion of the population (15.1 percent, up from 3.9 percent). Latino and Asian populations have increased dramatically and it's clear that in the future as well the U.S. population will become less and less white. Immigrants especially will be the labor force of the future, and thus the labor movement of the next upsurge. In 1960, only 6 percent of children were in immigrant families and more than two-thirds (71.4 percent) of those children were in families that had come to the United States from Europe or North America. In 1997, 20 percent of children were in immigrant families and more than three-quarters (75.7 percent) of those families came from Latin America or Asia. Among those who were twenty-five or older in 1940 (that is, the people who created the New Deal labor system), only a fraction over 10 percent were nonwhite or Latino; among those who were eighteen or under in 2000 (that is, those who will live under any newly created labor system), the proportion was more than 30 percent.[17]

In the rural South of 1940, black populations were tightly controlled and faced restricted social networks. Today, black, Latino, and Asian populations are more urban than the country as a whole. Because of housing segregation a large proportion of these populations are concentrated into restricted neighborhoods. Although ghettos (whether in central cities or suburbs) are a source of vulnerability—the schools stink, the cops treat residents with contempt, garbage isn't picked up—they also put large numbers of people of color in close proximity to each other with relatively little white presence. (Such neighborhoods are of course monitored by the police, but that only serves to increase the neighborhood's sense of group cohesion.) Because the same populations concentrated into these neighborhoods are also concentrated into certain (low-level, service sector) jobs, in at least some circumstances the density of social ties is significantly higher than the American average. This overlap between work and community has been central to many of the campaigns discussed here.

Also important has been the economy's increasing service orientation. The New Deal labor regime was developed around manufacturing; unions therefore sought to bargain wages and contracts on a national, not community, basis. The prototypical union site of the new millennium, by contrast, is a nursing home. The labor market is local, not national: a nursing home can't credibly threaten that if workers unionize it will shut its local site and ship people's grandmothers to Alabama (or Singapore). Moreover, the significant wage competition is not with nursing homes on the other coast, but rather with other kinds of (so-called) unskilled work in that community. In addition, any strike or job action will be extremely vulnerable to community, political, and media pressure (how can you do this to sick old people, they are the ones who will suffer, you should find another way to make your point). In order to succeed, the union needs to build strong ties with as many groups as possible.

The most recent factor promoting community unions is employers' neoliberal assault which has dramatically expanded contracting out and contingent labor. About one-quarter of the workforce holds some form of nonstandard employment and about one out of ten workers are independent contractors, on call, or working for temporary help agencies or contract firms.[18] Under New Deal system labor law, workers who unionize may bargain only with their direct employer. If Nike itself manufactures shoes, it's clear the company can afford to pay decent wages. But if Nike stops directly producing shoes, and instead contracts to other much smaller companies, those contractors may have tiny profits. Moreover, if a union campaign forces one contractor to raise worker wages, Nike may simply replace that contractor with a nonunion lower-wage contractor. Within the limits of labor law, the workers at the contractor have no way to hold Nike accountable—even if Nike's actions determine every detail of the employment situation. This situation coerces unions to become radical, innovative, and militant—the only way they can succeed.

These material conditions coerce workers and unions, but do not operate automatically. Their impact depends on human agency and direction, often driven by a social movement. Just as labor missed an important opportunity to connect with the women's movement, so too the 1960s and 1970s involved all too little connection between the labor and civil rights movements. Unions typically endorsed the goals of the civil rights movement and supported key acts of legislation; the UAW made substantial financial contributions. But unions (and white workers) resisted implementing policies that would end their own discrimination and their acquiescence in employer discrimination. A fusion of labor and civil rights would have had enormous potential, but only scattered instances began to realize that potential. Among the more noteworthy were Martin Luther King's support of striking sanitation workers in Memphis (the campaign he was engaged in when assassinated), DRUM (the Dodge Revolutionary Union Movement) and the League of Revolutionary Black Workers, and District 1199, a Left-led health and hospital workers union. District 1199 organized thousands of mostly poor black workers and was instrumental in making health care one of the fastest-growing parts of the labor movement. It explicitly combined "union power, soul power" and defined itself as a civil rights union, notably in its 1969 Charleston, South Carolina, campaign.[19]

Important as was the civil rights movement, the employer offensive (discussed in chapter 2) may be doing even more to push forward community unionism. Labor's post–World War II strategy relied on employer compliance with, and government enforcement of, New Deal labor law. Once employers began mass defiance of the law, and the government showed itself unwilling or unable to effectively implement the law, unions that stayed within the law became increasingly likely to lose. It took unions some time to recognize that they needed to find a way to win without relying on the law, or at least not on conventional

NLRB processes. Increasingly labor recognized that a timid, legalistic, and bureaucratic strategy wouldn't win and that the choices were therefore a mass movement or defeat. Many unions (and workers) became discouraged and stopped trying. But increasingly, if slowly and reluctantly, some unions chose militance. Employer resistance to the law *drove* unions to become more innovative and radical—which often meant community-oriented. The rest of the chapter examines examples of some of these campaigns, including Justice for Janitors in Los Angeles, self-organization by drywall tapers and by Richmark curtain factory workers, workers centers, and an innovative multi-union labor and community effort in Stamford, Connecticut. The first campaigns all centered among Latino immigrants, while most of those involved in the Stamford campaign are black. All these cases relied on community mobilization, but the degree of emphasis on community (roughly) increases from one case to the next.

Justice for Janitors in Los Angeles

Ideally, unions would strategically target key industries they believed not to be vulnerable to closings and organize the entire industry. This is exactly what SEIU did for janitors in Los Angeles. The union had once been strong, but had declined drastically: in 1978 Los Angeles janitor membership rose to five thousand but by 1985 it was down to eighteen hundred; the wage differential between union and nonunion workers also dropped sharply.[20] At the same time, Latino immigrants came to dominate the workforce, which also became increasingly female. SEIU, then headed by John Sweeney, decided to attempt to organize the entire industry, and by doing so to take labor costs out of competition. If all cleaning contractors are unionized no company need fear that it is at a competitive disadvantage because it is paying union wages. SEIU spent half a million dollars a year on the campaign; in its first two years it yielded only a handful of members, and had the project been terminated at that point it would have been judged a failure.

The union decided not to seek NLRB certification elections, but rather to use militant actions to force business to accept unions. In part this strategy was dictated by the structure of the industry. Technically, janitors are employed by cleaning contractors, who typically operate on short-term (thirty-day) contracts. If the union targeted a cleaning company and won the election the building owner could simply switch contractors; the (union) workers would be out of a job, the contractor could start another company with a different name, and nothing would have changed. Cleaning contractors (like garment industry contractors) had little power or accountability. The buildings, on the other hand, could not move across town; the building owners had the power to provide decent wages and were vulnerable to public pressure. Under NLRB procedures, however, the union had to deal with the cleaning contractor (who directly employed the workers), and had no legal basis for action against building owners (who technically counted as innocent bystanders). Moreover, in an election campaign the focus is on persuading the marginal, least committed, worker; by contrast, the Justice for Janitors campaign mobilized militant workers and used confrontational tactics. The aim was to build a different kind of union, one based on the civil rights movement and its tactics, rather than on a conventional election campaign.[21]

In place of NLRB elections, Justice for Janitors used strong background research, guerrilla legal tactics, "in-your-face" actions, and a mobilized rank and file. Although the union did not seek NLRB elections, it aggressively filed charges complaining of employer legal violations (and not just on labor issues). The union also provided information to, and demanded action by, state agencies charged with protecting worker rights (such as the Occupational Safety and Health Administration). Because cleaning was a small fraction of building owners' total costs, raising wages was economically feasible; because contractors operated on paper-thin margins, lawsuits could bankrupt them.

Justice for Janitors used demonstrations creatively, following an owner to his golf course and his favorite restaurant, then doing street theater or raising a ruckus. The union forcefully brought attention to the workers' issues; neither tenants nor the public could escape the sometimes confrontational actions. Building tenants complained to building managers; the tenants may have wanted the union to stop its actions, but the consequence was to increase pressure on building owners. On May 29, 1990, the janitors in upscale Century City struck. "We stormed through every single building in Century City, every single one. We had a lot of community people, it was about three or four hundred people. We went marching through the buildings, chanting and banging on drums, saying, 'What do we want? Justice! When do we want it? Now.' . . . The LAPD called a citywide tactical alert that day. They just completely freaked out." Two weeks after the strike began, at another such peaceful march and demonstration, the [pre–Rodney King] "L.A. police brutally attacked the marchers, seriously wounding several people and causing a pregnant woman to miscarry" and did so "in full view of the media, and recorded on videotape."[22]

The role of Latino workers, especially Central Americans, was key throughout the strike, and perhaps at no time more than in the aftermath of this demonstration. In addition to their shared work experience, the workers were tied together by family, friendship, and residential networks; once the union reached a critical point, all of these became a means of reinforcing union strength. As one organizer noted, for Salvadoran workers, "There, you were in a union, they killed you. Here, you [were in a union] and you lost a job at $4.25." Workers had generally been in the United States long enough to be committed to improving conditions here. When police attacked demonstrators, union staff worried that workers would be intimidated, but instead they became more determined than ever. "As one key rank-and-file leader put it, 'We Latino workers are a bomb waiting to explode.'" In the immediate aftermath of the Century City police attack, as workers prepared for still more militant demonstrations, the building owners and contractors capitulated and signed a contract. This became the crucial victory in a campaign that unionized eight thousand janitors. The union raised wages, though not dramatically, introduced good health benefits, implemented an expedited grievance process (which prohibits either side from using a lawyer), and introduced various immigrant protections.[23] Over a decade later not only is the union still using militant tactics and winning significant victories; in one study its 2000 strike was the most frequently mentioned example of promising labor actions,[24] and the union is launching a new campaign to unionize building security guards. (But see the final section of the chapter for a discussion of internal strife.)

Strikes to Organize and Latino Communities

The Justice for Janitors campaign was initiated and driven by the national union. Two other impressive organizing campaigns that also involved primarily Latino workers were initiated by the workers themselves, one in southern California among drywall construction workers and one in the Boston area among garment industry workers at a curtain factory. Both organizing drives used strikes before the union was recognized, both developed from community ties, both demonstrated impressive worker militance, and to achieve victory both needed support from other groups.

From the 1950s to the 1970s, the construction industry in California was highly unionized. For drywallers (who put up the plasterboard that constitutes the interior walls of most modern buildings) in southern California, into the 1970s essentially all commercial construction was unionized as was about 80 percent of residential construction. In the 1970s, however, in California as elsewhere, employers launched an anti-union offensive (see chapter 2), with by far the heaviest losses in residential construction.[25] Reflecting this national trend, drywall union losses in California were heavy and coincided with the increasing use of immigrant workers, especially Latinos. Native-born whites were 87 percent of drywallers in 1980, but only 43 percent in 1990, when foreign-born Latinos were 35 percent of the workforce. They were concentrated in the residential end, whose workforce, observers agree, was almost exclusively Latino immigrants. Although it would be easy to conclude that immigrant labor was a major factor explaining union decline, in most of the country immigration was not a factor, and union losses in California were only about the same as those nationally.

The leader of the strike, which also became an organizing campaign, was Jesus Gomez, who had been hanging drywall since 1975 when he was seventeen. In October 1991, three weeks in a row a contractor cheated Gomez out of sixty dollars, and in response he began organizing. He was an immigrant from the small village of El Maguey in Mexico. Although its 1990 census population was only fifteen hundred, that population was disproportionately female because "at least a few hundred" of the men from the village, bound together by close kin and friendship ties, worked in drywalling in California. A drywaller who accompanied Gomez during early organizing reports "That was the key, right there." Another organizer agrees: "That core group was a very vital, important thing. They were all friends, neighbors, relatives in some way or another." Within a few months the group was holding regular Saturday meetings attended by hundreds of workers. They met at a Carpenters Union hall, but union members and staff, who were "predominantly Anglo and fairly conservative," doubted that the effort could succeed. Thus it was as the "Movement of Drywall Hangers," an independent group, that they went on strike in June 1992.[26]

Precisely because the drywallers were independent, they maintained the rights listed in the U.S. Constitution; had they been members of a union, they would have lost free speech and association rights guaranteed to others. Had they been a union, they would have lost rights of assembly, for example, since they would have faced a "30 day legal limit on picketing for union recognition in construction (after which the Na-

tional Labor Relations Act requires that a petition be filed for a representation election)." The employers sought an injunction and filed unfair labor practice charges against the Carpenters, but the complaints were dismissed because the workers were independent, not affiliated with the
union. Milkman and Wong quote one executive complaining about the
inability to win an injunction: "If you belong to a union, now I have legal
recourse, now I can stop you. But as an individual there's no way to stop
you because it's your freedom of speech and so on and so forth. So you
get into a whole different ball of wax."[27]

The strike was extremely militant and initially effective. In El Maguey,
the village elders met, discussed the issue, and called on all residents to
support the strike. Some of the subcontractors, who were the direct employers of the drywallers, wanted to settle but the general contractors
(who controlled the construction sites and decisions about which contractors to use) were adamantly opposed. Some workers began drifting
back to work and subcontractors began hiring scabs from out of state; six
weeks into the strike the movement estimated that 30 percent of the
strikers had gone back, and employers said the figure was higher. Strikers led militant actions and the state cracked down hard; the severity of
the crackdown was undoubtedly related to race-ethnicity as well as to
the degree of labor militance. A month after the strike began, "149 drywall strikers were arrested leaving a job site in the Orange County town
of Mission Viejo on charges of trespassing and kidnapping—reportedly
the largest arrest in the county's history. They were all jailed, with bail
set at $50,000 per person." Some were in jail for ten days before they even
learned what the charges against them were. The strikers refused a plea
bargain, families of the strikers demonstrated outside the jail, the AFL-
CIO Regional Office established a Dry Wallers Strike Fund, pro bono legal assistance was offered, and eventually the charges were reduced.[28]

Across the country a few years later, Latino workers ran a somewhat
similar organizing campaign. A group of about ten workers at Richmark
curtain factory approached not a union but rather the East Boston Ecumenical Council (EBEC), a religiously based community organization.
EBEC and the Boston chapter of Jobs with Justice had developed a close
working relationship. (Jobs with Justice is a nationwide organization link-
ing labor and community groups, formed in 1987 at the initiative of a
group of unions.) As a result, the Ecumenical Council helped connect the
workers with UNITE, which had two bilingual organizers who had been
working with the Latino/a community on an industry-wide organizing
campaign for laundry workers. This drive, unlike the southern California
drywall campaign, therefore took place under the auspices of a union.

UNITE prefers a "blitz" strategy, trying to sign up as many workers as possible over a weekend, with workers and union organizers going together to visit workers in their homes. After an intensive weekend, Sunday night union supporters met and a local priest made an inspiring speech of support. Monday morning workers were leafleting at the plant gates.

The company's response was immediate: "six of the most pro-union workers . . . were fired on the spot." This was of course blatantly illegal, but is common (see chapter 2).

As the union organizers were in a church with the fired workers, filling out NLRB unfair labor practice charges and preparing for an extended legal battle, a remarkable scene was taking place inside the factory. Theresa, a seventeen-year-old worker, and one of the original organizing committee, was going up and down the plant talking to people, saying if they fired some then all should go out. "In a scene right out of the film *Norma Rae*, Theresa walked out with forty-two workers following her." This self-organized, unplanned walkout/strike was an incredible demonstration of the workers' courage, solidarity, and militance, but it also posed a terrible problem. As organizer Robin Clark explained: "The rest of the people were still in and a lot of those people didn't know what a union was yet. So the tricky thing was, what do you do when your strongest people are not inside talking to other folks?"[29]

The answer was: all the things you do in any good campaign. Workers inside the plant continued to be militant, and—as the union had taught them they had a legal right to do—during break times talked to other workers about the union and the need to stand up for the workers outside. Keeping to the pattern established before, when Lillian Carrerra did so, the supervisors pushed her out the door—and six of her coworkers followed her. Workers outside continued to make house calls, to picket, and to engage in other militant actions, including blocking a bridge.

In both these campaigns, without the self-organization and incredible militance of the workers and their families the strikes would never have happened; if that self-organization had stood alone, the strikes would have been crushed. In southern California, victory depended not only on the strikers' solidarity, but also on an innovative legal strategy pursued by the California Immigrant Workers Association (CIWA), an AFL-CIO-sponsored organization. While waiting for court hearings, one of the attorneys helping to defend strikers learned from them that they had been paid regular rates for overtime work; the strikers accepted this because they were pieceworkers, but the attorney knew that the Fair Labor Standards Act (FLSA) of 1938 specifically states that pieceworkers are entitled to overtime and explains how it should be calculated. CIWA not only helped workers fight injunctions, it also filed lawsuits over contractors' violations of the Fair Labor Standards Act and, in a more unusual move, used another provision of the law to ask the government to stop the sales of "hot goods" made in violation of federal labor law (that is, the overtime provisions). "The potential liability for the relatively small drywall firms involved was enormous, since the suits claimed not only back pay for overtime worked over the three-year statutory period by thousands of employees, but also double punitive damages and attorneys' fees."[30] One drywall executive explained, "We would have defeated the strike. It was the lawsuits."

Similarly, in Boston, a legal strategy was crucial: Richmark had clearly violated laws about homework, never even applying for the required permit, and was also violating the minimum wage law. A sympathetic state attorney general threatened criminal action. The union also began targeting customers, asking them to pressure the company to settle. On October 8, just two weeks after the strike began, members of the Jobs with Justice community board and other community supporters held a rally, attended by AFL-CIO president John Sweeney. To everyone's surprise, the company president invited them in and talked with them. After heated exchanges, he ordered them to leave but they refused to do so. Elaine Bernard, director of the Harvard Trade Union Program, explained: "The employer invited us in, but then he asked us to leave. We chose to stay. Essentially we want it understood that people are losing jobs because they've exercised their right to organize. We decided to stand up for that right."[31] The union threatened more rallies and the employer caved in, recognizing the union just three weeks after the drive began.

In southern California as well, reaching a settlement required the active involvement of a union, the Carpenters. Under the settlement, the lawsuits were withdrawn, wages raised to almost double the previous piece rate, medical insurance benefits provided, and the union accepted as bargaining agent without the need for a representation election. The employers insisted on a provision that in effect coerced the union to maintain control of the industry; if the proportion of work held by the union fell, then workers lost their medical benefits and the guaranteed piece rate.[32]

In both cases, the aftermath was much less satisfactory. The southern California drywall strike could have led to major transformations, but apparently failed to do so. "At the end of the strike well over three-fourths of the drywall trade was under union contract; five years later the union share had eroded to about 50 percent. Most of our interviewees—unionists and employers alike—blamed the union for this."[33]

This strike and organizing campaign took place in 1992, three years before the New Voice leadership took office. It's worth stressing both that the "old" labor movement engaged in innovative tactics—for example, the lawsuits initiated by the California Immigrant Workers' Association, funded by the AFL-CIO, were crucial to the victory—and that the labor movement did not follow up on a remarkable opportunity. Were such an opportunity to arise again, would today's labor movement do better? Possibly, but it's far from certain. For one thing, the decisions would be made not by central AFL-CIO leadership, but by the Carpenters—who withdrew from the AFL-CIO in early 2001.

For another thing, whatever the internal strengths of the union, larger forces can be determining, as was the case at Richmark. UNITE involved workers in negotiations and by doing so won a strong contract. The aftermath, however, shows a potential limit to even the most militant campaign: a little over a year and a half later, the company announced that it would close the plant because of "stiff overseas competition and high labor costs after the plant unionized."[34] As the final section of the chapter discusses, such outcomes may be particularly likely in some of the most militant campaigns, those initiated by the workers themselves.

Workers Centers

Justice for Janitors, the drywallers' strike, and the Richmark struggle all involved Latino immigrants, and in each case success depended in significant part on ethnic and community solidarity. All were highly innovative struggles, but each (eventually) fit within the bounds of unions-as-they-are. The growing movement of ethnically based workers centers—the Workplace Project on Long Island, La Mujer Obrera in Texas, the Chinese Staff and Workers Association on Long Island, Asian Immigrant Women Advocates in California, and several others—provides an alternative form of worker organizing. Workers centers are significantly different from unions as now understood and legally defined, although UNITE, the garment workers union, operated five workers centers for some years, starting its centers in 1990. The Stamford Organizing Project, discussed in the next section, combines many of the characteristics of workers centers with those of conventional unions.

The Workplace Project on Long Island, founded in 1992, works with Latino immigrants, about half of them from El Salvador (the nationality group that was most important in the Los Angeles Justice for Janitors campaign). It has about six hundred dues-paying members, about 15–20 percent of them active. Although the popular image of Long Island is one of affluent white suburbs whose residents all commute to New York City, perhaps as many as 400,000 Latino immigrants live on Long Island, most of them low-income workers in one or another part of the service sector. Jennifer Gordon, founder of the Workplace Project, argues that "the traditional union model of organizing workers in only one industry or with one skill has little applicability to the lives of most immigrant workers today" because Latino immigrants typically work at several different jobs in the course of a year.[35]

These low-wage workers—often with little English, often undocumented—face a variety of challenges when they fight for better conditions. The Department of Labor "had one inspector for approximately 7,000 private workplaces" and neither does it welcome reports of abuse. Gordon offers the example of a dishwasher paid less than the minimum wage who complained to the Department of Labor, only to be told that Spanish-speaking personnel are available for only three hours every two weeks and the case backlog is eighteen months. A group of the dishwashers approached three different unions, each of which told them the shop was too small and the chances of success too low to make organizing worthwhile.[36] Most union contracts are only available in English, and few union personnel speak Spanish. Unions sometimes collaborate with employers: one set of workers told The Workplace Project they were forced to change their names every six months in order to prevent them from qualifying for union benefits, since the union contract specified that after six months workers would join the union and would be paid union wages/benefits.

Initially many workers were drawn to the Workplace Project because of its free legal clinic for workers with job problems. One common problem is employers who don't pay wages at all, or pay less than the minimum wage. Through the years, the project has won judgments for many of these workers; this was also one of the major activities of UNITE's Garment Workers Justice Centers. When the Workplace Project filed cases with the Department of Labor, only 3 percent of the cases "resulted in even partial payment to workers." In the 234 cases the project pursued directly, it "resolved 71 percent of them, winning $215,000 for 166 workers." But the project soon realized that this approach, like a union servicing model, undercuts organizing. The workers who bring complaints are usually leaders; when their individual problems get resolved they may cease to be active. (And in order to get a resolution, the employer almost always insists on a confidentiality agreement so other workers won't learn what they are owed.) For that reason both the Workplace Project and UNITE prefer an organizing approach. At UNITE's center, a group of thirty to forty people might assemble, take a video camera, and go out to the shop to confront the boss: "We've had numerous complaints and have taken affidavits, this is illegal, we want it to stop." Such actions are often highly effective. They scare the employer, give workers a sense of power, show what collective action can do, improve conditions, and help reduce the cost advantage of nonunion establishments.[37]

Workers centers typically also offer a variety of classes (English, citizenship, labor rights) and social activities. At the Workplace Project "a nine-week night class in Spanish on labor law, organizing techniques, and labor and immigration history" is the gateway to all other project activity, from eligibility for the legal clinic to participation in committees to serving on the project's board. (The board of directors consists entirely of immigrant workers.) The course is not just a "know your rights" workshop: it is designed "to provide group opportunities for reflection that will lead to analysis and action." A student must "pay" for the course by signing up to "put at least ten hours of her time back into the organization and the community in order to teach others what she has learned and to involve more workers in the fight for rights at work."[38]

All the project's activity, including the current version of the legal clinic, centers around organizing. Gordon argues that service can help support organizing, but "it takes a lot of thought to create a service approach that actually does lead to organizing, as opposed to one that cuts organizing off at the pass."[39]

Perhaps the Workplace Project's most notable success was the passage of New York's Unpaid Wages Prohibition Act. Immigrant workers from several centers shared experiences and designed the act, which raises employers' fine for repeat nonpayment from 25 percent to 200 percent of the back wages owed, and makes nonpayment a felony rather than a misdemeanor. To win a legislative majority workers made in-person visits to Republican legislators and told their stories in Spanish with simultaneous translation.

Workers centers are clearly wonderful institutions and advance the interests of low-wage immigrant workers in circumstances where conventional unions have been absent. Workers centers embody the vision of a new paradigm, develop leaders, and create networks. But they also involve at least three significant limitations. First, almost all workers centers define themselves ethnically—for example, the Chinese Workers and Staff Association. That is both a strength and a limitation. It helps to create unity within a group but does less than a good union to confront differences across racial-ethnic groups. When it began, the Workplace

Project was only for those from Central America, then expanded "to the entire Latino community, because we realized that immigrants from many Latin American countries were working side by side all over Long Island; checking passports at our center's door would only reduce the potential for solidarity in the workplace."[40] That's fine if the workplace/community is entirely Latino, but what if the other half of the workforce/community is African-American, Asian, or white?

Second, it is difficult to institutionalize the gains of most workers center activities. For example, one of the Workplace Project's first major successes was its day labor campaign. Workers on street corners organized, formed committees, and set wages. No one would get in the truck until the contractor agreed to pay the set wage. The project raised the base wage on the corner from forty dollars to sixty dollars for an eight-hour day. This is reminiscent of the approach adopted by the Industrial Workers of the World in the early twentieth century, and it's easy to romanticize this no-contract-just-organize approach. Connected with this, the independent centers are often skeptical of, or outright opposed to, existing AFL-CIO unions: "A position paper written for the first national conference of a small consortium of a dozen workers centers, held in New York in June 1994" argued that workers should "organize not unionize."[41] Gordon, however, is very aware of the limitations of this approach:

> The workers who were elected to represent the corner on the committee were those recognized as leaders by the others on the corner—those who had the most skills, spoke the most English, were most respected. Those same people were also the first to get work each day. So as the day went on, the committee would fall apart. A similar process of attrition took place as the season went on—over time the workers on the committee often got permanent jobs.[42]

She concludes that "a stable contract has real advantages. Contracts are extraordinarily important in institutionalizing gains." To that end, the Workplace Project has cooperated with several unions, and helped their organizing campaigns.

Third, unions are self-financing from the dues of their own (often low-paid) members, but workers centers depend on foundations for funding. Their activity can be sustained only through the infusion of outside resources. Unions would be happy to have such resources, but foundations—even left foundations—are almost never willing to fund union projects. UNITE put resources into its workers centers in hopes that this "community-based strategy, properly implemented, can bring about an upsurge."[43] But given that the union's resources come from the dues of low-paid garment workers, and given that the rest of us in the society have not created the conditions for an upsurge, it wasn't economically feasible to sustain these centers in sufficient numbers for a sufficient period. Given competing demands for funds, UNITE closed down its workers centers. Independent workers centers can take on the tasks that they do only because they don't attempt to be self-sustaining, and because foundations are willing to fund them (but not unions).

Union and Community in Stamford

Stamford, Connecticut's multi-union project is probably the least known of the examples discussed in this chapter. It combines many of the advantages of workers centers with those of unions, and as such best indicates the potential for a new paradigm. In Stamford, four unions work together not just to address workplace issues, but also to lead community-wide struggles for better housing. The issue isn't simply how community ties and ethnic solidarities can help unions, but also how unions can help drive community struggles to improve the lives of the working class. In some ways the Stamford Organizing Project's approach is fairly conventional: it was instituted from the top down by the AFL-CIO, depends on it for continued funding, and usually operates through NLRB elections. But the project uses a range of organizing innovations and has a community-focused approach that has few (recent) precedents. If we undertake a thought exercise and imagine what would happen if any one of the examples in this chapter were to be multiplied fifty- or a hundredfold, the Stamford paradigm would probably involve the most thorough transformation of U.S. society.

Stamford is in many ways the most unlikely of locations for a militant and successful union drive, since it is not only an affluent bedroom suburb but also the headquarters for Fortune 500 runaways. Since 1970, eleven corporate headquarters have relocated from New York City to Lower Fairfield County, Connecticut, making it a home to more Fortune 500 companies than all but a handful of major metropolitan areas. (Only New York, Chicago, and Houston are ahead; Atlanta is tied.) Tiny Stamford (population 130,000) houses eight Fortune 500 companies. The median family income for Lower Fairfield County is $104,000 a year.

Based on past performance, this would hardly seem the most promising location for a major union mobilization. But labor can't revitalize itself unless it makes breakthroughs in new areas. So perhaps it makes sense that in March 1998 Stamford was one of the cities the AFL-CIO chose for an experiment in innovative organizing. Four local unions formally joined the project, committing organizers of their own and agreeing to work together to develop new models, and the AFL-CIO infused extra resources, including two-and-a-half organizers, a researcher, and an office manager.[44]

"Service economy" is often taken to mean high tech and financial services, just as "suburb" is often read to mean "white." But in Lower Fairfield County, 21 percent of the population is black or Latino. The four local unions in the Stamford Organizing Project represent the service sector, but these are low-wage workers, almost all people of color, mostly black, including nursing home workers (District 1199 New England), child care and municipal workers (UAW [autoworkers] Region 9A), janitors (SEIU 531, Justice for Janitors),[45] and hotel workers (HERE 217). Attention today focuses on economic globalization, but these jobs—like most in the United States—are not directly threatened by globalization. A large majority of the members, and an even larger majority of the activists, are women. Their approach, in sharp contrast to that of Kris Rondeau at Harvard, is aggressive and confrontational—an illustration that there is no one "women's" way to organize.

When the project began, the AFL-CIO Organizing Department hired a project director, Jane McAlevey, a white woman who had never worked as a union organizer. However, she had considerable experience in community organizing, and had been working for the Unitarian Universalist Veatch Foundation, which had funded many of the independent workers centers discussed in the previous section. In addition to hiring a staff and getting to know the relevant people in the four local unions, McAlevey undertook a power analysis of the community: who had what sorts of leverage, what were the resources the campaign could hope to activate, what were the forces it would have to confront.

The four unions varied in their internal strength, commitment to the project, and on-the-ground presence in the Stamford area. After the power analysis, the next step was for the project to assess the unions' existing strengths and members' priorities. Because workers typically worked more than one job and had families, and because members had not necessarily been active participants in the existing unions, the organizers began by talking to the already organized workers, trying to speak with as many of them as possible. Much of this was done one-on-one, sometimes on the phone, sometimes in person. Two of the questions in that survey were particularly important. First, organizers asked members about their community ties: What organizations did they belong to—the PTO, the BlockWatch, the NAACP, a church (and if so, which)? Second, organizers asked what issues most concerned the workers: What were the greatest problems they faced?

Housing

Over and over again, workers emphasized housing as their number one concern; it was also a priority for black ministers, one group of community allies the project hoped to work with. McAlevey emphasized that the unions' first priorities are to organize more workers and help them win decent contracts, but "housing was the single most talked about issue from every member and worker we talked to when we got here. 'What's the issue here in Stamford?' 'I can't afford to pay the rent.' Next worker: 'so what kinds of things happen here in Stamford?' 'I can't afford to pay the rent.' Next worker: 'I can't afford to pay the rent.' So this was our challenge." Traditional unions confine themselves to "wages and hours and working conditions." The Stamford Project unions continue to organize around those, but they also mobilize all community residents, not just union members, to fight for affordable housing.

A recent study by the National Low Income Housing Coalition concluded that in order to afford a market-rate two-bedroom apartment in Stamford, a worker needed to earn $21.27 an hour. Alternatively, at $5.15 an hour, a person would need to work 165 hours a week. (If the family could cram into a one-bedroom unit, 135 hours a week would do the trick.) This made Stamford the third most expensive place in the country; the wage needed to afford housing was higher only in San Francisco and San Jose.[46] It would take quite a union to win twenty-one-dollar-an-hour wages for janitors, nursing home aides, and hotel and child care workers.

Stamford has public as well as market-rate housing. Much of the public housing dates from the late 1960s, when the city razed a ninety-nine–acre block of downtown in an "urban renewal, Negro removal" project that destroyed block after block of working-class housing and cleared the way for the Fortune 500 company headquarters. Some of the housing units fit the stereotype of public housing—high-rise buildings—but some are scatter-site two-family houses surrounded by green lawns, with connecting backyards that fill with children after school. So many people want in that the waiting list for Section 8 public housing is filled up.

By the mid 1990s, the Housing Authority's goal was not to build more affordable housing, but rather to "rehabilitate" existing units: remove the tenants and improve the buildings, then privatize, rent at market rates, or convert housing to "moderate-income" units. Under federal guidelines, moderate income is defined as anything up to 70 percent of the area's median income; in Stamford, the $104,000 median income means that families with incomes over $70,000 are eligible for the refurbished housing.

Because union members and black ministers saw housing as their greatest problem, the Stamford Organizing Project unions decided they should make it a priority issue. The first union-led housing battle took place at Oak Park, a 168–unit complex of scatter-site housing with lawns and trees within sight of the ocean and within walking distance of downtown: perfect housing for young executives, and far too desirable to stay public housing, which should be unpleasant, depressing, and dangerous. In 1999, when the struggle began, rents ranged from $400 to $480 a month. Stamford's Housing Authority told the press that the "improvements" it was considering "could include anything from rehabilitation to demolition to new construction" and that although they had no concrete plans to privatize, they also hadn't ruled it out. Ed Schwartz, executive director of the Housing Authority, "told residents he couldn't promise rents wouldn't go up as a result . . . or that residents would return to the same apartments once renovations had been made," and in fact residents had suffered from both those problems two years earlier at the William C. Ward housing project.[47]

The Housing Authority's plans were disrupted by the unions' tenant organizing. Resident anger was already there, but so had it been in previous city displacement projects. The difference this time around came from union organizing. Union staff went door to door, telling people what the Housing Authority planned, hearing resident concerns, and organizing meetings for the tenants to plan a response. Equally important, many of the residents had recently been through union organizing drives where they were tested in struggle. They had learned how to develop a collective voice and stand in solidarity with each other, and also learned that organizing can win smashing victories.

When the Housing Authority held a meeting for tenants to elect two Oak Park residents to serve as token representatives on a committee to decide the future of the complex, the tenants turned out en masse and refused to play by the Housing Authority's rules. Such committees prevent collective solidarity, create divisions between committee representatives and other residents, make decisions through bureaucratic means in back rooms, and leave the tenant representatives outnumbered and isolated. The residents would have none of it: Tenant Association Vice President

Viola Clark "said that any changes to Oak Park should be decided by more than two residents on a committee. Any changes should be decided by an open forum, so all Oak Park residents and the entire city can have a say."[48] Marie Pierre, who had previously lived in the state-subsidized housing complex on Connecticut Avenue, had been driven out when it went private and the rent on a two-bedroom apartment shot to eleven hundred dollars a month. "We will not let you do to us what you did to Connecticut Avenue and Southfield Village," she said. A single mother of two children, she had recently become an 1199 member in a bitter contest at the Honey Hill nursing home, where five workers were fired before the union prevailed (winning the election, a first contract, and the return of the fired workers).

Two months later, 150 residents and supporters were back when they "electrified the usually low-key bimonthly Mayor's Night In session." The mayor kept them waiting for two and a half hours, outraging the Oak Park contingent by skipping over them to meet with others who had signed up for the session later. When the mayor finally did meet with the residents, clergy, union officials, and NAACP leaders, he refused to sign a letter promising that rents would not be raised or tenants displaced.[49] Two months later, the unions and residents had enough clout that Vice President Gore left a $400,000 fund-raiser in the fanciest part of town in order to meet with tenants, ministers, and union leaders.[50] Unrelenting pressure forced the city to back off; Oak Park has not been privatized and still provides affordable housing.

The spring after the Oak Park battle, in April 2000, two hundred people showed up for a hearing, normally attended by at most a handful, to consider the city's application for a "Hope VI" federal grant to "upgrade" yet another project, once again reducing the number of low-income units. The Housing Authority, having learned that stalling doesn't make the tenants go away (it just makes them angrier), suspended its normal agenda and created an open mike session for tenants and their supporters. The Housing Authority chair in effect deferred to the tenant leader, who had a prepared list of speakers, each of whom was articulate and to the point.

The first speaker, identified only as Julie, a tall, dignified, and imposing black woman, spoke eloquently about her situation. Her landlord had sought to evict her and one of her checks had bounced, giving him the excuse he needed to do so. Just at this time, her son had died, and the money she had saved for a new place to live went for his funeral. At first she stayed with friends in the Oak Park complex, but that put them at risk of eviction, so she and her remaining three children had moved out.

She had applied to every public housing project in Stamford, but the only place they could go was the homeless shelter, where they had been since December. (One-quarter of the Stamford homeless are working poor.)

The problem was not a lack of income, she said: as a member of District 1199 she earned twelve dollars an hour as a certified nursing assistant, but market-rate housing in Stamford requires an income of more than twenty-one dollars an hour. "Yes," she said with humor, "we could find housing in Bridgeport, but I don't want to move there. My kids are getting a pretty good education in Stamford; my daughter is taking college-level math. To survive school in Bridgeport, kids have to be good at fighting, and my kids don't fight that well." But staying in the homeless shelter posed terrible problems. In the shelter, any time the adult leaves, the children must leave as well. If she had to work on a school holiday, or if the school had a snow day, what was she to do? If the kids wandered the streets on their own, she'd be declared an unfit mother; if she missed work, she'd lose her job.

The last of the five tenant speakers, Joan Phang, was just as powerful. Her remarks—and audience comments throughout the meeting—made it clear that the tenants knew more about Stamford housing than did the members of the Housing Authority, and had a clearer plan for what could be done. The Housing Authority, she said, was not interested in fixing up apartments. Three years ago the authority received a Community Development Block Grant for twenty-seven thousand dollars to insulate the Oak Park apartments, which would have been wonderful, since the only problem with that complex was the lack of insulation. But the authority had never used that money and therefore had lost it.[51]

Now the Housing Authority was running an ad in the paper seeking to hire a public relations consultant to explain authority policies to tenants and the community. "You can save that money," she said. "If you do the right thing the community will support you and you won't need high-priced consultants." Moreover, fourteen units in Oak Park were vacant and boarded up, but "as we just heard, families need housing." If those units were fixed up, the authority could be collecting rent on them, but the authority didn't seem to want to do that.

She then read a statement to the commissioners and the assembled tenants. The statement committed the authority:

- to identify the vacant units in all of the projects within one week
- to fix the fourteen vacant Oak Park units within three weeks and to fill those units with families from the homeless shelter

- to fix all of the vacant units in other projects within two months, and place families in them

She concluded by saying that if the commission would sign the statement, the tenants would help them identify and fix the vacant units. The audience erupted with shouts, chants, and calls of "Sign the paper, my man, sign the paper." The Housing Authority, of course, was not prepared to endorse the tenants' agenda, however sensible it might have been.

But Is It a Union?

Sounds great. An impressive struggle. But what does this have to do with unions? How long can unions afford to subsidize housing struggles? Won't labor need to return to its core task, organizing workers at their place of employment? The answer to this is twofold.

First, labor unions have always taken on a range of other issues: supporting environmental legislation, helping to fund the student and civil rights movements, pushing for child care and health care (as discussed in chapter 3). One of the local unions in the Stamford Project, 1199 New England (an affiliate of SEIU), offers citizenship classes for its members and sponsors training programs that help members gain the certification needed for higher-level positions. Unions are and should be concerned with anything that can improve the lives of workers in general and union members in particular.

The Stamford Organizing Project unions don't take on every social issue. The project's criteria for involvement require that:

- the issue be widely and deeply felt by the members
- the issue ties back into why people need unions
- the labor movement can have a measurable impact if it joins the effort
- the issue is important not just in general, but to labor's key allies
- the campaign enables unions to expose or confront some of labor's main targets
- the campaign develops a positive image for labor (positive among those whom unions seek to organize, not among power brokers)

In Stamford the first issue was public housing; elsewhere such issues might include public transportation, toxic waste dumps, other environmental pollution, discriminatory employment policies, the quality and availability of child care or after-school programs, or a host of other issues.[52] In 2001 and 2002, for example, the Stamford project began to expand its geographic base, and in doing so focused on immigrants' rights issues. When the Connecticut Department of Motor Vehicles (DMV) attempted to impose new regulations denying drivers' licenses even to many legal immigrants, the project worked with ACORN to lead the organizing against this. Over seven hundred people turned out at two meetings. When two busloads of people showed up to a DMV hearing, they were turned away—ironically, because to gain entry to the hearing people needed to present a driver's license (or other government ID). People demanded entry and were sprayed with Mace. Publicity from this led to a new hearing. Several dozen legislators signed a petition saying that such changes should require legislation, and the attorney general rejected the DMV's proposed changes.[53] This focus on immigrant rights is part of a national movement within the AFL-CIO, which has officially changed its position to strongly support rights for all immigrants, documented or undocumented.

Second, however, and far more interesting: tenant (or immigrant) organizing *is* union organizing. For one thing, such organizing helps develop leadership, and that in turn develops the union's future capacity. In the Oak Park campaign, perhaps the strongest leader, Marie Pierre, had not been a key person when her nursing home organized just months before. "The thing that moved her, that touched her, were her children, but she's definitely a leader now and her union's better for it," explained AFL-CIO organizer Myrna Iton. Also, at meetings on public housing union organizers meet key workers, talk to people at unorganized facilities, and get to know the friends, relatives, and neighbors of organized workers.

Even more important, the housing and immigrant campaigns build a reputation for the unions. Consider what happened, for example, when the UAW launched a campaign to organize the city's child care workers. One of the keys to the success of the child care organizing campaign was the unions' reputation in the community, built through the Oak Park housing campaign. As Myrna Iton explained:

> We go in and talk to a group of workers in the child care center for example, who are mostly African American and poor and live in the projects, and they know who we are, there's no question about that. They've heard their pastors talk about the union and unionization for months, and they've seen the fights, very public fights, that union members have waged around public housing, and it's all fresh, they've seen it happen. So that's been a slam dunk.

In Stamford, many of the union members—be they child care workers, nursing home aides, or janitors—live in public housing. A standard part of many organizing campaigns is the house call—a visit to a worker's home to talk about the union. In the public housing projects, when union organizers started making these calls, they were met by an unusually friendly reception. Workers/tenants knew the unions fought for people like them, as a result of the housing campaign already had personal connections to union staff and members, and welcomed organizers into their homes. During 1199's campaign to organize the Atria assisted living facility, for example, Marie Pierre, a leader in the Oak Park housing battle and an 1199 member, but not employed at Atria, went on house calls to talk with Atria workers who lived at Oak Park. Stamford Organizing Project unions rely on these preexisting community connections.

Organizing Innovations

In Stamford, the union is the community and the community is the union. The coordinated group of unions identifies and takes leadership on the issues of most concern to the working poor—that is, to actual and prospective union members. In turn, the community relies on unions to fight hard on issues of importance to people of color and the economically marginal.

What's different here is not just the greater union involvement in the community, not just the expanded definition of what's of concern to unions, but also (and above all) the altered character of the relationship. The usual (best case) union approach is: "If a community group asks us, we'll make a donation or have a union official speak at the rally." The Stamford Organizing Project is entirely different: "These are our issues, they are priority concerns for our members, so our members are using the union to fight on these issues." The unions are not a minor auxiliary, part of a long list of support groups, but rather are the leadership, the force driving the campaign. Housing issues were of concern to Stamford's low-income population long before the AFL-CIO launched its innovative organizing project—that's why members identified the issue as their number one concern—but public housing tenants and people of color were consistently losing until the unions entered the fray. Now they are winning battles, though in the current political climate these are mostly defensive struggles to prevent the privatization of existing public housing.

In the fall of 2001 housing campaigns moved beyond the project-by-project defense to win an ordinance providing one-for-one replacement for housing demolished or taken out of commission. The ordinance covers both public housing and publicly assisted housing and provides that the replacement housing must be at the same level of affordability. The AFL-CIO has also made an extraordinary pledge: if the state will commit $50 million to affordable housing, the AFL-CIO Housing Investment Trust will match it with a $50 million line of credit.[54] That's a form of leverage that dramatically raises the stakes, catching the public's attention and putting the legislature on notice.

One of the keys to the Stamford Organizing Project, I concluded during my visit, is the simple fact that the four local unions and the AFL-CIO organizers all share office space. The organizers don't just know each other; they are constantly interacting, sharing experiences, dealing with the same problems. Without making a conscious effort to do so, they provide each other with ideas, community news updates, and organizing leads. That's all the more true since their members are related to each other, are neighbors, and go to the same churches. If an employer outrage takes place somewhere in town, if nonunion workers are angry and ready to organize, the organizers will hear about it. And of course public housing actions provide an opportunity for workers and organizers to see the range of nonworkplace connections, to discover that an 1199 nursing home militant is the neighbor and friend of a UAW child care worker. The strongest bonds are forged in struggle, but the simple fact of shared office space provides a base for developing a community perspective. Unions elsewhere could take a big step toward a community orientation simply by locating in the same space so that organizers buy each other sandwiches to eat at their desks, take coffee breaks together, and share stories about atrocities and acts of heroism.

In Stamford, of course, this shared approach is central to the project and all its actions, and is by no means accidental or fortuitous.[55] Ever since the project started and staff went out to talk with workers, they have not only asked what issues most concern the workers but also about workers' community connections: whether they belong to a church; what community organizations they belong to (PTO, Block-Watch, NAACP, etc.); if they are married, where their spouse works and whether he or she is a union member; and whether the member is registered to vote and actually does so. All that information is then put in a database, making it possible to determine how many union members live in this housing project or neighborhood, how many attend that church, and so on. When the survey was first proposed, one of the organizers objected: "We can't ask our members that, it's a privacy issue." But that person quickly came around since, as Myrna Iton notes, "The members actually loved it. They were fine. To them it was a natural way to deal with their concerns." Based on that community analysis, the unions are able to determine where they can and cannot exert power and leverage. In what neighborhoods or churches or community groups do they have a presence? (One thing the project quickly learned: by far the most important community connections are with churches.)[56]

Perhaps the single most impressive aspect of the Stamford Organizing Project, more so even than taking the lead on housing, is that instead of union staff building community alliances, if an issue arises workers use their preexisting community connections to mobilize to support each other and the union. The organizing staff help prepare and train workers to do so, but the message is carried by workers themselves—and as a consequence is far more powerful than anything that could be done by staff alone.

For example, if a worker is fired simply because she is a leader of pro-union workers, staff may file an NLRB complaint, but they don't rely on the government's official processes, which can delay justice for up to three years. Instead the union staff use the data base to determine which members attend the fired worker's church, and also make similar lists for all the other churches attended by members who work for that employer. The unions then bring together groups of workers from each church for discussion and training. First the group talks about workers' need for allies to increase their power and accomplish their goals, and then about the issue itself. The emphasis is on parishioners/workers/union members' personal stories and how the issue plays out in their lives—things like:

- Mary, the worker they fired, is one of the best workers in the place. The only reason they fired her is because she fights for the union. If the company gets away with this, no one is safe.
- Right now, to get health care for just one extra member of my family I would have to pay seventy-five dollars a week. If my kids get sick, they don't have health insurance. At our meetings it came out that no one—*no one*—can afford the copayment.
- At the nursing home, the employers forced us all to attend a meeting to hear their anti-union propaganda. And I mean *all* of us. No one was left on the floor; during the meeting one of the residents fell out of her wheelchair and was hurt.
- Three supervisors pulled me into an empty room and grilled me for an hour; I was so scared I was shaking. Next the group agrees what it will ask the pastor to do and engages in one-on-one role playing to prepare for the meeting.

The workers then arrange a group meeting with their pastor. (Depending on the size and membership of the church, the group may contain from three to fifteen workers.) Union staff can help prepare workers, and help them learn more about the issue, but as one organizer explained, "I can't tell them how to talk to their pastor, because they know them much better than I ever could. They have a relationship, and that's the whole point: that union issues should not be viewed as separate from people's lives, that this is what they are fighting for, that this is economic justice, not just a union issue."

The Stamford Organizing Project unions have a stunning record with this approach. The clergy have become involved in campaigns, speaking out from their pulpits, sending letters of support, showing up at rallies and picket lines, speaking at community hearings. In the process, clergy have learned much about their congregants' lives and the structure of power in Stamford, and as a result, many have become radicalized. At one rally prior to a planned massive strike, twenty-two ministers (and several hundred workers) attended and signed a statement of support. That enabled workers to win without needing to go on strike.

One telling example of this approach: union contract negotiations are typically held at a "neutral" site. But neutral for whom? Most contract negotiations are held in a "businesslike" setting, a hotel conference room, a location where managers are at home and workers are uncomfortable. (Many of these workers, after all, have friends or relatives working as maids and housekeepers in these hotels—or do so themselves as a second job.) Stamford Organizing Project contract negotiations always take place in (black) churches, a "neutral" setting where workers feel at home and (white) managers are uncomfortable. Frequently the minister comes at the beginning of negotiations to offer a prayer, a hope that everyone will do the right thing. You'd hate to be the public relations manager for a company that refused to negotiate in a church, but the setting almost inevitably alters the "balance of comfort" (and hence power), at least marginally.

The Stamford Project uses the same approach to politics. Union political persuasion does not come from campaign donations or staff lobbying. Instead, legislators and representatives are asked to meet with groups of their constituents who tell their own stories: this is what is happening in our organizing drive, here's what management is doing to us right now. Legislators, like pastors, are asked to take a stand: we want you to write a letter to the owner, to speak in our support at a rally, to walk the picket line with us. Politicians are politicians, but they are also human beings, and they respond. Of course, even a cynical politician may find it good politics to publicly identify with workers' compelling stories; it's more problematic for a politician to be bracketed with union staff and campaign donations. In Stamford the personal stories are backed by worker power: the unions' ability to turn out hundreds of workers on issues that matter. As with pastors, politicians get educated, become far more sympathetic to worker issues, and although "radicalized" might be too strong a term, step by step are led to take actions unheard of for most politicians.

Recently the Stamford unions have taken another step in member empowerment—a step that, like the others, is an innovation in today's standard union practice, but has a long history in the labor movement and in other kinds of organizing—the member organizer.[57] Some of the best and most active members have been trained to be organizers, to go on house visits with nonunion workers to talk with them about what it's like to be in a union. Each member organizer pledges to organize eight hours a month. They also meet together once a month to study, talk about economic justice, share experiences, and learn from each other. At a recent meeting, organizers from the nursing home union met with child care workers and housing campaign leaders: "A room full of women leaders talking about issues and it was really great." Although other unions have member organizing programs, Stamford is unusual in that rank-and-file activists from an 1199 nursing home meet with UAW child care workers and SEIU janitors. Asked if member organizers get anything for their eight-hour commitment, the answer was: "Power, man. They understand that the only way they are going to get better contracts is greater [union] density."

Assessment

Four caveats about the Stamford Organizing Project should be noted. First, a project strength is also a limitation: the workers do low-income service work. Those jobs are far more central to our economy than most realize—2.2 million health and nursing aides, 3.1 million cleaning and building service workers, 1.2 million child care workers—and many are among the fastest-growing occupations. Organizing them is clearly vital, and that's the goal of the Stamford Organizing Project. But the labor movement needs to find equally innovative ways to organize the far more numerous clerical, technical, and professional workers.

Second, most of this service work is done by people of color mainly women). Because Stamford is a mid-size (or small) city, and because most of the housing is extremely expensive, union members and nonunion workers doing the kinds of jobs the unions have targeted are heavily concentrated in a few geographic areas and housing projects. The actual and potential union members not only work at similar jobs, but often live in the same neighborhoods and are united by race or ethnicity. White workers are less subject to the ghettoization of housing, and consequently would probably be more dispersed. In addition, white workers might feel less of a sense of commonality and community,[58] and it's an open question whether their ministers would be equally willing to become involved in parishioners' struggles for economic justice.

It would be a mistake, however, to essentialize and assume that all workers of color share an immediate and unproblematic affinity, thus making solidarity automatic. Jamaicans may see themselves as having more ambition and drive than African Americans, citizens born in the United States may look down on immigrants, the documented may have problems with the undocumented, and language (English, Creole, or Spanish) divides workers from one another. For example, as people were preparing to leave a meeting of the member organizers—those most committed to unions and social change, who are therefore likely to have the most advanced consciousness—one important African American leader said, "I bet that idiot Ed Schwartz [the executive director of the Housing Authority] isn't even legal, I bet he's a goddamned immigrant, let's get him out of Stamford." Jane McAlevey, director of the Organizing Project, asked everyone to sit down again, and pointed out that the equally committed leader in the next chair was a Haitian immigrant. The African American leader responded, "I didn't mean if he wasn't from here, I meant if he was illegal we should run him out of town." This initiated a new round of discussion. Jane reports that among the people of color "the tensions are huge, but good unions are contributing to undoing the ethnic stuff, much more quickly than community groups."

Third, even within the terms of the project, some problems are obvious. Most glaringly, although the sign board in the building lobby lists four participating unions, no one was in the office allocated to the hotel workers, evidently no one has been for some time, and only a handful of hotel workers have been organized. That's a huge loss: hotel workers are demographically similar to child care workers or nursing home aides, live in the same neighborhoods and housing projects, are friends and relatives of the other categories of workers, and sometimes hold second jobs in the other industries. By failing to make a serious attempt to organize in the hotel industry, labor loses the advantage gained by worker networks and community ties. The hotel industry gap also undercuts union power, not only politically but economically, by maintaining a pool of exploited lower-wage workers. This highlights that the Stamford

Organizing Project adds an additional layer to, but does not alter, existing union structures. These remain four separate union locals, and in each case the Stamford contingent is only a small part of the total. The Stamford organizers have to answer to leaderships based elsewhere; certainly there is no multi-union council of workers to coordinate project activities.

Fourth, what the labor movement most needs are self-sustaining initiatives, but it's not clear whether Stamford will be one. The national AFL-CIO committed money to support the project for its initial period, but—as planned—has now reduced its funding. The hope was that local resources would support the project and the national AFL-CIO could provide seed money to other communities. Andy Levin, the national AFL-CIO official most responsible for initiating and supporting the project, thinks it is a "fantastic model" but that if Stamford is not able to sustain itself and become self-supporting then by one important criterion the project would be a failure.[59]

That said, the Stamford Organizing Project has been, and continues to be, a spectacular success: adding forty-seven hundred new union members,[60] winning strong contracts, defending public housing, building an impressive reputation in the community (among both friends and foes), drawing in pastors and political leaders. The gains so far are impressive, and the project's limits have by no means been reached. The labor movement needs to create one, two, many Stamfords.

Perils and Possibilities of a New Paradigm

Under the New Deal labor regime, the state was supposed to guarantee workers' rights. In theory, workers who wanted a union could file asking for a speedy election, conducted by a neutral government body (the NLRB) under rules of fair play, with violations swiftly punished. In the labor regime's waning years that is no longer true in practice. Employers make sure that justice is delayed, and so denied. Because violations of labor law, even the most blatant and outrageous, face minimal penalties, both in law and in public opinion, employer cost-benefit analyses lead them to violate the law and fair play.

In a world where the law is ineffective and rights are consistently violated, at least two (contradictory) responses are possible. Unions can adopt militant tactics and forge community alliances, or they can try to cut political deals with employers or politicians. Not surprisingly, unions are adopting both responses. John Sweeney began his AFL-CIO presidency by saying that he wanted to build bridges, but was also willing to block bridges if necessary (a reference to a militant Justice for Janitors action). He has been arrested at numerous demonstrations, but in his autobiography he also argues that the labor movement's "ultimate goal is a new social contract, by which workers will share not only in prosperity but in power."[61]

The approach that I've emphasized, and one main union thrust, is using militant tactics, publicity, and community alliances to protect workers' rights without relying on the NLRB's normal processes and procedures. In this approach, union campaigns may well use the state, filing lawsuits and challenging employers in regulatory bodies, but filing a lawsuit is just one of many ways of bringing pressure to bear. Worker rights are won, if they are won at all, by mobilizing enough community support and publicity; the strength of the movement, rather than the effectiveness of state legal processes, becomes the key to success.

Union staff by themselves can't bring that pressure to bear even if they want to do so. Unions, and especially union bureaucracies, don't have the public standing that commands attention and respect. The unions with the broadest-based, most militant campaigns, taking on the widest range of issues, are the ones most able to adapt to the new realities.

The new reality reverses the old approach that argued unions could succeed only if they narrowly confined their attention to wages and benefits and working conditions. Today it is often the case that in order for the labor movement to mobilize significant pressure, it must show that the issue is more than "just" a union issue. Usually it's not enough to show that it is a worker issue. Violations of workers' rights, especially if the workers are affiliated with a union, rarely grab the public imagination. Unions that attempt to mobilize media attention and popular sentiment are usually unable to do so unless the campaign also involves racial-ethnic inequality, or the environment, or sexual harassment, or the safety or quality of some service/product (such as health care). Most union campaigns do involve such issues. Where once unions saw those issues as distractions, increasingly they become vital elements of success.[62] That reality helps change the balance of power inside unions, strengthening the hand of those who wish to build a broader and more progressive labor movement.

At this point, the labor movement—and any movement for a progressive cause—is trying to swim against the tide. It takes hard work just to stay even, and in the aftermath of these campaigns workers have often experienced reversals. If the approaches described here remain isolated they are likely to be crushed and to be remembered, if at all, as curiosities. But if the tide turns, these approaches could produce not only numerical gains, but a qualitative shift in the character of the labor movement, a shift that would change laws, the culture, and our understanding of what a union is and does.

To date, the most significant successes with this approach have been in campaigns involving people of color. But elements of the approach are now used in a wide range of struggles. Jobs With Justice pioneered this orientation and many of the specific tactics, but the AFL-CIO has now put out a booklet about organizing community campaigns, and its weekly report on union organizing victories almost always notes those that were won using "card check" campaigns. In this approach, a community campaign pressures the employer to agree not to insist on a normal NLRB election, but rather to stay neutral and agree to accept the union if it can show that a majority of workers have signed cards asking for union representation.[63] Typically the card check is conducted by a neutral outside body, for example, a group of ministers, community, and political leaders. Sometimes that group is constituted specifically for that one campaign and sometimes the cards are taken to a permanently constituted Workers Rights Board, an innovation introduced and given reality by Jobs With Justice.[64] In effect, this neutral outside body does what the National Labor Relations Board is supposed to do: it guarantees that workers' rights are protected. Employers fear public condemnation by these community leaders far more than they do NLRB action. The toughest part of the campaign is pressuring the employer to accept such a decision-making process. The union's aim is to make it difficult for an employer to explain why he/she is unwilling to trust Reverend Jones and Mayor Smith.

Even with these tactics, it is an open question the extent to which the campaigns are democratic and worker-controlled. Critics argue that even in the Justice for Janitors campaign, workers were *mobilized* but not *organized*. That is, the union made use of workers' militance for key actions, but the campaign was not controlled by workers. In such campaigns, angry workers are "turned out" but don't learn the skills needed for a successful campaign, don't develop their own leadership, and don't participate in a meaningful way in making decisions. In a critique of an article by Steve Lerner, lead organizer for the Los Angeles Justice for Janitors campaign, Mike Parker and Martha Gruelle call this approach "militancy without democracy."[65] Critics point out that not long after the Justice for Janitors campaign, the local was taken over by an opposing caucus and the national SEIU responded by putting the local into trusteeship. Most of the insurgents were people of color, and most of the Justice for Janitors organizers were Anglo white. It would be easy to paint this as about race-ethnicity or rank and file versus staff. Some left accounts have presented the issue that way; others, who will only talk off the record, see the issue as more complicated and confused, with no clear heroes. But no matter what, there's something wrong when the labor movement's model campaign results in the national union not being willing to accept the election results in the local that's just been revitalized.[66]

The Justice for Janitors campaign may have been initiated from the top, but the campaign's success unequivocally depended on worker militance, a claim it would be harder to make for SEIU's home care campaign. This 1999 Los Angeles victory was labor's biggest numerical gain in more than fifty years, bringing in seventy-four thousand workers. It too was an impressive campaign, also forging impressive alliances, but with success more reliant on politics than worker-to-worker contact. Home care workers are personal attendants receiving (prior to unionization) minimum wage to care for the elderly or disabled in their homes. They are paid by the state, but hired and fired by those they care for; almost half of home care workers are family members of those receiving care. Because such workers are scattered in thousands of worksites and never come together, organizing faced a huge challenge. Because home care workers provide vital individualized care for people for whom they care deeply, a strike was not an option. Three factors were crucial to the campaign's success. First, SEIU was willing to stay with the campaign for more than a decade. Second, the campaign built an impressive alliance between home care workers and the disabled/elderly consumers, a considerable challenge given that the consumers were also the people who hired, fired, and disciplined the home care workers. Third, thanks in part to the consumer-provider alliance, SEIU was able to exercise political leverage to define an employer of record that made the workers able to unionize.[67]

The California home care campaign depended on political alliances more than worker militance, but it was a real campaign, reaching and involving thousands. In 2002 New York hospital workers struck a flat-out political deal with Republican Governor George Pataki; it will be some years before it's clear what was won and what was lost in that deal. What Pataki gained was clear: the endorsement of the 210,000–member union, famous for its ability to turn out its mostly minority membership. That endorsement helped undercut Carl McCall, the Democratic nominee and an African American; it also made it credible for many other unions—such as the Teamsters, Laborers, and building trades—to endorse Pataki. The union won $1.8 billion in state money to finance raises and pay for recruiting unionized health care workers and Pataki backed a significant increase in New York's minimum wage. The union also won language intended to provide employer neutrality in future organizing drives, although the bill was not as strong as the union had hoped. The final language specifies that employers who receive state money (notably, hospitals and nursing homes receiving Medicaid money, but with language that covers all employers) may not use the state money to oppose union organizing. The union had sought a provision requiring employers who receive state money to pledge to stay neutral during organizing drives. The actual language permits employers to oppose unions as long as they can show they did not use any state money to do so. Employers present this as an accounting problem, not as changing their response to union organizing. The Communication Workers (CWA) have won the stronger language that the New York hospital workers sought— but CWA did so through strike action, or the credible threat it would go on strike if not granted this language in contract negotiations.

These two different strategies—developing worker militance and community alliances versus seeking a social contract with politicians or employers—are related to the extent to which unions rely on a top-down versus a bottom-up approach. Frances Fox Piven and Richard Cloward argue that unions (as well as other poor people's movements) make significant advances only when driven by a mass upsurge from below. In their brilliant book, *Poor People's Movements: Why they Succeed, How they Fail*, they argue that organizers need to learn that "whatever the people won was a response to their turbulence and not to their organized numbers." The correct approach, they believe, is to "escalate the momentum of the people's protests," recognizing "that efforts to build organizations are futile" because the organization either serves to co-opt the insurgency or itself gets crushed.[68]

That may be true in a period of mass upsurge, but that's not the current situation; should unions simply wait for an explosion? In some ways, on a small scale, that has been the dominant approach in most unions: wait for a "hot shop," where workers are angry and eager for a union, then organize it. But isolated pockets of insurgency are totally different from a society-wide mass movement. The problem with the "hot shop" approach is that a union ends up representing a nursing home here, a grocery store there, some bus drivers a few miles down the road.[69] The union doesn't represent a large enough share of any industry to exercise significant leverage on its wages and working conditions, so workers win only minimal improvements. (Alternatively: the union wins substantial advances, the employer becomes uncompetitive, the worksite closes or moves elsewhere.) At least as important, under current (employer-dominated) conditions, few groups of workers show the self-organization and militance of Richmark or the California drywall tapers. If unions wait for such situations, little organizing will take place, unions will continue to decline, and workers will lose power. Both the Los Angeles Justice for Janitors campaign and the Stamford Organizing Project were introduced from the top, by a national union grouping, on a large enough scale that workers could gain the power to significantly improve conditions.

Kim Voss and Rachel Sherman's research directly challenges the Piven and Cloward argument. Based on a careful study of northern California, Voss and Sherman argue that today the key to both the level of organizing activity and the use of innovative tactics is pressure from above (typically from the national union) rather than an upsurge from below. Workers get mobilized because an organizer activates and channels them. Local unions undertake organizing in significant part because the national union pressures and rewards them for doing so. The most effective organizers are those with past involvement in nonlabor social movements.[70]

Voss and Sherman's research reminds us that mass insurgency does not magically appear. In the Great Depression of the 1930s, material conditions may have made people desperate, but leftists organized and led many of what we now celebrate as popular outbreaks. When I was a child, my father taught me that the Montgomery bus boycott began because an old woman was just too tired to move. In fact, Rosa Parks was an officer of the NAACP and had attended the Highlander Center; her refusal to move to the back of the bus was carefully planned in advance. This is precisely what would be predicted by resource mobilization, the most influential theory in the sociological study of social movements.[71]

The arguments and evidence presented by Piven and Cloward, juxtaposed with those of Voss and Sherman, outline a contradiction. A true contradiction means there is important truth on both sides, and the tension cannot be resolved through an unproblematic choice.[72] In many circumstances outside organizers and pressure from above can help workers mount militant campaigns that otherwise would never take place. Without Jane McAlevey and the other union organizers, Stamford might have high levels of discontent, but neither workers nor public housing residents would be as mobilized or as successful as they are at present. Workers are developing skills, leadership, and consciousness that they would not otherwise have developed. The Justice for Janitors campaign was possible only because hundreds of workers were willing to engage in demonstrations and civil disobedience. But the campaign would never have happened if John Sweeney had not authorized spending large amounts of money on an untested approach that took a long time to show results. At the same time, established unions have often stifled change. Labor has made big advances *only* in periods of upsurge, and the same is true for other social movements (African Americans, women, gays and lesbians). And every such period of upsurge has been driven by rank-and-file activism. I may be a crazy optimist to believe that we are on the verge of a new period of upsurge, but that's at least an arguable position. It would be delusional, however, to believe that a smart and committed staff can by themselves draw up and implement plans for a society-wide mass movement, or even for a dramatic increase in the number of union members. Voss and Sherman are probably right that at this time much of the activism comes from the top down, but that's another way of marking how little is currently happening. For labor to regain its once strong standing there will need to be an upsurge. The key basis for evaluating labor's current activities is the extent to which they make an upsurge more possible.

5

Neoliberal Globalization

Forces and processes associated with globalization fundamentally shape the world we live in. No account of labor's current weakness and potential regeneration can neglect the topic. In the United States from 1899 through 1963, import content as a proportion of finished manufacture was never more than 3 percent; in 1971 it was still only 9 percent. Today the value of manufactured imports is equal to 69 percent of the sector's GDP. Not only is world trade more important, but the technical and cost barriers to world interactions are dramatically lower than they once were. The cost of a three-minute New York-to-London telephone call fell from $188 in 1940 to $31 in 1970 to $3 in 1990 to under half a dollar in 2002.[1] When we ask how the world of today differs from that of the 1930s, globalization is clearly one of the most consequential differences.

But what is "globalization"? Is it sharing music and ideas, enjoying foods from around the world, and utilizing the World Wide Web? By that standard, most people in the United States would endorse globalization. Is it taking steps to address global warming and adopting policies that show concern for every person on earth? The most vocal advocates of "globalization" would oppose such policies. Or does "globalization" mean that business and profit must be all-determining, that any law that helps workers or the environment must be abolished?

Business and conservative advocates have seized control of the term "globalization." The debate is usually framed as "globalization: yes or no?" with those opposed to "globalization" cast as modern-day equivalents of flat-earthers, people putting their heads in the sand in hopes that doing so will stop "progress." But, despite what Thomas Friedman of the *New York Times* would have us believe, the meaningful debate is not about whether or not this is and will be one world—at least since Columbus, *that's* been settled—but rather what will be the terms of engagement, who will control the process, for what ends will it be pursued, and by whose standards will it be evaluated? Are we seeking global justice or the worldwide triumph of business neoliberal policies?

Neoliberal policies—that is, those that promote reliance on the market and a questioning of government—have been thoroughly integrated into the institutions regulating globalization, so much so that it is often difficult to think about globalization separate from its neoliberal variant. In the United States neoliberal policies are advocated by both Republicans and New Democrats. The alternative viewpoint—usually called "anti-globalization" by business and the media—promotes global justice for workers and the environment. The contest between these two competing visions can be divided into three stages: business's mobilization and increasing triumph from the 1970s to the late 1990s, the post-Seattle period (1999–2001) when global justice forces began to redefine the debate, and post-9/11 when everything has been in abeyance.

An old joke tells of a man returning a broken rake to his neighbor. In his defense he argues (1) I never really borrowed it, (2) besides, it was broken when I got it, and (3) anyway, there's nothing wrong with it. Advocates of neoliberal globalization argue in similarly contradictory ways: First, that globalization is a neutral, inevitable, unstoppable process which has nothing to do with politics or human will. Second, that these are desirable policies, the only ones that can guarantee our country's prosperity, and that business and conservatives deserve a lot of credit for introducing them. Third, well, maybe these policies aren't so good for most people in the United States, but they are needed to aid the underdeveloped world. Every one of these business claims is demonstrably wrong.

The structure of this chapter differs somewhat from that of the others, because the political-economic framework both created labor's difficulties and must be changed if labor is to advance. Policies that may initially seem to have nothing to do with labor actually structure the options and determine what is possible. More background is therefore needed in order to understand the challenge labor and its allies face, and the sorts of approaches that need to be considered to develop solutions. The first half of the chapter considers and refutes each of the three arguments made by the advocates of a business-driven globalization policy. The last half of the chapter considers three of the options labor can take to advance workers' interests: capital controls, international labor standards, or building cross-national labor solidarity.

Inevitable and Apolitical?

Business apologists claim that globalization in its current form just happened; no one pushed for it, no one sought to shape policies to promote their self-interest or class interest. According to Thomas Friedman: "I feel about globalization a lot like I feel about the dawn. Generally speaking, I think it's a good thing that the sun comes up every morning . . . But even if I didn't much care for the dawn there isn't much I could do about it."[2] Because globalization is an inevitable accompaniment of modernization and economic development, no one should try to fight it. The only debate is how to adapt to it.

But there are alternatives to the neoliberal framework of globalization through commercialization; consider the (fully global) Internet. Because it's a spectacular success, companies today are of course attempting to take it over and shape it to their purposes, but the Internet and World Wide Web are global but not (yet) neoliberal. Key steps in the development process were pushed by researchers, university-based personnel, and idealists. Its creators relied on public rather than corporate funding, and their aim was to facilitate communication and connect people with one another, not to enrich themselves. The Internet and the Web are powerful forces bringing people together globally. By no means can the Internet be said to be open to all on equal terms, but once plugged in to the Internet there are few limits to where someone can go. Anyone may not only receive messages, but post them to others. A person with little wealth or power can create a web site accessed by tens of thousands around the world. This model of globalization contrasts sharply with the World Trade Organization (WTO) model that all decisions must be made in terms of what is best for business.

Much of the debate about globalization "presupposes an 'original condition,' a starting-point for the process, in which the world is made up of distinct and self-sufficient national economies, each under the jurisdiction of an independent nation-state." But movements of goods, people, and ideas go back many thousands of years, at least since modern people swept out of Africa some sixty thousand years ago. Although the term "globalization" is new, the phenomena to which it refers have long been discussed and studied. "States have always had to respond to and been constrained by external actors. Their autonomy in terms of their real capacity to formulate and implement public policy has almost in-variably fallen short of their formal claims to sovereign national power."[3] People living in small or weak states have no trouble understanding this: the intellectuals and workers of Panama or Nicaragua (or for that matter the Netherlands) are under no illusion that their states or economies are, ever were, or possibly could be autonomous and self-sufficient. How-ever, both intellectuals and ordinary citizens in hegemonic states, such as the United States, or former hegemonic states, such as Great Britain, have much more difficulty understanding or remembering this, and may become angry or engage in victim-bashing when events force them to recognize the limits to sovereignty.

The implicit argument—rarely made explicit, because once it's brought into the open its ludicrous character is almost self-evident—is that "globalization" requires that local democracy be abolished in favor of decision making by unelected bodies such as the WTO (dominated by representatives from the world's richest countries acting on behalf of the most powerful businesses). Neither these organizations nor globaliza-tion in its neoliberal form appeared through some magical, apolitical, technological imperative. As Frances Fox Piven, Leo Panitch, and others have emphasized, globalization is a politically instituted process. "As *The Economist* [perhaps the world's leading business magazine] put it re-cently, those 'who demand that the trend of global integration be halted and reversed, are frightening precisely because, *given the will, govern-ments could do it.*'"[4]

It's taken many years for business and its political allies to build the ne-oliberal version of globalization; each step in the process required a new set of decisions. One key element was dismantling capital controls; the United States pushed hard for this to be the policy of both national gov-ernments and the International Monetary Fund.[5] Perhaps the most cru-cial neoliberal step was the creation of the World Trade Organization. In 1994, business neoliberals thought that GATT (the General Agreement on Tariffs and Trade) wasn't strong enough, because it applied only to trade in goods and because it had weak and ineffective mechanisms for resolv-ing disputes between nations. So they strengthened their particular ver-sion of globalization by creating the WTO, which covered trade in serv-ices as well as goods, and they instituted new rules requiring member nations to accept its jurisdiction and obey its decisions. Countries that fail to do so promptly are subject to fines and trade sanctions imposed by the WTO. When the WTO investigates disputes and imposes penalties, the decision is made by a totally unrepresentative body meeting in secret, with the deliberations not open to the public even after the fact.

The WTO not only rules on tariffs, but also on "nontariff barriers to trade," that is, any governmental policy (at whatever level: federal, state, local) that limits "free" trade. When the United States passed regulations requiring that fishing nets be modified to reduce the likelihood that they would ensnare (and thus drown) endangered sea turtles, the WTO ruled that this was a "nontariff barrier to trade" and the United States was forced to abandon the regulation (and the sea turtles). The Ethyl Corporation has sued Canada, arguing Canada has no right to ban a harmful gasoline additive; Metalclad has sued Mexico, arguing Mexico has no right to deny Metalclad a permit for a toxic waste disposal site; and the United States has argued France has no right to ban entry to hormone-treated beef.[6] Neither the creation of the WTO, nor such rules and rulings, are inevitable.

For workers, unions, and environmentalists, such treaties pose serious problems. Neoliberals act as if we must either operate on these rules or entirely cut ourselves off from the world economy, thus eliminating coffee and bananas from our diet, and never hearing records or seeing films produced outside our borders. Such a claim, implicit in much of what neoliberals say, is ludicrous. Because WTO decisions are made out of the public spotlight, through the workings of bodies whose officials are not politically accountable (or even recognized by the public), it may seem that the neoliberal version of globalization is the only possibility. But the fact that a decision is hidden, or the alternatives are never presented or debated, does not mean that the decision is technically necessary or inevitable. Quite the reverse: the decision must be made in secret precisely because it could not withstand public scrutiny.

Good for the United States?

Forced to admit that the neoliberal variant of globalization is by no means inevitable, but is instead a politically instituted process, proponents of the neoliberal variant of globalization have a fallback position: Even if globalization isn't inevitable, we should support it because it's good policy. Globalization, Thomas Friedman tells us, "is the engine of greater long-term prosperity for every country that plugs into the globalization system."[7] Neoliberals say that we must therefore abolish all impediments to the free market and accept complete free trade both inside the United States and with all the rest of the world. (Not quite all: neoliberals make exceptions for corporate welfare, tax breaks, and export subsidies.) Otherwise, they say, our nation's economy will stagnate, consumers will pay inflated prices, incomes will go down, and everyone will suffer.

If "prosperity" refers to conditions for most of the population, this is simply wrong. Neoliberal globalization has been good for profits and wealthy individuals, but for few others. This can be seen by comparing two periods: the welfare state (or Keynesian or social democratic) policies that prevailed in the 1950s and 1960s, and the increasing neoliberalism of 1973 to the present. From the end of World War II to the early 1970s, the United States, most European countries, and most of the Global South (also called "the underdeveloped countries" or "the Third World") pursued at least mildly social democratic policies involving strong government intervention in the economy. In much of the world—although notably not in the United States—key industries were nationalized. Social welfare systems were created or expanded. And typically a compromise, or at least modus vivendi, was reached between the labor movement and the capitalist class, a compromise that extended to both company and government-level policies. For example, Richard Nixon, a conservative Republican, announced that "we are all Keynesians now," a statement that was consistent with his economic policies—which included support for creating the Environmental Protection Agency, the Occupational Safety and Health Administration, wage-price controls, and what was in effect a proposal for a guaranteed annual income. Business generally accepted these policies both because of the strength of unions and because, given a relatively closed economy, business relied on increasing working-class incomes to support the growth of a mass-based consumer economy.

Before 1973, governments regulated transfers of capital or currency from one country to another (the so-called Bretton Woods system).[8] Such regulation is needed in order to maintain a strong welfare system, protect the environment, and pursue most other people-oriented goals. Suppose a megabillion dollar corporation can say, "We moved our official headquarters to the Bahamas (although we only have four employees there), and we now count all our profits as coming from there; therefore we have no U.S. profits and don't need to pay any taxes." (Not so long ago this would have been illegal; today it is an increasingly common corporate tactic.) If there are no controls on a corporation's ability to move its capital from one country to another, it can (on paper) claim that all its profits come from whatever country will give it the lowest tax rates.

Since the early 1970s, the United States and most other countries have increasingly adopted neoliberal policies, deregulating both their national economies and all international economic exchanges. Government intervention in the economy has been drastically reduced. As president, Ronald Reagan declared that government was not the solution, government was the problem. In Europe, nationalized industries have been sold; in the United States, regulated industries have been deregulated, and government services have been contracted out to private firms. In this way, a market logic comes to dominate even the provision of government services. The market, rather than strengthened international institutions, becomes the force regulating global activity, with FedEx and UPS as the new post office and a host of private banks and securities firms in place of an effective global regulatory institution. Social welfare programs have been curtailed everywhere, since their cost has increased and their benefits (to business) decreased.[9]

These policy changes, made with relatively little public awareness, much less debate, have had profound consequences. Once, foreign currency exchange was about paying for trade (or tourism); now it's mostly about speculation. "It is estimated that, in 1971, just before the collapse of the Bretton Woods fixed exchange rate system, about 90 percent of all foreign exchange transactions were for the finance of trade and long-term investment, and only about 10 percent were speculative. Today, those percentages are reversed, with well over 90 percent of all transactions being speculative."[10] This dramatically increases the amount of money involved, which no longer bears any meaningful relation to the actual flow of goods and services. The effects of that reverberate throughout the economy, strengthening the hand of those who want to restructure other institutions. As a consequence "international financial pressures are felt by small and medium sized firms operating in the home market, and not only by large companies operating internationally."[11]

Neoliberals would have us believe that these post-1973 policies have produced economic success, and that if we want to increase economic performance we need to further extend and strengthen neoliberal globalization. But in fact the economic record is clear: from 1945 to 1973, the "bad old days" of currency controls, capital controls, strong unions, frequent strikes, and government regulation, the economy boomed and prosperity was widely shared. During the period of neoliberal globalization, on the other hand, the economy has stagnated and inequality increased. In the United States, using constant 1999 dollars for all comparisons, from 1949 to 1973 average family income more than doubled, from $19,515 to $41,935; moreover, incomes during this period became more equal, so those at the bottom benefited even more. In the next quarter-century, from 1973 to 1999, incomes went up much more slowly, and much of the increase was because so many more married women were working. Moreover, incomes during this period became substantially more unequal, with the largest gains going to those at the very top. If incomes had increased as fast in the neoliberal period as they did during the welfare state period, the average 1999 family would have had an income of $97,623 instead of the actual average of $48,950. It takes some nerve for neoliberals to claim their policies are necessary for economic success.[12]

Help the World's Poor?

If the neoliberal version of globalization is not inevitable, and if it has a poor economic record in the United States, perhaps it nonetheless helps promote development in Africa, Asia, and Latin America. Maybe the U.S. economy has been stagnating precisely because globalization is promoting the development of the Global South. Such thinking makes sense only if we assume that there is a fixed quantity of production and wealth; in such a zero-sum world, a gain for any group must be counterbalanced by an equal loss for some other group. For more than twenty years, as U.S. wages stagnated, such views have become more widespread, entrenched, and a part of accepted common sense.

But that's not how capitalism operates. Even Marx recognized—and celebrated—capitalism's enormous productivity, and the liberatory potential of these increases in production. Over 150 years ago he described what sounds like the globalization of today:

> The bourgeoisie cannot exist without constantly revolutionising the instruments of production, and thereby the relations of production, and with them the whole relations of society. . . . The need of a constantly expanding market for its products chases the bourgeoisie over the whole surface of the globe. . . . The bourgeoisie has through its exploitation of the world-market given a cosmopolitan character to production and consumption in every country. . . . All old-established national industries have been destroyed or are daily being destroyed . . . The intellectual creations of individual nations become common property. . . . From the numerous national and local literatures, there arises a world literature. . . . [The bourgeoisie] has created enormous cities, has greatly increased the urban population as compared with the rural, and has thus rescued a considerable part of the population from the idiocy of rural life. . . . The bourgeoisie, during its rule of scarce one hundred years, has created

more massive and more colossal productive forces than have all preceding generations together.[13]

Remarkable as U.S. growth was in the post-1945 period, the economic development of the Global South during this same period was still more incredible. "In statistical terms, the Third World's economic achievements of the three decades 1950–80 are a story without parallel in world development history."[14] The South's record during this period surpassed that of Europe during the nineteenth century from 1820 to 1900. "The South did this in half the time at twice the growth rates" and did so despite having a population five times as large as that of Europe in the nineteenth century.

Economic growth of this kind is not simply a statistical abstraction; consider some of what it meant for people's lives. In Brazil, from negligible levels in 1950, by 1980 76 percent of all households had radios, 55 percent had televisions, 50 percent had refrigerators, and 22 percent had automobiles. Or consider literacy. Europe's literacy rate is estimated to have been below 25 percent in 1850 and below 50 percent in 1900.

The corresponding level of literacy in the South was about 30 per cent in 1950. By the 1980s, however, it had risen to 50 per cent in Africa, 70 per cent in Asia and 80 per cent in Latin America. More significantly, despite all the shortcomings both in the data and in the quality of education imparted in developing countries, the North-South educational gap narrowed spectacularly during these decades of relative prosperity.[15]

Public health also improved dramatically, with life expectancy in the Global South increasing "from around forty years in 1950 to sixty years by the mid 1980s," an extra twenty years of life for the average person.

One of the reasons for the economic development of the Global South was that those who dominated U.S. and European business and politics wanted to forestall revolution or the appeal of so-called Communist parties. More than a third of the world's population was in this "Communist" bloc, which had a major presence in Europe (Eastern Europe, Russia) and Asia (China, parts of Korea and Vietnam), a minor presence in the Americas (Cuba), and, in one variant or another, substantial political appeal in much of the rest of the world. Communist parties were significant political forces in France and Italy. At one point or another over a forty-year span an impressive list of countries accepted aid from, or maintained friendly relations with, China or the Soviet Union. Competition with the Communist bloc constrained the United States to see that benefits were widely distributed to the Global South's population; anything less would have weakened the United States in its competition with the Communists. As Robert McNamara explained:

> Too little, too late, is history's most fitting epitaph for regimes that have fallen in the face of the cries of the landless, unemployed, marginalised and oppressed, pushed to despair. As such, there must be policies designed specifically to reduce the poverty of the poorest 40 per cent of the population in developing countries. This is not just the principled thing to do, it is also the prudent thing to do. Social justice is not only a moral obligation, it is also a political imperative.[16]

For most of the Global South the explosive economic growth of the post-1945 period of social democracy ended under the impact of neoliberal policies, although rapid growth continued in Asia. "In Latin America, after a sustained rise in the previous three decades, per capita incomes fell by 10 percent in the 1980s. In Sub-Saharan Africa, per capita incomes fell on average by as much as 25 per cent during the same period."[17]

The political (and economic) conclusion from this is crucially important but—remarkably—seems to be almost completely missing from the conventional wisdom of globalization discourse: economic prosperity for one region (whether North or South) does not come at the expense of the other. Rather, the same set of social democratic policies brought economic growth to both North and South, and the neoliberal policies that have created stagnation for average workers in the North have also created hardship in the South. Rather than a trade-off between workers of the two regions, the policies that benefit one also aid the other. For economic policy, the conflict is not so much that between the Global North and South, but rather that between capitalists and workers.

How Damaging Is Neoliberal Globalization?

Neoliberal claims about the origins and benefits of globalization don't hold up, and the neoliberal form of globalization hurts workers both North and South. But just how significant is globalization for workers and unions? Many commentators argue that the effects of globalization overwhelm most other factors and are (almost?) all-determining. These analysts seem to imply either that there isn't much labor can do, or that labor needs to focus almost all its energy on addressing globalization.

Once again we need to analytically separate globalization (the world-wide spread of ideas and economic development, based on interchange and interaction) from neoliberalism (the abolition of government regulation and all other barriers to the unchecked rule of business and the market). Most people support globalization and oppose neoliberalism, so business and its allies have tried to blend the two and insist that to have globalization we must also have neoliberalism. If labor is to develop a response (the focus of the last half of this chapter), it needs to determine the source and seriousness of the problem.

Even without neoliberalism, globalization would have significant effects on the U.S. economy, but neoliberalism is far more important. Globalization is, of course, one of the factors that has helped strengthen neoliberalism and maintain it in place. The combination of globalization and neoliberalism has devastated manufacturing unions. But neoliberalism, even without globalization, has had similar effects on many other sectors of the labor movement. At this point it may not be possible to disentangle neoliberalism and globalization, but the independent effects of globalization per se may not be the primary issue. There's every reason to believe that the effects of globalization will spread to new areas of employment. Despite that, outside of manufacturing much of U.S. employment is not particularly vulnerable to being moved elsewhere, but *is* vulnerable to other forms of neoliberal policy such as privatization, deregulation, and contracting out.

The effects of globalization are of course uneven: for some industries it is devastating and inescapable, for others it has little or no direct impact. Consider table 5.1, which gives a tentative assessment of the relative impact of globalization on various sources of employment, and the number of employees in each area. The table uses broad categories which are useful for a first approximation, although there is wide variation within some categories. In manufacturing, for example, the garment industry is largely based outside the United States, but the tobacco consumed here is manufactured almost exclusively inside this country; the auto industry is somewhere in between. Within the business services category computers and data processing are vulnerable to globalization, but temporary help is not. Moreover, globalization can exercise a substantial effect on an industry by means of a change of ownership, the importation of another country's labor practices, and so on, even if employment in the

Table 5.1. Vulnerability of the U.S. Economy to Globalization, by Sector

Employment sector	Number of sector employees (in millions)	Total for category (in millions)
Highly vulnerable (imports more than 50% of domestic)		18.9
Manufacturing	18.4	
Mining	0.5	
Somewhat vulnerable (imports 15–20%)		7.7
Transportation	4.4	
Agriculture	3.3	
Minimally vulnerable (imports less than 5%)		93.3
Communications	1.6	
Public utilities	0.9	
Finance, insurance, and real estate	7.5	
Hotels	1.9	
Personal services	1.3	
Auto repair	1.2	
Business services	9.7	
Amusement and recreation services	1.8	
Health services	10.1	
Legal, educational, and social services	6.5	
Wholesale trade	7.1	
Retail trade	23.1	
Government (federal, state, and local)	20.6	
Total employment accounted for in table		119.9
Total U.S. employment		135.2

Source: Statistical Abstract of the United States 2001, calculated from tables 609, 641, 1283, and 1306. No major employment category had imports between 21 and 49 percent or between 6 and 14 percent.

sector stays almost exclusively U.S.-based. (This is probably true for the communications industry, for example.)

It's important to remember that at issue is the extent to which the employment, not the employer, must be based in the United States. Foreign firms can purchase U.S. hotels, but if the hotels are in the United States, so must be the employment. Similarly, the issue is not the country of origin of the employee: a large fraction of private household workers may have been born outside the borders of the United States, but the work itself must be performed here. Responsive unions should be able to organize U.S.-based workers, whatever their country of origin, and whatever the nationality of their employer.

Not only is two-thirds of employment (by this calculation) relatively insulated from globalization, but that is even more true of the fastest-growing jobs. Of the thirty occupations with the largest job growth, I would classify only four as vulnerable to globalization: systems analysts, database administrators and computer support specialists, computer engineers, and hand packers and packagers. Job growth for these four occupations from 1996 to 2006 was projected to be 1.2 million. Excluding general managers and top executives as not relevant to a union analysis, the other twenty-five occupations with the largest job growth all appear to be relatively insulated from the pressures of globalization. These occupations include (from most to least job growth) cashiers, registered nurses, retail salespersons, truck drivers, home health aides, teacher aides and educational assistants, nursing aides (including orderlies and attendants), receptionists and information clerks, secondary-school teachers, child care workers, clerical supervisors and managers, marketing and sales supervisors, maintenance repairers, food counter and fountain workers, special education teachers, food preparation workers, guards, general office clerks, waiters and waitresses, social workers, adjustment clerks, short-order and fast food cooks, personal and home care aides, food service and lodging managers, and medical assistants. Job growth for these occupations was projected to be 6.9 million.[18]

Globalization has been devastating in the manufacturing sector, especially in the old-line industrial unions that had some of the best wages and benefits and sometimes provided a model of progressive labor militance. Given this, employers can routinely threaten that if workers vote for a union, the owners will close the plant and move it abroad, and this is a powerful weapon in the assault on unions. Kate Bronfenbrenner's study, conducted for the NAFTA Labor Secretariat, showed that in manufacturing, where it is particularly credible to threaten closure and plant relocation, employers threatened closure in 62 percent of all union organizing campaigns, and unions won only 23 percent of the manufacturing campaigns where employers threatened closure.[19]

But even in relatively immobile industries such as construction, health care, education, and retail, employers threatened to close in 36 percent of campaigns. Employers routinely threatened "that the employer might go out of business or have to contract out work if the union succeeded in its collective bargaining goals." Globalization alone simply cannot explain the decline of union membership or the growth of contracted-out labor. For example, from 1975 to 1999 the number of members of the vulnerable-to-globalization auto workers, steel workers, and machinists declined 42.5 percent (from 2.9 million to 1.7 million). But leading construction unions, which are relatively immune to the (direct) effects of globalization, declined just as fast as the auto, steel, and machinist unions: by 47.7 percent over the 1975 to 1999 period (from 1.6 million to under 0.9 million).[20]

There are alternatives to the neoliberal form of globalization, and the next sections explore some of those. There are no easy solutions, however, because neoliberal assumptions have been structured into the institutional fabric of economics, politics, intellectual life, and popular discourse. That means the transition from the current regime to something else is likely to be difficult.

A solution seemingly requires one of four things, all equally unlikely:

1. Impose codes of conduct to hold corporations to standards enforced by monitoring and publicity
2. Control capital, creating policies that discourage corporations from leaving the country, and thus make it possible to enforce U.S.-specific labor standards and to establish effective fiscal policy
3. Regulate labor conditions internationally through some official agency such as the United Nations or World Trade Organization
4. Develop global class solidarity, either with a single world union for each industry, or with strong alliances between unions around the world

In practice, unions are pursuing all four, some mix of all is likely to be needed, success on one makes it easier to succeed on the others, and it seems exceptionally difficult to win a significant victory in any of these areas. Advance on any of these fronts will require a strong social movement; absent a movement the likelihood is that neoliberal globalization will become even more firmly entrenched. Codes of conduct will be discussed in the next chapter, and so are omitted here; the rest of this chapter looks at the other three approaches to controlling neoliberal globalization.

Capital Controls

Both unions and governments try to set limits on corporations, requiring them to pay for overtime, promote workers on seniority instead of management whim, pay taxes, control pollution, or pay a minimum wage. Corporations try to limit union power and elect compliant politicians so they can avoid ever having to confront such policies. But if the policies are adopted, corporations try to evade them. Perhaps the most powerful way they do so is to pick up and move; often a corporation can defeat a policy simply by threatening to relocate. In the United States corporations are treated as having an absolute right to relocate, for any reason or no reason, but European countries have imposed a variety of restrictions, from needing government permission to increased tax rates.[21] Without capital controls (or a global regulatory body) it is difficult to provide adequate social welfare benefits, protect the environment, or pursue an expansionary fiscal policy. Although neoliberals often claim capital controls are destructive, international capital controls of various sorts operated effectively for a quarter-century after World War II, so clearly they are compatible with a booming world economy.

One advantage of capital controls is that they can be imposed nationally, although even they would be more effective if they were adopted by several countries. Because capital controls are national policies, they could also be the focus of democratic political agitation and be raised as issues in elections. At least for a country as large (in area, economy, and population) as the United States, unilateral action is a feasible alternative, but without a doubt in the 1980s and early 1990s "'the focus on nation states derive[d] primarily from a pragmatism born of a total inability to conceive, let alone construct, a meaningful political process at the global level.'"[22] Post-Seattle, with the emergence of a global justice movement, attention shifted to global actions (see below).

Economists and policy wonks have developed a host of mechanisms that would impose costs on speculative transactions and move the economy toward more regulation and control of capital. For example, Nobel prize–winning economist James Tobin has devised a proposal (dubbed by others the Tobin tax) to impose a tiny tax on all foreign exchange transactions. Suppose the tax is one-half of 1 percent, either for buying or selling. An investor who buys a foreign bond, holds it for a year, and then cashes back into the home currency, will pay a tax of 1 percent. Similarly, companies that use foreign exchange transactions only when paying for actual movements of goods and services would experience minimal tax consequences. If an investor trades currencies once a month, however, the tax becomes 12 percent, and if the investor is a pure speculator, trading currencies once a day, the tax becomes 365 percent a year, a level sufficient to discourage most speculation. Tax policies are a time-honored way of promoting or discouraging certain kinds of behavior. If business behavior did not alter, or changed only modestly, the Tobin tax would also generate enormous amounts of revenue that could be used to meet human needs in the Global South, to protect the environment, or to address other pressing needs. By one mid-1990s estimate, a Tobin tax of one-quarter of 1 percent would raise $200 to $300 billion a year globally.[23] Capital controls of various sorts could reduce employers' ability to threaten that if workers unionize the company will move to another country.

International Labor Standards

Since the early 1990s the labor movement and many other groups have focused on introducing international standards; that has been the defining approach of the post-Seattle global justice movement. Such standards could apply to labor (the focus here), the environment, or other issues; the basic principle is that the World Trade Organization should be as concerned about fair trade as it is about free trade, as concerned about promoting a better world as it is about protecting profits.

Through the 1980s unions' primary response to trade was to favor protectionism for any industry faced with significant competition from imports. Protectionist policies have historically been associated with racism, nationalism, and xenophobia.

The U.S. labor movement has increasingly moved away from protectionism and now favors international labor standards. Critics sometimes describe this policy as "disguised protectionism," but its political implications are worlds apart. Instead of demanding that "foreign" goods be kept out, the labor movement now supports the free international movement of goods and services provided that they are produced in countries that honor certain basic labor rights. The entry of goods would be restricted only if they had been produced by forced labor or by workers whose attempts to organize were repressed. Politically the message is not "Americans against foreigners" but rather "worker rights against employer repression." This promotes a very different sort of movement, with promising alliances, and raises issues usually excluded from mainstream politics.

These labor standards already exist in the form of conventions agreed to by (many of) the countries that are members of the International Labor Organization (ILO). The ILO's "core" standards are as follows:

- Freedom of association—workers and employers to have the right to establish and join organizations of their own choosing without prior authorization (ILO Conventions 87 and 98)
- Freedom from forced labor (ILO Conventions 29 and 105)

- Minimum age for the employment of children (ILO Convention 138)
- Freedom from discrimination (ILO Conventions 100 and 111)

It's important to recognize that these "are universal standards in the sense of being independent of a country's level of economic development." That is, any country, rich or poor, can guarantee its workers' right to organize, prohibit forced labor, and so on. Nothing in these conventions requires the payment of any particular wage.[24] If these standards were accepted there might be huge wage disparities between Indonesia and the United States, but even were that the case, the AFL-CIO would favor permitting goods of Indonesian origin free entry to this country.

These standards are so modest that it might seem every country would support them. To the contrary, the U.S. Congress has (so far) refused to endorse the labor conventions providing for freedom of association. Probusiness members of Congress fear that the U.S. government would be found in violation of ILO Convention 98, which declares that "workers shall enjoy *adequate* protection against acts of anti-union discrimination in respect of their employment" (my emphasis). The United States acknowledged as much in its 1999 report to the ILO when it stated "there are aspects of this [U.S. labor law] system that fail to fully protect the rights to organize and bargain collectively of all employees in all circumstances." A Human Rights Watch report concluded that in the United States "millions of workers are expressly barred from the law's protection of the right to organize." U.S. labor law is designed to protect long-term, full-time, nonsupervisory, rule-bound workers with a single employer; that is, "the rights of a worker who is fast disappearing." Even when workers are theoretically covered by the law, Human Rights Watch notes, "the reality of NLRA enforcement falls far short of its goals" with "weak and often ineffective" remedies and enforcement "often delayed to a point where it ceases to provide redress."[25]

Human Rights Watch points out that "labor rights violations in the United States are especially troubling when the U.S. administration is pressing other countries to ensure respect for internationally recognized workers' rights as part of the global trade and investment system."[26] For U.S. labor one benefit of international standards might be the need to improve U.S. labor law and its enforcement. Despite the United States' own failure to ratify the ILO conventions, at least during the Clinton administration the U.S. government—pushed by the AFL-CIO—was a leading force promoting the adoption of international labor standards.

The most vocal and visible opposition to international labor standards came from the leaders of Third World countries, such as Prime Minister

Mahathir of Malaysia, who has "argued that the pro–Social Clause lobby will undermine the comparative advantage of developing countries in low labour costs" and thereby "retard economic development."[27] It is also true that most of the rich (that is, OECD) states supported such standards and the majority of Third World governments were intensely hostile. But that ignores the internal dynamics, both North and South. The international labor movement generally supported standards, although with hesitation and reservations; employers, including those in the United States and Europe, opposed them. Since the prime minister of Malaysia is the most frequently quoted opponent of international labor standards, it is worth quoting the position of the Malaysian Trades Union Congress:

> We want a world trading system that puts the human being at the centre of economic activity. We say that if the world's companies can have common global rules, then so, too, can the world's workers. . . . We believe that an open, transparent and multilateral system of examination of unfair labour practices can only benefit workers of all countries. The obvious, best way of achieving this would be to take the main standard-setting conventions of the International Labour Organisation and build them into the WTO.[28]

Given the support of the dominant nations of the North, including the United States and the European Union, it would seem to follow that labor rights guarantees should have been adopted. But although the United States government has publicly promoted such standards, it has never put its weight behind meaningful and enforceable standards. The only standards that governments have supported, even rhetorically, have been those that are unenforceable. The greatest victory for labor standards was the December 1996 Singapore meeting of the WTO, which called for "a commitment to the observance of internationally recognized core labour standards" and named the ILO as "the competent body to set and deal with these standards."[29]

Although ILO rules might sound like a solution, in practice such standards would be toothless; only WTO rules would be enforceable. This is because of the enormous differences between ILO and WTO rules. ILO conventions are almost entirely voluntary. When an ILO convention is passed, each member state must submit it to its legislature for ratification, but there is no obligation to ratify the convention (even if it involves "core" standards), and conventions are not backed by a workable enforcement mechanism. On the other hand, "It is a condition of membership of WTO that members automatically accept the jurisdiction of WTO dispute settlement panels." The offending country can be penalized with tariffs on other areas of trade.

That is why labor, environmentalists, and a broad coalition of other groups are fighting to see their concerns incorporated into the World Trade Organization rules. The logic is simple: worker and environmental concerns should have the same priority and protections as profit and property concerns. WTO rules explicitly prohibit any rules about *process*, about the way the goods are produced, that is, whether workers are exploited. There is a total lack of parallelism: property rights are carefully specified with effective enforcement means provided, and labor rights are omitted entirely. As Elaine Bernard has argued:

> The WTO says its purview does not include social issues—only trade. So it claims to be powerless to do anything about a repressive regime selling the products of sweatshops that use child labor. Yet let this regime use the same children in sweatshops to produce "pirated" CDs or fake designer T-shirts, and the WTO can spring into action with a series of powerful levers to protect corporate "intellectual property rights." So, it's really not a question of free trade versus protectionism, but of who and what is free, and who and what is protected.[30]

Even in treaties that appear to address labor rights, minimal sanctions are involved and enforcement is implausibly difficult. For example, the Clinton administration negotiated NAALC, the North American Agreement on Labor Cooperation, but workers' rights to freely associate, organize, and strike were excluded from the dispute settlement procedures that could end in fines or sanctions.

> And even where sanctions were contemplated, for example, when there has been a "persistent pattern" of failing to enforce laws relating to health and safety, child labor, or minimum wages, the procedures were so convoluted that the chief Mexican negotiator felt safe in assuring Mexican entrepreneurs that it was highly improbable the stage of sanctions would ever be reached. . . . In striking contrast, [NAFTA's] chapters on intellectual property and investment are tightly drafted and contain clear sanctions for violations and a detailed mechanism for settlement of disputes. Furthermore, they are incorporated into the main body of the agreement.[31]

As things currently stand, these are structural differences. At present, the treaties themselves contain no effective mechanisms for enforcing labor rights, but contain powerful procedures for protecting property rights. Unless the treaties are modified, even prolabor governments or prolabor WTO representatives would be unable to do much.

Business and its (academic and media) apologists argue that "There is No Alternative" (TINA, as it was called in South Africa) to their version of globalization, which they present as the neutral unfolding of the objective historical forces of progress. But that claim is fraudulent: look at the way rules were carefully and self-consciously formulated to privilege property rights and ignore human rights. As currently structured, there is almost no outlet for democratic input into the policies that determine our lives. But, despite that, the South African liberation movement taught us "There Must Be an Alternative" (THEMBA). Every limitation is also a strength: precisely because there are no inside-the-system forms of recourse, if people want to make changes, the only available option is to build a militant and participatory movement—such as that forged in the streets of Seattle.

The Battle in Seattle

On Thanksgiving Day 1999 few Americans had even heard of the WTO, much less knew what it did. The Seattle WTO meeting, or rather the protests against that meeting, dramatically increased public awareness. On its opening day, the WTO was unable to convene because protestors blocked the streets, confining ministers and high officials to their hotels. A wide coalition of environmentalists, church groups, and labor created alliances and a movement that only a few years earlier would have seemed inconceivable. The spirit of the day was best captured in one demonstrator's sign, "Teamsters and Turtles, Together at Last." Young demonstrators in turtle costumes protested a WTO ruling that U.S. legislation to protect sea turtles was an unwarranted infringement on "free trade." Perhaps as many as fifty thousand marched in the streets, six hundred civil disobedience demonstrators were arrested, and a handful of anarchists smashed store windows. Police fired rubber bullets, wooden dowels, and so many rounds of tear gas that downtown became a disaster area.

For years the labor movement had been working to redefine the issues and to build alliances with a range of other social movements. Seattle was a spectacular demonstration of the successes of that strategy. In 1992 Pat Buchanan (along with Ross Perot) framed the trade issue for public debate, and his populism was nationalistic, xenophobic, and bordering on racism and anti-Semitism. It would be easy to imagine an AFL-CIO rally with a Pat Buchanan message, but that's emphatically not today's

labor movement. Instead of "Buy American" labor's message was res-
olutely internationalist. For the early 1990s NAFTA debates, the language focused on nation and race; the key issue was whether the United
States would gain or lose jobs. By Seattle in 1999 labor as well as others
framed the debate in terms of class and rights, not only in the United
States but around the world. As the *Seattle Post-Intelligencer* reported,
"On stage at the rally were dozens of U.S. workers . . . who had lost
work when their plants moved to poor countries. Beside them were
workers from Third World countries who have won jobs in U.S.-owned
factories but are making less than a dollar an hour and are desperate to
organize unions in their countries." Not only were they on stage together, but the crowd was ready for a left message: "A Ford maquiladora
worker got a huge response at the AFL-CIO rally when she shouted,
'Long Live the Zapatistas!'" John Sweeney told the National Press Club,
"The debate isn't about free trade or protectionism, engagement or isolation. The real debate is not over whether to be part of the global economy, but over what are the rules for that economy and who makes
them."[32]

To a surprising degree, labor's message got out through the media,
and I think the reason for that is the nature of the protest coalition and
the "man bites dog" character of the alliances. Given the range of groups
that were there—Earth First!, the Ruckus Society, anarchists, church
groups, Teamsters, Longshoremen, Steelworkers, and a host of others—
it's remarkable that a spirit of good feeling and common cause prevailed.
That sense of camaraderie was captured by Jeff Crosby of IUE Local 201
and the (Massachusetts) North Shore Labor Council, who titled his report, "The Kids Are Alright." As he noted:

> The labor movement basically piggy-backed on the courage of the young
> environmentalists and anti-sweatshop and church activists. Without the
> direct action, which disrupted the WTO, the labor march would have re-
> ceived a 90 second clip on the nightly news. . . . Then again, without the
> tens of thousands of union members, it would have been easier to write
> off the young protesters as flakes, people who aren't worried about basic
> issues like having to earn a living.[33]

Before that day people would have expected many of these groups to oppose each other, but the events created a sense of alliance and common
purpose, a hope that next time even more could be done. Nor were the
Seattle protests a one-time phenomenon; they initiated a mass movement. Labor's response has not consistently been as good as it was in

Seattle; the record has been uneven, but U.S. labor remains a member of the loose global justice alliance, even if with significant backsliding (see chapter conclusion).

Cross-Border Organizing and Labor Solidarity

If one way to check business power and protect ordinary people is regulation by government, national or global, another is to build power through (union) solidarity, national or global. Business is far more globalized than labor; many corporations have operations in dozens of countries. Labor is organized globally, but the organizations are weak and limited. Fourteen International Trade Secretariats (ITSs), such as the International Metalworkers Federation (the other IMF) or the International Transport Workers Federation (ITF), serve as federations of national unions, and are loosely affiliated with the International Confederation of Free Trade Unions, dominated by Europeans with social democratic orientations.[34] National unions join and participate in one or more of these international secretariats, but historically these loose federations have been restricted to information sharing, diplomacy, and policy. Until recently they rarely became involved in on-the-ground union campaigns and (at least in the United States) barely registered on the consciousness of most union leaders or staff. If labor were satisfied to hold an occasional symbolic protest or send a letter of support/inquiry, the existing ITS would provide a mechanism.

But in current circumstances symbolic protests won't do the job and the role of the trade secretariats is being transformed. National unions are most likely to seek out the relevant ITS when faced with a tough employer that they can't beat inside their own country, as the Steelworkers did in the Ravenswood strike.[35] Unions increasingly launch international campaigns, although it's still rare, and happens primarily when a struggle is already in trouble. But successful campaigns have been mounted; this section examines three, each of which strengthened labor both in the United States and overseas.

Garment Workers in Guatemala

The garment industry in Central America exploded during the 1980s with the creation of free trade zones. "From Caribbean Basin nations alone, textile and apparel exports to the U.S. rose from $512 million in 1984 to $3.6 billion in 1993 . . . , while U.S. employment in the sector simultaneously dropped by more than 25 percent." This also led to huge increases in the number of Central American shops and workers. In Guatemala the number of maquila factories went from 41 in 1985 to 480 in 1994, by which time they employed more than 100,000 workers. The workers were primarily women, many unmarried, and they were paid extremely low wages. (In Guatemala the minimum wage in the 1990s was $2.80 a day.) Employers were given a free hand in suppressing unions, with the assistance of the government if needed. As a consequence there were virtually no functioning garment workers unions: in Guatemala "by the end of 1993 only six out of more than 300 maquila factories had managed to form a union, and only one had managed to negotiate a limited contract."[36]

In Guatemala one of the best plants was run by Phillips Van Heusen, the world's largest shirtmaker. Better conditions meant that the plant had lower turnover, and this enabled the workers to form closer ties. From 1989 on there were almost continuous efforts to form a union. At various points the workers received help from U.S. unions (especially UNITE, the garment workers union); from the relevant ITS, the International Textile, Garment, and Leather Workers Federation (ITGLW); and from citizen action type groups, especially the U.S./Guatemala Labor Education Project (US/GLEP). In the United States, unions prefer to organize in relative secrecy to avoid triggering an employer anti-union campaign. But in Guatemala during the brutal repression of the 1980s, if employers suspected undercover union activity, death squads might simply assassinate those believed to be union leaders. Paradoxically, therefore, union leaders "had come to rely on visibility as protection, fearing that a more clandestine action would engender an army response. During the 1980s, increased publicity and international attention had buffered paramilitary attacks."[37]

The successful drive, however, adopted a modified version of the secretive "blitz" organizing strategy favored by UNITE in the United States; Guatemalan labor activists were more willing to adopt this tactic because of the 1996 peace accords, which reduced overt repression. An underground campaign identified leaders, did training, built small groups inside the plant, and laid a groundwork. Then, on the 1996 U.S. Labor Day weekend, explained Teresa Casertano of ITGLW, "We organized all those leaders and got cars and drivers and take-out food, and for three days straight, every hour it was possible to go to somebody's house, we were signing up co-workers." Even so it was difficult to reach the 25 percent threshold that would make it legally necessary for the company to negotiate with the union. Workers were understandably fearful, and union leaders were reluctant to identify all the supporters because some workers wanted to remain secret. The union needed 166 workers to make the 25 percent cut-off, and apparently exceeded that. On the first Monday in September, 100 of the 620 mainly women workers came in T-shirts emblazoned with the name and the logo of the union. "Meanwhile, in the United States, where it was Labor Day, supporters were already on the streets leafleting stores that sold Phillips Van Heusen products, urging the company to bargain with its workers."[38]

The campaign's ultimate success required much more than one good weekend, of course, but it continued to depend on the one-two punch of a strong worker base in Guatemala combined with support activity in the United States. Management used the normal anti-union tactics: posting armed security guards (in a country where death squads had recently had free rein), framing union supporters on theft charges, challenging the union's 25 percent support level, and so on. One lever that the labor forces used was the threat of U.S. trade sanctions against Guatemala for labor rights violations under the U.S. General System of Preferences. The threat meant that the company no longer had a (totally) free hand in dealing with its workers and union, nor could the government simply ignore illegal activity, since the United States might impose sanctions that would cost all Guatemalan employers, not just Phillips Van Heusen. Under this pressure, the Guatemalan labor minister found Phillips Van Heusen guilty of assorted labor law violations.

If Guatemalan workers had not stood firm, the entire campaign would have collapsed. But given that worker base, the key turning point came in the United States. Incredibly, one of the owners of Phillips Van Heusen was on the board of Human Rights Watch and was scheduled to co-chair a November fund-raising dinner. The United States/Guatemalan Labor Education Project planned a protest at that event; to avoid that embarrassment, a deal was struck, and two investigators from Human Rights Watch went to Guatemala. They "concluded that the union did indeed have support from one-fourth of the workers and that the confusion over documentation reflected the union leaders' desire to protect members from very credible threats of harassment." The company owner personally went to Guatemala and in August 1997 a new contract was approved. It provided for "reasonable wage increases (11 percent the first year, 12.5 percent the second), a grievance procedure, clearer rules on wage rates, and a guarantee that current employment and production would be continued as long as productivity was sustained. The union also won increased subsidies for transportation, lunch, and children and the right to a public presence in the factory."[39]

In labor circles, much has been made of this victory, but few other cases will offer such welcome targets. Almost all brand-name companies operate through contractors, thus buffering themselves from labor troubles. Virtually no garment executives sit on the boards of human rights organizations—or care much about their companies' records in this area. Even with these advantages and an effective campaign in both Guatemala and the United States it took a year for the final campaign (not to mention the preceding seven years of failed campaigns)—and the plant closed only a little more than a year after the union contract was signed.[40]

All of that said, this campaign, and a few others with generally similar characteristics, show that international solidarity can make it possible to win even under difficult conditions. If labor were able to win international labor standards, enforceable through the World Trade Organization or some other mechanism with teeth, it would become dramatically easier to organize workers in the Global South. International economic issues are often posed as "us" against "them," with "them" understood as everyone in Guatemala or Singapore or Indonesia, and "us" as everyone in the United States. But in this case, as in most others, the real "us" is workers, and employers are "them." Workers in Guatemala were helped: they received union wages and benefits. Workers in the United States were helped, because a union in Guatemala reduces (though by no means eliminates) an employer's incentive to move production there.

Teamsters' UPS Strike

In the last case, U.S. unions and labor-support groups used their power to assist Central American workers; in this one, European and other unions assisted U.S. workers.

The 1997 UPS strike was the most impressive U.S. labor victory in many years. At a time when most strikes are smashed, and most unions fear the risk of a strike, the Teamsters took on a huge and highly profitable corporation, fought on an issue of principle—that part-time workers deserved better pay and benefits as well as promotion to full-time jobs—and won. The three most important reasons for that victory were (1) the Teamsters' carefully prepared comprehensive campaign, (2) the solidarity of the workers, and (3) the overwhelming support of the U.S. public, support that increased as the strike progressed, despite the inconvenience many suffered.[41] In a strike where a great deal was done right, international solidarity may not have been the decisive factor, but it was one additional source of labor strength. Labor's international leverage was unexpected; management usually relies on its global reach to give it an advantage in any confrontation.

UPS has major operations in sixteen European countries; in Germany it employs eighteen thousand workers. But the vast majority of UPS's employees are in the United States, and the U.S. Teamsters (also known as IBT, International Brotherhood of Teamsters) represent two-thirds of UPS workers worldwide.[42] Because of the relative weight of the U.S. operation, unions in other countries had a stake in the Teamsters negotiations.

More than a year before the U.S. contract was to expire, the Teamsters went to the relevant International Trade Secretariat, the International Transport Workers Federation (ITF), and "requested a special informal meeting for ITF affiliates to discuss problems they were experiencing with UPS." Seven countries were represented in June 1996, and in February 1997 a further meeting shared highly detailed information about UPS. The ITF created a World Council, planned a World Action Day, and circulated a global corporate code of conduct. "On May 22, 1997 [a little over two months before the strike], the Council organized more than 150 job actions and demonstrations at UPS facilities worldwide as part of the action day." These actions took place in eleven countries; in Italy and Spain brief work stoppages took place.[43]

Another meeting of the World Council was scheduled to coincide with Teamster negotiations in the United States, and to be held in Washington at the site of the negotiations. "The IBT asked Council members to come a day early and to join its negotiators at the bargaining table with UPS. In a show of solidarity, IBT negotiators introduced each of their 'international guests' to management negotiators. After the World Action Day protests, the implied threat was unmistakable."[44] The council also created a structure, including an English-speaking "Internet steward" in each country, with each steward to produce a monthly news report (of no more than a page) and to translate highlights of the other countries' reports so they could be widely circulated. The council also vowed to pursue UPS anytime it relocated work to avoid unions, and to assist organizing efforts in the new country.

In many ways UPS was more vulnerable in Europe than in the United States. Because UPS controlled 80 percent of the U.S. market, competitors lacked the short-term capacity to take its business. In Europe other companies were much more important, as were national postal services, so UPS was at risk of permanently losing its customers. The ITF encouraged nontransportation unions to pressure the companies they dealt with "to drop UPS services for the duration of the strike." The Teamsters and the World Council also "asked European public-sector unions to appeal publicly for their members who were customs officers and labor inspectors to give greater scrutiny to UPS packages and UPS workplace-safety standards during the strike. Such public pronouncements could create apprehension among UPS customers that in part use express package services to *avoid* delays at customs."[45] Because the U.S. labor movement is weak, these forms of cross-union solidarity are rare in the United States, but in some countries they can be extremely important.

European union assistance to striking U.S. Teamsters was a wonderful act of solidarity, but it wasn't just an act of charity. If 185,000 unionized U.S. workers couldn't stand up to UPS, what were the chances of a few thousand workers in one or another European country? Conversely, what better time to stick it to UPS than when it was vulnerable and its resources stretched thin? As a consequence, in the United Kingdom, where sick-outs are legal, workers developed "Brown Flu" [UPS is known as Big Brown], and Brussels workers took the occasion to launch a wildcat over long-standing health and safety grievances. Although the Teamsters and ITF focused their efforts on Europe, mostly spontaneous actions took place elsewhere in the world. "For example, in India, where UPS delivers by rail, the railroad union responded to the ITF's call for solidarity by refusing to transport UPS packages during the strike. In the Philippines, the Civil Aviation Union organized a motorcade of 100 cars that surrounded the UPS subcontractor in Manila, preventing the transport of packages for a day."[46]

Web-Led Solidarity Actions

In 1995, when five hundred dock workers in Liverpool, England, refused to cross the picket line, the Mersey Docks & Harbours Company fired them. Six thousand miles away in Oakland, California, Ellen Starbird, an instructor in the Laney College Labor Studies Department, had just introduced a course on computers and organizing on the Internet. She urged students "to select a project with workers who were doing similar work in a different country, or, in some cases, doing the same work overseas that the student had done before losing his job." One of the students decided to focus on the Liverpool dock workers, but could only reach them by phone. The student coached the Liverpool dockers on how to use e-mail and establish a web page; Liverpool workers established a web site and began active use of the Internet. Two years later, on September 28, 1997, the *Neptune Jade*, a Mersey-loaded ship, arrived in Oakland, California, where at shift change times (5 A.M. and 5 P.M.) it was "greeted by a picket line of community activists, retirees, and students, called out by Internet invitation from Liverpool."

Although the ILWU (International Longshore and Warehouse Union)

Oakland dock workers' contract contains a no-strike clause, workers may—without reprisal—refuse to work if there is a "bona fide health and safety hazard." The Oakland dock workers refused to cross the picket line, arguing that the loud and boisterous picket line posed such a hazard. The company demanded instant arbitration but the arbitrator "ruled that the size of the crowd constituted a health and safety risk." In the next four days, an arbitrator was called to the scene six more times. "Twice a ruling was made that the crowd had thinned to a level of safety and thus there was no bona fide health and safety danger." Even when that happened, dock workers honored the picket line, sacrificing a day's pay. The company sought an injunction (denied) and was granted a temporary restraining order. But "the crowd had swelled in defiance of the judge's order, and it now included mayoral candidate Jerry Brown, the former Governor of California." The dock workers continued to honor the picket line, despite the restraining order.

The ship left the port and then tried to sneak back in, but the pickets were still there.

> On day four the ship set sail for San Francisco Bay, then went up to Vancouver, Canada. It became a point of honor among longshore workers to refuse to unload her. The *Neptune Jade* crossed the Pacific, and at Kobe and Yokahama, Japan, the dock workers likewise refused to unload the Mersey Dock cargo from the *Neptune Jade*. Finally the ship was sold to a Taiwanese company, cargo still in her hold.

The Mersey Corporation returned to the bargaining table three months later; the Liverpool dockers were eventually offered twenty thousand pounds each and the option of returning to work. The Oakland dock company filed two contradictory lawsuits: one against the dockers (arguing the picket line was safe and they should have crossed it) and another against community organizations seeking millions in damages (arguing the picket line was so threatening that no one could cross it). The community organizations (including the Laney College Labor Studies Club) and all individuals known to have participated were subpoenaed and ordered to name everyone they knew who had attended the demonstration, and all of their political affiliations. After a further long struggle, these suits were also defeated. The process of struggle strengthened academic freedom, community mobilization, and student labor action; among other things it led to a strong antisweatshop campaign.[47]

If international working-class solidarity is to develop, it will emerge from a series of campaigns that simultaneously advance the material interests of workers in two or more countries, rather than from workers in one country doing a favor for workers in another. Those campaigns will also create a consciousness that the important dividing line is not "everyone in the United States" against "everyone in Brazil" (or China, or Mexico, or Indonesia). Rather, workers in both countries have common interests, and these interests are opposed to those of employers; in fact, often the same employer is creating the problems for workers in both the United States and Mexico. Such struggles remain unusual, and most rely heavily on leaders and staff rather than rank-and-file workers. But these campaigns are becoming more common. For example, unions are creating company-specific global networks, bringing together Northern Telecom or General Electric workers from around the world. Unions are also sending organizers to work with sister unions in other countries, to learn from each other's organizing approaches and to offer concrete aid. Three organizers from the U.S. Communication Workers lived with union families in Britain for four months while working on British campaigns to unionize cable companies (that also provided phone service). When UNITE was organizing a large firm in Quebec, a significant minority of the workforce—potentially enough people to be the margin of victory or defeat—were from Bangladesh. The staff organizers were not effective in reaching these workers, in significant part because language posed a major barrier. Organizers were brought in from Bangladesh—arriving in thin saris in midwinter, but making all the difference. Increasingly, both unions and labor conferences are bringing together rank-and-file workers doing similar work in different countries. For example, the Labor Notes conference brings Daimler-Chrysler workers from Germany to meet with their counterparts in Detroit.[48]

Global Justice

If we make an analytic distinction between globalization (worldwide interchange of ideas and economic products) and neoliberalism (a set of policies abolishing all impediments to the unchecked rule of the market), then it is clear that neoliberalism and not globalization is the problem. Under any circumstances, globalization would have expanded dramatically in the late twentieth century. Because this expansion took place during a period when business and its allies dominated economically and politically, not just in the United States but in many other areas of the world, neoliberal principles were deeply and thoroughly embedded in major institutions. "Globalization" has thus become one of the primary means of advancing a neoliberal agenda. The alternatives are posed as: globalization or antiglobalization. "Globalization" is understood as what we now have—rules for the world economy based exclusively on what is good for business, but disguised as the impartial logic of the market. The only alternative the media acknowledge is presented as "antiglobalization": opposing economic advance, and (sometimes) hostile to advance for the Global South.

But this is a false dichotomy; the alternative to the current form of neoliberal globalization is a democratic process that considers workers and the environment rather than worshiping business profits. That's the principle behind the campaign for international environmental and labor standards. With such standards we can improve conditions for the vast majority of the population in both the United States and the world. To illustrate this point, let me take what might appear the most difficult challenge: the environment. The argument is made that if production in the Global South advances, this will damage the environment, contributing to global warming and pollution, that advances for the rest of the world would require reductions in U.S. consumption. This would only be true if there were a fixed and invariant relationship between the level of material comfort and the degree of global warming and pollution. In fact, however, some production practices are much more damaging than others; environmentally superior technologies and practices are currently available and unused. The United States builds highways and fills them with SUVs; France has TGV trains traveling 185 miles an hour. As a consequence of these and similar practices, for any given level of economic output, France produces far less pollution than the United States. If we made the environment a priority, we could develop much less damaging ways to meet our energy needs and produce our goods. What keeps us from doing so is not minimum wage workers in Indonesia and street children in Brazil, but rather the decisions of corporate executives—both their decisions about how to produce the goods and their ability to dominate the political system. The issue is not globalization per se, but rather neoliberalism and its political dominance.

The labor (and environmental) movement(s), in the United States and around the world, will need to advance on multiple fronts: cross-border organizing, international labor standards, and controls on capital. It seems extremely difficult to make significant gains on any of these fronts. It is hard enough to organize in one country. For workers to understand the need for solidarity that extends beyond borders, and coordinate effective action, will be far more challenging. The decision whether or not to adopt international labor standards, what these should be, and how they should be enforced has—at least to this point—been decided by appointed bodies operating in secret, creating treaties not subject to amendment by Congress. In politics, business is overwhelmingly dominant, such that almost no elected candidate is willing to confront it. Winning controls on capital is impossible unless a majority of politicians are prepared to face a fierce political confrontation.

Any effort to change the system faces two problems: not only the power and dominance of neoliberal views and institutions, but also the huge differences among the opponents of the current system. Structural location influences both interests and power. The North has power over the South, men over women, whites over other races, union workers over nonunion workers, nongovernmental organizations over the unorganized, and so on. At various points in U.S. history men have supported equal pay for women—as a means to keep them from being employed at all. Many in the Global South are worried that international labor standards (or capital controls or environmental protection) will be promoted on the basis of high principles but shaped in their details to harden inequalities and assist the world's most privileged workers.[49] An important part of the struggle for a new system will take place *within* the groups opposed to neoliberalism. No single action will address all concerns and solve all problems. Even if labor (or environmental) standards were adopted, getting them enforced would be a further struggle, and even with such standards, winning victories will require both courage and creativity by large numbers of people.

Before the November 1999 Seattle protests against the World Trade Organization, it seemed impossible that neoliberalism could be successfully challenged or that allies with such different views, strengths, and structural positions could bridge their differences and work together. That changed significantly in the span of a week, a first-step demonstration of the meaning and impact of upsurge. The movement that so forcefully announced itself in Seattle was not a one-hit wonder. From Thanksgiving 1999 to September 11, 2001, the global justice movement grew by leaps and bounds. World leaders could not meet without confronting thousands of demonstrators demanding that economic decision making consider not just profits but also the environment and workers' rights. Even more impressive, labor remained an important—if somewhat shaky—part of the coalition protesting unchecked globalization, although its stance on Permanent Normal Trade Relations with China reverted to nationalism.

The 9/11 attacks changed everything. Attention turned to other issues and challenges to the status quo were seen by many as giving aid and comfort to "the enemy." As a result, no post-9/11 global justice demonstration had one-tenth of the numbers that had been routine. Labor became much more cautious about its participation, and unwilling to be associated with militant confrontation—but the same could be said about most college students. Important elements of labor also became more protectionist and willing to invoke nationalist arguments; simultaneously parts of labor chose short-term jobs over long-term environmental protection. Although specifically global justice demonstrations did not revive, an impressive antiwar movement sprang up when war with Iraq threatened. In an unprecedented step, the AFL-CIO Executive Council adopted a mild anti-war statement and numerous unions made stronger statements. On February 15, 2003, more than ten million people in more than four hundred cities around the world marched to prevent war. Coordinated worldwide demonstrations on such a scale are totally unprecedented. The internet and e-mail were the foundations for connections and coordination at a speed and with a range never before seen. A spirit of internationalism infused the marches: people identified with the demonstrators in other countries and opposed their own governments. Those demonstrations are a model for what the labor movement needs to do. The connections and the culture they created will make it far easier to build future actions of a similar scope.

The global justice movement has also opened a new front, a first step in creating counterpower—although this new initiative has received very little attention in the United States. Instead of creating yet another large demonstration against a meeting of world leaders, the 2001 World Economic Forum in Davos, Switzerland, was paralleled by the first World Social Forum in Porto Alegre, Brazil. The World Economic Forum brings together the heads of state of the world's most powerful economies, along with the leaders of many of the world's largest corporations, and thousands of their support staff. Held in a part of Brazil governed by the Workers' Party, the World Social Forum was explicitly conceived as an alternative. It brings together the representatives of nongovernmental organizations (NGOs), unions, and social movements. The organizers expected two to three thousand people; in 2001 an estimated eight to fifteen thousand attended, in 2002 there were perhaps fifty thousand, and in 2003 one hundred thousand from over one hundred countries, making connections, strengthening networks, and creating common projects. To much of the world this was an important event—not only to the social movements, but even to the media. The U.S. media barely acknowledged the forum's existence, and few Americans participated (an estimated one hundred in 2001 and four hundred in 2002).

In the United States, at least, it might seem that people—in and out of the labor movement—are no longer as prepared to act for global justice, but there is a saying in the labor movement that "the best organizers are the bosses." That is, if an employer is treating workers respectfully, incorporating them in decision making, being understanding about family and personal problems, and paying decent wages and benefits, it's unlikely that workers will want to organize a union. On the other hand, if the employer's actions constantly create anger, humiliation, and resentment, workers will want a union (whether or not they succeed in organizing one). The institutions and mechanisms of neoliberal globalization—the WTO, NAFTA and the proposed FTAA (Free Trade Area of the Americas), the proposed MAI (Multilateral Agreement on Investment), the secret and antidemocratic character of all decisions—may be the best organizers for a new upsurge. The actions of global economic institutions like the WTO create the material basis for a broad coalition uniting environmentalists, labor, and those concerned about the Global South, since the WTO's actions harm all these movements. Because the WTO, NAFTA, FTAA, MAI, IMF, and World Bank are so completely undemocratic and so closed to any but the elite, there is little room (at least at present) for reform within the system. The consequence is that, unless people are prepared to submit to the neoliberal juggernaut, these various movements must unite and must engage in protests that go outside the system and challenge business as usual. Many progressive organizers in and out of the labor movement made extraordinary efforts, but it was the WTO itself that was most responsible for the amazing coalition and militant actions of Seattle's demonstrations.

The 9/11 attacks shifted the immediate agenda. But the underlying problems won't go away. The global justice movement helped lay the foundation for the global peace movement; the strength of the worldwide peace movement in turn makes further global alliances more likely. Economic difficulties and unilateral military action are likely to revive interest in democratic governance to meet people's needs. Through its involvement in both anti-war and global justice coalitions, labor has created linkages that might draw it into an upsurge led by others, or enable it to activate connections if labor were mobilizing on a relevant issue. Historians may look back on the period from 9/11 to the Iraq war as a hiatus equivalent to the gap in the civil rights movement between the Montgomery bus boycott and the 1960 student sit-ins.

6

Code of Conduct and Living Wage Campaigns

On campuses everywhere, students have demanded that their colleges or universities adopt Codes of Conduct pledging that T-shirts, sweatshirts, and caps bearing the university logo not be made in sweatshops. Under pressure, some colleges have agreed to accept independent monitoring to ensure that the workers producing college-logo goods are adults, not children, are paid a decent wage, are working reasonable hours, and have a right to organize to protect their own interests.

Cities and towns across the country have adopted living wage ordinances, promising that city employees, and the employees working for contractors doing city business, will be paid not just the minimum wage, but a living wage. "Living wage" definitions vary from place to place, but the basic principle is: enough so that a full-time year-round worker can support a family at the poverty line. A modest demand and immediately comprehensible benchmark, but also a substantial advance: in 2002, the federal minimum wage was $5.15 an hour, but a living wage would need to be at least $8.63 an hour.

These campaigns are among the most exciting harbingers of what might be a new direction for labor and a component of a new labor upsurge. Although the campaigns differ in many ways, significant similarities tie them together. These campaigns share three strengths that indicate their potential, but the campaigns also are united by their vulnerability to a significant peril.

The first strength of these campaigns is that they benefit low-wage workers who have generally been beyond the reach of the labor movement. Unions have not been able to organize sweatshop workers, in this country or abroad, and have trouble organizing most minimum wage workers. If the labor movement is to fight for social justice, it needs to in-volve and represent the bottom of the workforce as well as more privi-leged workers.

Second, these campaigns are often *movements*, generating an energy, excitement, and sense of mission that are all too rare in today's unions. As a result, participants develop innovative tactics and adopt militant approaches, often capturing the public imagination.

Third, more than almost anything else, these campaigns create a fu-sion between labor and other groups and social movements. The anti-sweatshop movement focuses on labor issues, but the participants are overwhelmingly students. Living wage campaigns focus on raising workers' wages, but not through a traditional union strategy; the coali-tions that promote these ordinances meld labor, community, and reli-gious groups. More than simply alliances, the groups' issues and activi-ties interpenetrate so thoroughly that it would be difficult to categorize them as one rather than another.

These three strengths create the potential for a radically different labor movement, one whose organizational basis would differ from that of to-day's unions. The struggles discussed here show the potential, as yet un-realized, for the construction of entirely new organizational forms. In the early 1930s, as workers attempted to unionize the auto industry, thou-sands of workers wanted a union—but the electricians were sent to one union, the machinists to another, the unskilled to a third, and it was im-possible to develop a serious drive.[1] The victories of the 1930s required the creation of a new form of union (which had already existed in some scattered fashion): the industrial union uniting all the people at one worksite, regardless of their particular craft and including the unskilled with no craft. The new form of union did not emerge easily; it split the existing labor movement, to the point of causing a fistfight between two union presidents on the floor of the national AFL convention. The new form was created by people in struggle, not by labor leaders, though John L. Lewis of the Mineworkers played an important role in creating the CIO and supporting the new forms of organizing, forms (and unions) that were anathema to many of the old AFL leaders. And as CIO unions created new forms, AFL unions responded by changing them-selves, and growing just as fast as the CIO unions did. Similarly, today, in the follow-up to living wage campaigns, unions often try to organize one or another group of low-wage workers, sending some to the Hotel Workers, others to the Service Employees, and still others to the Food and Commercial Workers. Just as the CIO of the 1930s reorganized boundary lines, perhaps a new upsurge will create new organizational forms, new ways of exercising leverage, and a new conception of what is and is not labor. Perhaps all of a community's low-wage workers will be in some unified entity that will include community groups as well as unions. Perhaps we will see the emergence of forms that are even more difficult to conceive, ones uniting workers and students.

This impressive potential is, however, accompanied by a significant peril. To this point, all the struggles considered in this book have not only been for workers and about workers, but also by workers. To the extent that other groups joined in the struggle, they did so in solidarity with workers, rather than *on behalf of* workers.

The labor movement can be understood in at least two fundamentally different ways. In one conception, the labor movement is about raising wages and winning benefits for workers. If the goal is to raise workers' wages and benefits, then other organizations and individuals can do it for workers. Union staff, living wage coalitions, student antisweatshop activists, or perhaps even employers can bring benefits to workers. If workers' conditions improve, it can be argued, what difference does it make how this happens?

In the other conception, the labor movement is about empowering workers—giving them a voice, a capacity to influence the circumstances of their own lives. Democracy is extended from the polling place to the workplace, from occasional days in November to the routine of everyday life. Instead of organizations and activities being run by professionals and managers, workers demonstrate and develop their own ability to democratically decide what they want, make tough choices, and carry out creative actions to exercise power or influence, all through organizations that workers create and control.[2]

In the first model, it's not a problem if workers are dependent on others; in the second, the key is that workers become subjects, the agents deciding what matters to them and controlling their own fate. If we consistently and one-sidedly do things for others it is because they are seen as not fully capable beings. (Or, alternatively and in very different circumstances, because they have power over us.) Thus parents take care of their children. But if a healthy eighteen-year-old does not know how to tie his or her own shoes because their parent always does it for them, our reaction is not that this is a wonderful parent who will do anything for their child. Rather we feel that the parent has created an unfortunate dependency that will harm, rather than help, the son or daughter. If other people do things for workers, if workers don't develop the organizations and capacity to do things for themselves, then they remain forever dependent. Partly it's an issue of whether the outside groups want the same things for workers that workers would want for themselves. More fundamentally it's a question of whether organizing builds people's long-run capacity to take control of their lives and circumstances. Workers need not just a solution to today's problem, but also to develop the capacity to defend themselves and exercise power tomorrow and the day after. When Karl Marx drafted the rules for the First International, the first sentence was: "The emancipation of the working classes must be conquered by the working classes themselves."

Events of the next few years will determine the extent to which these movements can develop their enormous potential while avoiding the peril of making workers dependent. The movements themselves, or at least significant elements within them, are well aware of, and actively working to address, the potential problem of substituting for workers rather than empowering them.

Living Wage Campaigns

The minimum wage reflects the balance of political power rather than being set by some neutral or objective criterion. It is not determined as a fraction of the average wage nor on the basis of what it costs to maintain a minimally adequate standard of living. In contrast to many of the matters of most concern to the rich and powerful, when the minimum wage is increased the act covers only specified years, rather than establishing a formula that provides automatic increases as the economy develops. Victory, if and when it comes, consists of one or two or three specified raises ending a year or two or three in the future. At the end of that period, a new struggle is required. In contrast, benefits for corporations and the rich are often based on formulas requiring automatic increases, and the same is true for Social Security payments. Because no rule requires that the minimum wage be adjusted, for many years (e.g. 1981–90, 1991–97) it was not.

One of the signal victories of the New Voice labor movement was its successful campaign, against all odds, to raise the minimum wage despite a Newt Gingrich "Contract on America" Congress. Increasing the minimum wage to $5.15 an hour is a substantial improvement, but even at this wage a person who works full time (forty hours a week, say nine to six, with an hour for lunch) all year round (fifty-two weeks, five days a week) would earn only $10,712 a year. In 2001, however, the poverty line for a family of four was $17,650.[3] Working at the minimum wage, even if paying no taxes and receiving free child care for all work hours (two impossibilities) a worker would need to work sixty-six hours a week to bring a family of four up to the poverty line. Realistically that means that two full-time minimum wage workers, assuming they paid Social Security taxes and had child care expenses, would be below the poverty line. And the official poverty line is itself disgracefully low; a National Research Council study found that the majority of researchers say the official poverty level needs to be raised.

The concept of a living wage, rather than a minimum wage, is that a person who works full time year-round should be able to support a family at least at the poverty line. In 2002, for a family of four (assuming the worker paid no taxes), this required a wage of at least $8.63.[4]

In current political circumstances, it appears "utopian" to imagine that the minimum wage could be established at that level, but through the 1960s and 1970s the minimum wage was almost high enough so that one full-time worker could support a family of four at the poverty level. In 1969, one full-time minimum wage job left a family of four about 10 percent below the poverty line; today such a job leaves a family 39 percent below the poverty line. Imagine what would have happened if workers in 1968 had had the political clout to establish a rule-driven minimum wage. In constant 2000 dollars, the 1968 minimum wage would be $7.92 per hour. But if progressives had been able to enact a sensible rule, the minimum wage would be still higher, because U.S. productivity has increased substantially since 1968, and the normal assumption is that wages should increase to reflect productivity increases. (Note that doing so does not increase workers' share of national income, it only enables workers to stay in place, rather than having all the benefits of productivity increases go to owners.) As Robert Pollin and Stephanie Luce point out in their excellent book, *The Living Wage*, if we had the 1968 minimum wage adjusted for productivity increases and for inflation, the 2000 minimum wage would have been $13.80. This is not an imaginary figure or something the economy could never afford: it would simply keep us where we were in 1968, with adjustments for productivity. If we wanted to enter the realm of the hypothetical and politically delusional, imagine what would have happened if, since 1990, the minimum wage had increased at the same rate as executive pay. From 1990 to 2001, CEO pay increased 571 percent. To keep pace with that, the 2001 minimum wage would have needed to be $25.50 an hour.[5]

The living wage concept embodies two politically brilliant principles. First, rather than arguing about the minimum wage, where people's thinking is stuck in what they've known for the past many years, it introduces a new concept, the living wage, which has no necessary relationship to the minimum wage.[6] Second, not only does the wage have a compelling name, but it is based on a formula that is difficult to oppose: Shouldn't a person who works full time be able to keep a family above the poverty line?

Trying to introduce these principles into American political debate, and recognizing that (at the moment) labor and community groups are not strong enough to win this for the society as a whole, the living wage movement has aimed to win limited victories, in hopes of creating a movement and spreading the living wage to more and more workers. By the summer of 2002, eighty-five municipal living wage ordinances had been passed and another seventy movements were active. Even after 9/11, living wage ordinances continued to advance.[7] Although there is considerable variation among them, most provide that all city employees and all employees paid out of city funds (including contractor employees) should be paid a living wage. Sometimes they also cover the employees of any company benefiting from a city tax break or subsidy (airports, sports stadiums, etc.).

The business community attacks living wage ordinances as economically impractical and misguided, but supporters' economic analyses are far more rigorous and thorough than those of opponents, in large part due to the efforts of Bob Pollin and his associates Stephanie Luce and Mark Brenner. The living wage forces have won the battle of ideas and credibility—which does not by itself win the war, but is a valuable tool in any struggle. Because the early living wage ordinances applied only to city employees, and to the employees of companies receiving benefits from cities, they covered far fewer workers than a minimum wage law. The Los Angeles city ordinance adopted in March 1997 set the living wage at $7.25 an hour, required twelve paid days off per year, included health benefits of $1.25 per hour, and covered public employees, firms holding service contracts worth more than $25,000, firms holding concession agreements with the city, and the subcontractors of covered firms. Rather than covering all employees of these firms, it covered only those working on city contracts or concessions. As a consequence, the plan was estimated to raise wages for 7,626 workers. By comparison, in Los Angeles County (not just the city), an increase in the minimum wage to $6.50 an hour would have raised wages for 870,513 workers, more than one hundred times as many people. In consequence implementing narrowly drawn living wage laws is not especially expensive.[8]

So are the victories only symbolic? Six responses are in order. First, symbolic victories are also important. Shining a spotlight on the issue and generating discussion of these ideas is itself a signal accomplishment, as is forcing politicians to take a public stand. If the concept of a living wage gets established in people's minds it becomes a powerful force, a roadblock to many business initiatives.

Second, even if the living wage ordinance for Los Angeles "only" applies to seven or eight thousand workers, to those workers it is a major victory; few union organizing campaigns win benefits for so many workers.

Third, the initial victory can be used as a wedge, with follow-up campaigns asking why other workers should not be entitled to the same coverage. This has happened in Portland and New York City, and living wage campaigns are spreading on college campuses (see below).

Fourth, a living wage ordinance is a huge preventive measure. Assuming it applies not just to city employees, but also to city contractors, the existence of a living wage undercuts much of the rationale for privatizing and contracting out. Contractors will still be paying less than the cost of wages (and benefits!) for unionized city workers, but the gap will have been narrowed; if the cost difference is small enough, privatization won't be worth the battle it would involve.

Fifth, a large raise for the lowest-paid workers often leads to a wage bump for those just above them. Nelson Lichtenstein reports that at the University of Virginia, a living wage would apply to only a few hundred workers. The vehemence of the university's opposition comes in significant part from the fact that the target living wage is almost as much as is earned by many of the (women) clerical workers at the university. If a living wage were implemented the university would feel compelled to raise their pay to maintain the distinction between (mostly white) high school–graduate clerical workers and (mostly black) cafeteria workers.[9]

Sixth and most important, however, living wage campaigns forge new coalitions and bring benefits to groups of workers that are hard to reach through conventional NLRB election campaigns. Not only are low-wage workers highly vulnerable to employer pressure; such jobs typically have extremely high turnover, so an employer who stalls long enough can replace much of the existing staff with a new anti-union workforce.[10]

Living wage campaigns break with the New Deal labor system and embody a different paradigm. In place of employer- and worksite-specific campaigns supervised and controlled by the state regulatory and court systems, they substitute community-wide coverage, won through a political process, mass mobilization, and a public relations campaign. For city ordinances, by far the most common, victory ultimately depends on a vote by elected officials. At universities, the sites of what may become a new round of campaigns, victory depends exclusively on mass mobilization and community pressure. The spread of living wage campaigns wins benefits for a different set of workers—many of them young or people of color—and does so through a different set of mechanisms than those of the New Deal NLRB system.

The coalitions and alliances forged in these struggles are significant in themselves. Labor unions are typically a crucial part of these coalitions, but only a part, and not necessarily the most important part. Religious groups, especially black and Latino churches, are usually vital, as are community groups and organizations such as ACORN. In Chicago, for example, the living wage coalition had seventy-eight members, about half of them unions, one-third community groups, and one-sixth individual elected officials.[11] Forging the coalitions and carrying through the campaign teaches the participants a great deal about each other.

Los Angeles's campaign was a model in building such new alliances. CLUE (Clergy and Laity United for Economic Justice) not only supported the living wage campaign, but became actively involved in the hotel workers' struggle to win wage increases through their union contract. Led by Reverend Jim Lawson Jr. (who was also a key figure in Nashville's 1960 sit-in movement), ministers initiated a "Java for Justice" campaign. Wearing large cardboard signs that said "Sign the Contract," groups of three to eight CLUE members would have coffee in the upscale hotels, then visit the manager to urge that he sign the union contract.[12]

The living wage approach has many strengths, but it also has significant limitations and drawbacks. First among these is that "it is not clear how many workers have actually received the higher wages mandated by the laws."[13] When unions run conventional campaigns, in about 25 percent of the cases an election victory never leads to a first contract. There's no reason the living wage should be different: passing the law doesn't mean it gets enforced. In many cases, movements initially assumed that if the law is on the books that takes care of it. But as a result of this assumption, as Andrea Cole of the Greater New Haven Labor Council said, "We don't know anything. We basically dropped the ball. It was a big mistake, not being involved."

Paradoxically, the more opposition a living wage movement encounters, the better. With conventional NLRB election campaigns, the faster they take place the better; employers stall in order to give themselves time to pressure, harass, and intimidate workers, and experience shows that the longer employers can stall, the worse the union's chances. The employer has the ability to isolate workers and subject them to unbearable pressure. Living wage campaigns are different, because the key to success is not the workers at any one specific workplace, and in fact is not even the low-wage workers themselves. Employers can't directly control the lives of those involved in the campaign. This reverses the relationship to timing and opposition: experience indicates that living wage campaigns are most successful when they encounter significant opposition, thus requiring the labor-community forces to forge a stronger coalition and more fully educate the public. If a campaign wins easily and quickly it is less likely to build a base for effective enforcement.

The problem in enforcing living wage ordinances is closely linked to what I see as their most important limitation: the success of such campaigns does not depend on reaching and mobilizing the low-wage workers themselves. In fact, they are typically minor participants in, or entirely missing from, campaigns. New Deal–system, NLRB union certification elections succeed if and only if the union side is able to win the votes of a majority of the bargaining unit. This is both a weakness and an incredible strength. With most political and community groups, people affiliate with the group because they agree with its goals. Since membership depends on agreement on the issues, and since few such groups enroll as much as 1 percent of the population, the groups recruit among those who already share most of their views; it's not cost-effective to attempt to persuade those with alternative perspectives, and little effort is made to do so. To win NLRB elections, however, unions must win support from a majority of a defined bargaining unit. Unions therefore require workers to engage, and find common ground with, those who differ from them in age, sex, race, religion, culture, family situation, job situation, political views, and in a host of other ways. The campaign can be heavily influenced by staff and outside forces, but ultimately the workers must decide.

Living wage campaigns—and, for that matter, a whole host of similar forms of political mobilization—depend on the ability to generate publicity and pressure; that is, to make it politically costly to oppose the initiative.[14] If 500 people show up at the Los Angeles City Council meeting, that is a huge show of force, even though it represents less than one-tenth of 1 percent of the Los Angeles workforce. Five hundred people might represent 10 percent of the workers who would be covered by an ordinance, but if 500 attended probably at least 450 of them would be members of community groups, faith-based activists, students, workers, or staff who would not be covered by the ordinance. It helps if the campaign can present a few articulate workers from the target population, but few politicians would care to challenge the group as not including a majority of the workers. Enlisting clergy, mobilizing student activists, or lining up sympathetic reporters is more important to the campaign's success than winning the participation of another fifty or one hundred targeted workers. The campaign is under no compulsion to enlist the workers and is not answerable to them. The center of the campaign is not the workers but rather the staff of participating organizations. They are the people who are able to turn out numbers of activists and to enroll high-visibility participants or create media-worthy symbolic actions. The campaign is not waged in solidarity with the workers, but rather on their behalf. I don't want to romanticize union election campaigns, and to imply that the workers are always in control, but there is a qualitative difference between the typical union election campaign and the typical living wage campaign.

The Prehistory of Antisweatshop Actions

Sooner or later, living wage campaigns usually win, in part because they are in the public sector. It's been far harder to make advances in private sector sweatshops. One early victory was by a workers center, Asian Immigrant Women Advocates (AIWA), in a campaign to get back pay for twelve Chinese immigrant women cheated by a contractor who had been making dresses for Jessica McClintock. The campaign featured memorable full-page ads in the *New York Times* ("Jessica McClintock Says: 'Let Them Eat Lace'") and a year-long campaign of rallies and public pressure.[15] Another campaign, which ultimately became of enormous importance, targeted Nike, again relying on clever ads and savvy media presence. Jeff Ballinger's two-page article in the August 1992 *Harper's* showed a photocopy of a worker's pay stub and Ballinger's commentary on it. The worker, Sadisah, earned fourteen cents an hour; during the pay period she had worked sixty-three hours of overtime, for which she received a two-cent-per-hour bonus. Ballinger calculated that "the labor cost for a pair of Nike shoes selling for eight dollars in the United States was about twelve cents." The anti-Nike campaign did not take off until 1996, when it was boosted by Bob Herbert columns in the *New York Times*, and even more so by the explosion of publicity over Kathie Lee Gifford.

The popular TV show host had lent her name to a line of Wal-Mart clothing. Charles Kernaghan of the National Labor Committee testified at a hearing of the Congressional Democratic Policy Committee that the clothing was made in terrible conditions, by workers as young as fourteen. With him was worker Wendy Diaz, fifteen years old, who had worked making Kathie Lee clothing since she was thirteen. She testified that she had to work from 8:00 A.M. to 9:00 P.M., and sometimes was forced to work all night.

> The supervisors insult us and yell at us to work faster. Sometimes they throw the garment in your face, or grab and shove at you. The plant is hot like an oven. The bathroom is locked and you need permission and can use it twice a day. Even the pregnant women they abuse. Sometimes the managers touch the girls, our legs or buttocks . . . We have no health care, sick days, or vacation.[16]

The testimony gained its media visibility not from the fact that *workers* were being exploited, but rather because Wendy Diaz was female, a person of color, and above all young; the media (and public) rarely are concerned by the exploitation of adult male workers. Kathie Lee at first claimed she was innocent, but broke down crying on her own TV show, soon vowed to clean up the situation and actually took steps to do so. Because of the publicity over this incident, both the media and the public were more interested in and sensitive to other stories about sweatshops, which increased Nike's vulnerability.

Global Exchange helped arrange a tour by an Indonesian Nike worker dismissed (with twenty-three co-workers) for "daring to demand that their employers pay the minimum wage" according to a Bob Herbert column in the *New York Times*. New reports exposed further Nike abuses and led to a string of hard-hitting Doonesbury cartoons. Nike claimed it was now paying minimum wage but "a few weeks later more than ten thousand workers at a factory making Nike shoes in Indonesia burned cars and ransacked the factory's offices over the company's refusal to pay the new minimum wage."[17]

These sustained campaigns hurt Nike's image and its profits. In fiscal 1998 its profits were down 49 percent from the year before. "Nike stock fell 39 percent in 1997 while the market as a whole rose more than 20 percent."[18] The campaigns may have had only modest success in improving conditions for Nike's workers, but the blow to its profits did not go unnoticed by other corporations. A new verb has entered the advertising and corporate public relations worlds: "to be Nike-ed" is to have your labor practices questioned and your good name attacked, with consequences for the bottom line. Today's shoe or garment manufacturers make money not through production, but rather via advertising and a brand name. The companies with identifiable logos prefer to do all of their production through subcontractors in a framework controlled by the brand-name company and with the lion's share of the profits flowing to it. The problem for corporations, however, is that the more identifiable their brand name, the more vulnerable they are to exposure. Now that the precedent has been set and the public is on the watch, if the word gets out on e-mail networks or articles are run in the media, the better-known the company the more likely word is to spread. This makes the employer side vulnerable and gives the worker side leverage, but so far it has not resulted in significant and sustained gains for workers.

The campaigns targeting Jessica McClintock, Nike, and Kathie Lee Gifford dramatically raised public awareness of sweatshops and the exploitation of workers. All these campaigns were driven almost exclusively by media exposés. There was much less organizing on the ground and few efforts to win a systematic change in labor practices except through an employer's voluntary adoption of higher standards in order to avoid future embarrassment. The student antisweatshop movement, by contrast, took the issue to a higher level through on-the-ground mass mobilization to force the adoption of codes determined by (or at least negotiated with) the demonstrators, rather than those adopted at the discretion of the manufacturer.

United Students against Sweatshops

Sweatshops were in the popular consciousness in 1996 at the inception of Union Summer, and some student groups were beginning to make an issue out of their universities' relationships with Nike.[19] The next step came in the summer of 1997, when "interns at UNITE! [the garment workers union] designed the first organizing manual for [what became the student antisweatshop] campaign and brought the idea to Union Summer participants and campus labor activists around the country."[20] Over the next two years this seed developed into the biggest student movement since the South Africa divestment struggles of the 1980s.

The student antisweatshop movement is often portrayed as students using their leverage as consumers. In one sense that's absolutely correct, but it also misses a crucial aspect of the campaign: students did not focus on individual decision making, but rather used their collective power and their standing as members of their universities' communities, in effect asserting a democratic right to decide what sorts of goods would bear the university standard. Apparel with college and university logos is big business, $2.5 billion a year.[21] Students argued that their colleges or universities should not use sweatshop labor. How could anyone wear a university logo with pride if they feared the clothing had been made in sweatshop conditions? In order to uphold their own ideals, the universities needed to guarantee that their names were associated only with sweat-free goods.

For the United States, scholars typically define a modern sweatshop as a factory or homework operation that violates two or more significant labor laws. Typically that means it pays less than minimum wage, or fails to pay the overtime wages required by law, or skips town without paying wages at all, or seriously violates health and safety laws. In a 1998 Department of Labor survey of garment firms in Los Angeles, 61 percent were violating wage and hour regulations. In a 1997 survey, 54 percent of the firms had health and safety violations that could lead to serious injury or death, and 96 percent were in violation of some regulation.[22]

Even the largest and best-known companies may use and benefit from the worst of sweatshop conditions, so universities that wanted to be sweat-free couldn't just buy caps and sweatshirts from well-known companies. Consider what is probably the most notorious example of sweatshop labor, the Thai slave workers in El Monte, California, a workshop exposed in an August 1995 raid by state and federal officials. The compound was surrounded by barbed wire; the workers, all undocumented immigrants from Thailand, lived eight to ten in a room and worked an average of eighty-four hours a week for $1.60 an hour. "The garments they sewed ended up in major retail chains, including Macy's, Filene's and Robinsons-May, and for brand-name labels like B.U.M., Tomato, and High Sierra." In fact, the El Monte compound was placing its goods through front shop D&R, and D&R was supposedly being monitored to ensure its compliance with the highest standards. The monitoring was not by some fly-by-night outfit, but rather by the largest monitoring firm in California—which failed to detect that a large quantity of work was being sent out.[23]

In the summer of 1998 student activists from thirty schools founded United Students Against Sweatshops (USAS) and a delegation went to Central America to talk to workers and meet with members of activist and human rights groups. In the spring of 1999 the antisweatshop movement took off, with sit-ins at Duke, Georgetown, Wisconsin, Michigan, North Carolina, and Arizona, all of them victorious, winning varying degrees of university commitment to avoid any future use of sweatshop labor for college-logo goods.

At the next USAS conference, in July 1999, some two hundred students gathered from more than a hundred campuses across the nation. The problem they faced was: What next? How could the movement go beyond raising consciousness and holding militant demonstrations in order that it could have an impact on the actual conditions of sweatshop workers? That is, if students were winning, what should they be demanding, and would their current demands accomplish their purposes?

The obvious solution was monitoring, but that was a demonstrated failure. The most extensive recent experience with garment industry monitoring came under what should have been unusually favorable conditions: a California program imposed by the government under the threat of severe sanctions. In the 1990s the Los Angeles office of the U.S. Department of Labor rediscovered, and began to enforce, the "hot goods" provisions of the 1938 Fair Labor Standards Act.[24] Under this New Deal–era law, the government may seize goods manufactured in violation of federal law if those goods enter into interstate commerce. Therefore, goods made in sweatshops that fail to pay minimum wage or overtime are subject to seizure. In order to avoid having their goods seized, manufacturers agreed to pay the back wages owed; recidivist corporations agreed to monitor their subcontractors in preference to the other penalties the Department of Labor could have imposed. Because these corporations "are presumably making a good-faith effort to monitor their contractors, they are exempted from lawsuits or the seizure of hot goods when violations do occur."[25] Note, however, how kindly corporations and their executives are treated: even repeat violators, implicated in stealing thousands of dollars from low-wage workers, do not face jail. Rather, they simply promise to be sure it doesn't happen again.

We have one careful study of what such monitoring has involved, that by Jill Esbenshade, and the results are extremely discouraging. Even a program imposed under government threat—and seizure of goods is a much more meaningful threat than filing a normal regulatory complaint—is only minimally effective. On the one hand, monitoring is a huge operation, involving hundreds of corporations (most of them cooperating "voluntarily," sixty as a result of signed agreements). "Monitoring has become a multimillion dollar industry. Private compliance firms conducted more than 10,000 audits in 1998 in Los Angeles alone. This is about ten times the combined number of investigations carried out by the state and federal enforcement agencies."[26]

Does monitoring eliminate abuses? Not even close. In a survey that looked only at registered contractors (the ones least likely to have serious abuses), of the monitored shops, in 1996 only 58 percent were in compliance with applicable laws, and in 1998 only 40 percent were in compliance.[27]

Companies choose their own monitors, and monitors are paid by the companies; monitoring, as Esbenshade argues, is a privatization of the government's regulatory function. Reports are sent to the manufacturer, although the manufacturer may force the contractor to pay for the cost of the monitoring. In order to stay in business monitors must be hired by manufacturers, and are therefore under pressure to compromise their strictness: "For instance, one monitoring firm had a policy of conducting all unannounced visits, but changed this when clients demanded announced visits." Since manufacturers are paying the costs, they pressure to hold down the number of audits. Although workers are sometimes interviewed, the employer knows which workers are being interviewed and the interviews are not effectively confidential. Many of the monitors are themselves anti-union and see monitoring as better than a union; one key proponent of monitoring told Esbenshade that now "workers don't need to organize, they don't need to pay dues," and that monitoring provides "stronger forces" than the union. (By this, however, he meant stronger forces to guarantee the payment of minimum wage and overtime, apparently the only benefits he could imagine garment workers wanting or getting.) Because the goal of monitoring is to prevent the company from being embarrassed, a monitor at the largest monitoring firm in Los Angeles "explained that he considered armed guards a plus in terms of a given factory's rating because guards prevented the entrance of muckrakers."[28]

Because of the demonstrated problems with industry-financed monitoring, students and labor advocates want to be sure that business does not control the process, that monitoring is truly independent. But more: USAS and labor advocates do not want the process exclusively controlled by any outside group, however well-meaning. USAS wants workers themselves to play a leading role, in part from a commitment to empowering workers and in part from a pragmatic recognition that workers are everywhere. Workers know the conditions firsthand and are vitally concerned day after day, but any monitoring system will be episodic and the monitors may lose their passion. Moreover, it will be much easier to deceive monitors than to deceive the workers, the people experiencing the conditions.

In July 1999 the students of USAS decided to create their own mechanism, the Workers Rights Consortium (WRC). Universities were pressured to join the WRC instead of (or in addition to) the Fair Labor Association, an industry-created association. While the Fair Labor Association board is dominated by garment manufacturers, the WRC board contains no manufacturers. David Unger, a sophomore at Cornell University, explained that "we don't want to have an antagonistic relationship with manufacturers. At the same time, we don't want them involved in running the organization that is supposed to be monitoring them."[29]

The WRC does not certify factories or companies, instead seeking full disclosure. "The WRC seeks to open up conditions in the apparel industry to public scrutiny and respond to the needs of the workers sewing licensed products for institutions of higher education."[30] USAS insists that companies producing college-logo goods must publicly disclose the names and addresses of the factories producing the goods so that non-governmental organizations (NGOs), human rights groups, and unions can check whether production is meeting the standards specified in the college's Code of Conduct. The WRC makes all reports of factory investigations public, but affiliated colleges and universities that are directly affected by a report receive the report in advance of its public release. The WRC also aims to conduct "trainings for workers at collegiate apparel factories to inform them of their rights under college and university Codes of Conduct. Our goal is to establish a mechanism for workers to bring complaints about violations to the attention of trusted NGOs and, through them, to the WRC."[31] That is, USAS and the WRC are self-consciously working to create a system that will empower workers, rather than a structure where others benevolently take care of workers.

Because our political system is business-dominated, the laws and the courts say that the brand-name manufacturer (the only entity that consumers can target) has no legal liability for the actions of its contractors. Manufacturers use contractors to produce the goods, although the "manufacturer" may own the material from beginning to end, and the contractor may be making the goods by prearrangement with every detail specified, including a price per garment that *requires* workers to be paid less than minimum wage. If workers attempt to unionize, the theoretical employer is the contractor, but organizing the contractor will accomplish nothing, since contracts are short-term. "Manufacturers have the ability to quickly move production from one plant or country to the next. Contractors have no reputation to protect, few assets, and are extremely mobile."[32] No matter how tightly manufacturers control contractors, no matter how little choice or autonomy contractors have, no matter if the manufacturer in practice demands the creation and use of sweatshops, legally this has nothing to do with the brand-name manufacturer. USAS and the WRC are trying to make an end run around the courts and Congress, where business hegemony remains strong, to reach out to the public, which hates sweatshops and does not want to be associated with them. If it becomes possible to identify the products produced in sweatshops, no college or university will want its symbol identified with a sweatshop; if this can be extended beyond college-logo gear to all clothing, consumers will boycott those products. Whatever the legal liability, the moral case will be compelling.

College Codes and Workers on Campus

Monitoring, disclosure, and certification are ways to help vulnerable low-wage workers improve their conditions and gain their rights. In some circumstances, as at U.S. colleges and universities, a direct worker-student alliance and a union offer an even stronger route. Colleges and universities are nonprofit, dedicated to promoting humane values and fostering free speech, operating from fixed and identifiable locations, with work and finances accessible to students and the public, subject to public pressure, and with comparatively strong financial positions. For all those reasons, colleges should be both model employers and neutral in worker organizing campaigns. But colleges often deny workers a living wage and a right to organize; participation by other members of the university "community" may be encouraged, but from workers it is resisted. By themselves workers find it difficult to improve their situation; in alliance with students, faculty, and the public, tens of thousands of workers could win victories and begin to create a model for a new sort of labor movement.

Antisweatshop struggles have usually been led by students but focused on workers in faraway places, whom students rarely if ever meet. The campaigns discussed in this section are a logical next step to antisweatshop activity, working with low-wage workers on the campus itself, the people who serve the food and clean the buildings for students (and faculty). In practice, these workers are often a world apart from the students they serve. One young AFSCME organizer, Elizabeth Kennedy, recognized this by pairing students with janitors to work alongside them on the night shift, describing it as in some ways the equivalent of a Global Exchange tour to a foreign land. The students loved getting to know campus janitors, and then wrote op-ed articles for the campus newspaper describing the work and conditions.

By far the most common student campaigns for college workers are living wage struggles. At thirty-four campuses, including Johns Hopkins, the University of Virginia, Brown, and Harvard, members of the campus community, mostly but by no means entirely undergraduate students, have demanded that the institution pay a living wage. With students (or their parents) paying more than thirty-five thousand dollars a year, and some workers paid as little as thirteen thousand dollars a year for full-time work, the contradictions are glaring. In 1999 Johns Hopkins, the largest private employer in the city of Baltimore, became perhaps the first to accept the need for a living wage, though the administration did so on its own terms (by 2002 it would bring workers to the

1998 living wage level). In the spring of 2001, Harvard students occupied an administration building to demand a living wage. After three weeks, although it would not promise to pay a living wage, Harvard agreed to create a commission to consider doing so, and on this basis the students ended their occupation; workers did subsequently get a raise.[33]

Students at Fairfield University and at Wesleyan University, both in Connecticut, have gone further, helping janitors to organize a union and win a first contract. This section focuses on students at Wesleyan, who built a worker-student alliance that shows impressive potential—and also shows some possible pitfalls.[34]

Despite the "university" in its title, Wesleyan, located in Middletown, Connecticut, is primarily an elite liberal arts college, one of the ten most selective such institutions in the country, and one with a significant progressive presence. The food service workers are not only unionized, but have a militant, participatory, activist, articulate workforce—a model union in all kinds of ways. In the aftermath of the first Union Summer, the twenty-plus students who had participated formed a SLAC (Student Labor Action Coalition). In a situation that is all too rare, that SLAC has remained vibrant ever since. The students are allied with Wesleyan's food service workers—the workers, for example, have demanded an improvement in the quality of student food, and students have fought changes in workers' schedules—and have supported area workers.

As a direct result of the janitor-student campaign at Fairfield University, in the spring of 1999 a student in the Wesleyan SLAC began investigating the situation of Wesleyan janitors. Wesleyan students learned that the university used to employ unionized janitors, but in 1989 had contracted out some of its cleaning services. In the fall of 1999 the contractor, Initial Cleaning, employed twenty-nine janitors, whose pay started at $6.50 an hour; only five of the janitors had worked long enough to earn more than $8.00 per hour, and even they had no benefits. If the workers had been hired as physical plant Wesleyan employees, they would have started at $11.62 an hour and worked up to between $14 and $17 an hour.[35] Of the twenty-nine workers, only four spoke fluent English; two were Polish-speaking, and the remainder were Spanish-speaking. The students approached SEIU 531, a Justice for Janitors local, and proposed to work with the union to organize the janitors.

Not all unions would respond well to such a student overture, but the students built a close working relationship with the union, especially with Kevin Brown, the secretary-treasurer of the local. Before proceeding he wanted the students to find out how many janitors were involved, because the union could not afford to commit resources unless there were at least twenty to thirty workers. According to Olivia Debree, a student who took the lead in the organizing campaign, once it was established that there were twenty-nine workers, Kevin "was immediately receptive. I think we took him for granted, the extent to which he would commit to things, come to our meetings at ten o'clock at night."[36] At the beginning "it was a lot of him telling us how to proceed, what we didn't know. There were some places where we disagreed with him about what to do, but for the most part we agreed, and he also gave us space to make decisions on our own. He was very good about that, which we also took for granted."

Because our society has a weak union culture, because most colleges— never mind high schools—teach students little or nothing about labor organizing, and because even progressive unions usually operate from a conventional model, the students weren't aware of alternative organizing models. Several of the students I spoke with expressed regret that the organizing campaign did not do more to empower workers and put them in control of the campaign. As Olivia Debree noted, "One thing that Kevin failed to do was teach us basic organizing models, like forming an organizing committee of workers and then allowing them to do all the organizing. We never did that. It never dawned on us to do that. Instead we would just go talk to workers individually."

Almost every member of the SLAC spoke at least some Spanish, but few were so fluent that language was no problem. Some janitors worked during the days in dormitories, others at night in academic buildings. As Abe Walker, a first-year student during the organizing campaign, explained:

> We'd approach the worker by trying to sort of ease into it by talking about general working conditions and wages and trying to get a sense of where they are at. Get a sense of what they think of their job, what they think of their boss, and then from there try to identify a few problems, a few hot issues. Often that would be wages. Sometimes that would be a problem with the manager. But just try to get a sense of what's the most important thing for them. And then from there sort of lead into the solution, which is organizing.

Kevin Brown of the union had given the workers a sheet with basic information about the union and union authorization cards. The students "went with a twofold purpose, to get that card signed and to tell them about the union."

In doing so the students encountered many of the same situations as in any organizing campaign, but with some important differences that provided advantages to the students. Most important, union organizers would never have the kind of access to workers that students had. It would be difficult for a cleaning company to fire or discipline a worker for talking to a student, and impossible for Wesleyan or the cleaning company to bar students from the buildings. (Union organizers, of course, are routinely barred from company property.) The cleaning company ran an anti-union campaign, but for the most part it was mild and ineffective and did not scare the workers. As one of the key workers, Norma Mercedes, explained, "In life, you win or lose—if someone's scared to fight, if they don't start fighting because of fear, then there's no alternative."[37]

Workers would sometimes ask the students why they were doing this. "I said: We think that the school we go to should pay people living wages, and that workers should have a right to organize a union if they wanted to. We put it in terms of holding the university accountable." Some of the workers were immediately enthusiastic and actively worked to recruit other workers; one "very charismatic guy" was especially supportive, came to student USLAC meetings, spoke to other workers, and got many to sign cards.

The campaign began to pick up momentum after some key workers joined and recruited other workers. It accelerated after the union had a clear majority, reaching more than 80 percent support by the end of the fall. As soon as there was significant support, meetings were set up at the union hall in Hartford (about a twenty-minute drive from campus). Students consulted with workers to find a good time for meetings, "because they all had second jobs, they worked on Saturdays and stuff." The first meeting was attended by seven workers, about 25 percent of the workforce; the largest meeting was attended by ten or twelve workers. A rank-and-file Polish worker from another location attended meetings to translate for the two Polish-speaking workers. One early focus of the meetings was a power analysis:

> Workers wanted to blame the cleaning company, and only the cleaning company, and it took a long time before workers would understand and incorporate the university into that power dynamic. That was one of the things that Kevin explained at the first union meeting. I remember him drawing this diagram at the first union meeting, making it clear where the leverage points were, and that his approach would be to put pressure on the university and not the cleaning company.

In late November Initial, which operated other unionized sites, agreed to do a card check recognition, and scheduled a meeting for workers, students, and SEIU 531 to present evidence that a majority of workers had expressed support for the company. Three days later Initial called the union to cancel the meeting because the Wesleyan director of human resources had urged the company to pursue a National Labor Relations Board (extended delay) election process. Within three days fourteen hundred students, a majority of the student body, had signed a petition supporting the janitors, and food service workers—at their own initiative—created and signed a similar petition.

Students also demanded an immediate meeting with the president, Doug Bennett (formerly the head of National Public Radio). At the meeting students told Bennett what had happened, and he reportedly responded, "That sounds off the wall." Students gave President Bennett a specific deadline. On deadline day the university issued a statement indicating that the director of human resources had merely "expressed his professional opinion" and that this did not constitute intervention by Wesleyan. One student reported that "from what I understand Bennett was furious" that the director of human resources had intervened. In the next couple of weeks a worker and two students presented Bennett with a petition, signed by a majority of the workers, asking Wesleyan to pay a living wage and stay out of unionization efforts, and numerous students and faculty sent e-mails defending workers' right to organize. Not long thereafter, in late December, with Wesleyan's neutrality established, the contractor accepted a card check and recognized the union.

In any campaign, union recognition is a key hurdle, but winning a first contract is crucial. In January and February 2000 negotiations—attended by union staff, workers, and students as well as by company representatives—advanced only slightly. The union invited all workers to attend negotiations, but few workers did so, in part because of scheduling difficulties. Initial, of course faced a problem: unless Wesleyan agreed to increase its payments, it would be difficult for the company to raise its wages significantly.

When students returned for the spring semester, therefore, a campaign mobilized to pressure Wesleyan to support a living wage for all Wesleyan workers, including the newly unionized Initial workers. During the fall semester students had gone to meet with middle- and lower-level administrators, in order that students could "introduce the idea to administrators who were going to have some kind of influence, and us be the ones to introduce the idea, not have the president tell it to them." In February the students started a faculty petition, eventually collecting signatures from more than half the faculty. They also mobilized alumni (mostly recent alumni, because that was who they knew) and parents.

Students wrote numerous letters to the student newspaper, and went to a wide range of campus organizations to inform them about the campaign and secure their endorsement. USLAC argued that the disgracefully low wages for Latino/a janitors were a form of institutional racism, and student-of-color groups agreed.

A large rally was held in mid-February, and was well attended by both students and workers even though it took place as a blizzard was beginning. "We organized in no way that I've ever seen anybody organize on this campus. We were doing basic things, but just extremely thoroughly." Almost every member of USLAC had a role in the rally; workers as well as students spoke, and the crowd marched on the president's office, having arranged the demonstration to take place during his office hours. Students were demanding not just a first contract for janitors, but also that the university adopt a Code of Conduct. The eight demands for a Responsible Code of Conduct were put on large poster sheets, one demand to a sheet, and explained to the crowd.

Students mailed informational packets to all members of the Board of Trustees, and went to open trustee functions where they stood quietly and handed out leaflets. Then on the final day of the trustee meetings students protested so loudly outside that the trustees offered students a chance to present the workers' concerns in return for quiet so the meeting could be continued. (That meeting took place at half past eight on a Saturday morning the day after spring break began; it took a pretty committed group of students to stay around and get up early in order to have an impact.)

All these activities were crucial preparation, but students had "realized in September that an occupation would be happening at some point, because we knew they [Wesleyan, Initial] would never agree." In December people in the union had suggested that it might be time to take strong action. The students said, "No, we really disagree with you about this. We need to build more support in the community. People aren't going to take us seriously unless we do that."

The occupation was planned carefully. The students talked to core workers about it immediately after a union meeting; they waited until the end of the meeting because neither students nor key workers trusted a couple of the workers who had attended. The workers "thought it was really funny that we were going to do this, and also they were really excited. They thought it was great." Students explained the demands to the janitors; all of them understood the demands about the union contract "and some workers understood about the code, but most of them didn't." In advance, students directly told about fifteen of the workers, that is, about half of them, about the coming occupation, but the word spread quickly to other workers as well. (Amazingly, however, it did not leak to Initial management or Wesleyan administrators; clearly both workers and USLAC students guarded the secret well.)

Students planned every aspect of the occupation both creatively and with attention to detail, occupying the Admissions Building on April 4. This was during the period when prospective students must decide which school they choose to attend, and when hundreds of high-school students and their parents visit the school (and head for the Admissions Office). Because of deportation and other issues, no workers were official participants in the occupation, but in advance the workers "chose two worker representatives to have cell phones during the occupation so we could call them and tell them how things were progressing." At first about twenty-five students went in, twenty-two of whom had decided they were going to be arrestable.

Word of the occupation spread quickly, not only through word of mouth but also because far in advance students had publicized a massive rally for that afternoon, to be held outside the Admissions Building. "Lots of workers came to that rally and spoke, the most of any of our events. I don't know exactly how many, probably ten or so. And they were all smiles, it was great."

That night the number of occupying students grew to forty, and several workers came in, "but it was more like they sat in on meetings rather than participating. Partly that was because meetings were in English; we had people translating for them." One of the most militant workers was the person whose job it was to clean the Admissions Office building at night, so he was in the building for legitimate job purposes, also serving as an informal guard while students slept.

The next day students met with President Bennett, who gave in much sooner than students expected. By night everything was settled—the union contract was signed and Bennett had agreed to meet to negotiate a Code of Conduct—and the students left. "And I remember actually after we won, going around. Because when we left the office it was like 10:30 at night, and we left and saw workers and told them what had happened, and people were just ecstatic." The contract raised workers' wages to $8.10 an hour to start, increasing to $9.10 after one year, and provided benefits and a grievance procedure. As a side benefit of the occupation, janitors employed by another subcontractor, who cleaned a different part of the campus, also received union recognition and a contract.

Over the next month, the student negotiating committee and two members of the faculty spent more than twenty hours negotiating a Code of Conduct with President Bennett. The code was to govern all future Wesleyan employment, whether direct or through subcontractors. The students won almost every element of their proposal. The code has eight provisions:

1. a living wage, for the fall of 2000 defined as a minimum of $8.15 an hour in wages and $10.20 an hour in total compensation;
2. a weak provision on unionization and freedom of association (see below);
3. safe working conditions;
4. nondiscrimination;
5. a guarantee that if the university changes service contractors existing employees are to be offered positions;
6. all workers to be notified of the code, and a Code Compliance Board (consisting of two students and one faculty member) to enforce it
7. the code to apply to all contractors who bill the university fifty thousand dollars or more per year; and
8. provisions for future changes.

What the students were not able to win was agreement that Wesleyan would insist all its subcontractors accept card-check recognition; on this the president (or perhaps the trustees) put their foot down, a fact that is no surprise to any union organizer. This issue for a time divided the students, who considered launching either a hunger strike or a new building occupation, but in the end they settled for what they had achieved— unionization and a living wage for janitors, a living wage guarantee for all future workers, and job protection in case of changing contractors.

Paternalism or Empowerment?

No campaigns do more than living wage and antisweatshop struggles to show the potential for a dramatic shift in the labor movement. The 1930s expanded the conception of "union" from just skilled workers to everyone at a workplace and from white to multiracial. Living wage and antisweatshop struggles hold the potential for a new paradigm, one that further expands the notion of "union," or perhaps replaces "union" with "labor movement." These struggles go beyond a single worksite or employer to make the issue of concern to the entire community, whether the community is a city or university. This further broadens who is included and the focus of solidarity, building coalitions that reach beyond all the usual bounds (of race, employer, skill), implicitly creating a class struggle of (almost the entire) community against employers. Moreover, these campaigns have often been social movements, involving mass demonstrations and a willingness to go beyond what the system defines as acceptable.

At the same time, however, these campaigns have the potential to remove responsibility and control from the people most concerned, the workers themselves. Typically living wage and antisweatshop struggles directly involve few if any of the workers to whom the new policies would apply. The course of the struggle depends on students or community activists; they decide what the priorities should be and they are the ones involved in a transformative process of struggle. The workers who will benefit may not even know a struggle is under way; they are not involved in decisions about priorities, and they do not learn and grow during the struggle. In practice this is sometimes true of ordinary union campaigns as well, but if union certification requires majority support, ultimately it must be the workers who decide. Even more than bureaucratic unions, therefore, living wage and antisweatshop struggles have the potential to become a form of benevolent charity: other people doing things for workers who do not develop their own capacities or their ability to engage in future collective action. Gay Seidman notes that consumer boycotts are blunt instruments—hard to turn on, and even harder to turn off, thus potentially damaging workers even after an agreement has been reached. She also argues that boycotts typically leave control in the hands of affluent and well-educated activists in advanced industrial societies, who determine which struggles should be privileged and which issues selected; however much such activists may aim to empower workers, the workers themselves cannot make these decisions.[38]

If this new form of struggle were to become others doing things for workers, it would undercut the greatest, most democratic premise of the labor movement: that workers have both the right and the capacity to get together, organize, decide for themselves what is in their own interests, and then go out and fight to win. Employers may claim to be concerned about workers, may even think they are doing what is best for workers. Well-meaning allies, whether social workers, lawyers, nongovernmental organizations, or student movements, may intend to defend workers. Government regulators may enforce laws to protect workers. All of those are valuable, but none can substitute for workers getting together and deciding on their own priorities, for workers developing the power to stand up for themselves rather than having one or another external protector take care of them.

Any group, *any* group that argues that it acts *on behalf of* workers, and that therefore workers do not need to organize and select representatives of their own choosing, is not to be trusted. Whatever good it may do in the short run, in the long run it will undercut worker power and promote goals and strategies that differ significantly from those the workers themselves would choose. If men decide what is in women's interests, if whites decide what is in black people's interests, if employers—or human rights organizations—decide what is in workers' interests, the process is fundamentally undemocratic and cannot lead to the kind of society we are striving to create.

The mechanism by which workers get together, decide on their interests, select representatives to speak for the collectivity, and mobilize worker solidarity/power is a union. That's what unions are. Unions in practice often fall short of this ideal: the staff substitutes for the workers and acts (as it sees it) on behalf of workers, few workers participate, the union is ineffective. Labor needs to revitalize itself and create a social movement, but if the social movement is one that displaces and attempts to substitute for workers it will undercut the very premises for which it hopes to stand.

It's instructive to compare and contrast the Stamford Organizing Project with living wage and antisweatshop campaigns. All build impressive coalitions and extend the struggle well beyond politics (or labor) as usual. All focus on improving conditions for low-wage workers, most of whom are people of color. All are prepared to engage in militant actions and do so when the occasion calls for it. But there is a huge difference in who takes the lead and how the coalition is built. Living wage, antisweatshop, and Code of Conduct struggles are built primarily by students, union or community staff, or religious organizations with a social conscience. Many of those taking the lead are affluent and well-educated. In Stamford, the workers take the lead on essentially all actions, and workers reach out to those with whom they are already involved. Thus the Stamford Organizing Project does not involve any rabbis, not because there are no liberal rabbis in Stamford (there probably are), but rather because none of the workers attends a synagogue. Since Stamford mobilizes clergy by asking workers to contact their ministers, the Stamford Organizing Project has made no effort to involve the clergy of affluent congregations. Unions' mobilizing relies on workers' own power, networks, and resources, on their broad community, not on support from the outside. This contrasts sharply with student-led antisweatshop struggles.

Living wage and antisweatshop struggles simultaneously show the burgeoning strength and the existing limitations of new labor-based movements. On the one hand, business thoroughly dominates politics, so that the minimum wage is disgracefully low and gets raised only incrementally after great effort. On the other hand, activists have created a new concept, the living wage, that has captured the popular imagination and has won victory after victory. On the one hand, garment manufacturers are legally permitted to disclaim responsibility for the sweatshop conditions they foster, to hide their involvement and responsibility, and to monitor themselves when caught stealing from workers. On the other hand, the antisweatshop movement has succeeded in exposing this behavior; manufacturers are far more worried that consumers will hold them morally accountable than they are about (weak) government enforcement.[39]

If our country were serious about ending these abuses, we could institute a program to empower workers and make them partners with the government in the regulatory process. If the law mandated the creation of a democratically elected worker committee at each worksite, if that committee had the ability to monitor compliance and report violations of basic laws, and if those judgments stood until such time as all appeals were concluded, we could quickly solve the sweatshop problem. The same would be true if workers received real and effective guarantees of their right to form unions free of employer harassment or interference. But of course at the present time it appears utopian to propose such policies in the United States, never mind in Central America or Indonesia.

The movements discussed in this chapter have the potential to create a new paradigm, and participants in the struggle are self-consciously aiming to do so. The antisweatshop students of USAS created the WRC not as a new form of monitoring, but as a system of disclosure and verification, trying to open up the process and to provide means for workers (and others) to know what is happening and to initiate change. The students of Wesleyan struggled not on behalf of faraway workers, but for and with low-paid campus workers. Wesleyan students were much more involved with workers than is the case in most student labor campaigns, and as such that campaign offers a different model and a limited exception to the concerns voiced here (but see below). That was so for at least two reasons. First, the students were working to improve conditions for workers on their own campus. Second, they were trying to win a living wage by means of *a union*, and as a result necessarily became involved and worked with low-wage workers to a far greater degree than in many living wage or antisweatshop campaigns.

Nonetheless, these movements have the potential to reproduce, or possibly even exacerbate, the tendency of others to substitute for workers, with students (or living wage activists), like union staff, taking actions for workers instead of helping workers to gain their own voice and power. That was true even at Wesleyan University, where Olivia Debree and other students are self-critical about the campaign and its consequences:

> I think actually in retrospect, that because of the way we organized we kind of reproduced this power relation, between people who have money, have an education, and those who don't, and us telling them what they needed. . . . The consequence to the way we organized them, and our taking this role between the workers and the union, between the workers and the university, is that the way it is right now is that when there's a problem, the workers come to the students, they don't come to the union, they don't initiate their own plans and then go to the university about it. It's created a situation where the workers are dependent, when I don't think that they would be in this position if we had taken some other route.

Kevin Brown, the union organizer, agrees this was a problem: "The weakness of the campaign was that worker leadership did not develop as it should have. The presence of the students meant that workers had a crutch, and they used that crutch."[40] A continuing struggle in building strong unions is not to create a division between workers and "the union" as if the union were an outside force, as if employers were right that "the union" is a third party. In a different form of organizing, workers not only say "we are the union" but mean it, because they have collectively made decisions, have acted in solidarity with each other, and know that "the union" is what they do together even if they sometimes act through representatives.

At Wesleyan University many outcomes are still possible, but because the students are self-critical, because the students' goal is to empower the workers, there's evidence that workers are developing their own power, that a year after winning a contract workers are more capable of taking the lead than they were immediately after the contract victory. To begin with, instead of students going to workers, workers now come to the students much more than during the unionization campaign, "mostly about problems with the union," for example, the difficulties in having the health insurance kick in. In an unfortunate (but not atypical) situation, no one at the union health insurance office spoke Spanish, so workers asked students to call the health insurance office and speak to them. It's still the case that some workers "have been confused about whether or not the students are the union representatives. These workers definitely don't see themselves as the union. They definitely get the distinction between a representative and themselves."

At the same time, however, there has been a change. When workers first had complaints about the union, they wanted students "to talk to the union for the workers" but "now it's more of 'can we go confront so-and-so as students and workers? We want students to witness this, so that they know what we said.'" Students report that after winning the contract "there's definitely more solidarity among the workers." It remains to be seen whether over time the Wesleyan janitors' union will become more bureaucratic and staff-driven or whether workers will gain confidence and develop solidarity, in part because of their ability to draw on the support of students.

Living wage and Code of Conduct campaigns draw in new participants, build new coalitions, and reach workers that the labor movement would ordinarily find it difficult to reach. Kevin Brown, the SEIU organizer, feels that the Wesleyan University janitors campaign made a significant advance beyond a simple living wage, because it was done in conjunction with workers and a union: "These students were sophisticated enough to see that unions are the best vehicle to make changes that don't get eliminated six months later." It is highly unlikely a conventional union would have been able to organize these workers. The students spent incredible amounts of time, all unpaid, to bring about the victory; I'd estimate over two thousand hours of unpaid student time in addition to all the time, energy, and resources put in by paid union staff, in order to organize twenty-nine low-wage janitors. From an economist's dollars-and-cents perspective this may not have been a rational expenditure of time and effort, and certainly it's not something that unions could afford to do on a paid basis.

But such a campaign holds promise as a model of what might be involved in a future labor upsurge. SAWSJ (Scholars, Artists, and Writers for Social Justice) has proposed a Code of Conduct for colleges and universities. Colleges that sign the code would pledge to pay all workers a living wage, be at least neutral in dealings with unions, practice affirmative action, protect academic freedom, be environmentally friendly (to both workers and the community), and not use prison labor. Colleges and universities are major employers; faculty may be the most visible employees, but the number of janitors, food service workers, clerical employees, and maintenance workers is substantially greater than the number of full-time tenure-track faculty. If labor could build movements on campuses around the country, with faculty and students working with maintenance and clerical workers, it could benefit millions of workers and create a new model for the labor movement. Nor are colleges and universities the only institutions where such campaigns would be feasible—imagine child care center campaigns that mobilized parents and the feminist community, hospital campaigns relying on those who had been patients and on their families, recycling center organizing that mobilized environmentalists, or any campaign where workers at one worksite stood up for the rights of others in their community. Once campaigns succeeded at these institutions the coalitions could expand to new areas.

Whatever the law provides, if we—and this "we" must be much more than those now in unions—could create a movement that stopped employers from violating worker rights, suddenly tens of millions of workers would organize and push for better conditions. Thousands of times each year a worker is fired simply because he or she stood up for the union during an organizing drive. The media don't even bother to report most such firings. Imagine what would happen if the next day (or the next week) a thousand people showed up to block the entrance, leaflet the public, and in general make it clear that until the worker got his or her job back there would be "no business as usual." If labor could regularly mount such responses, whether or not the laws and the courts changed, workers would regain (at least some of) the rights that the law once promised, but which in practice have been taken away. No one can tell what the future may bring, but Code of Conduct and living wage campaigns show the potential for such movements—movements that could transform the character of the labor movement.

7

A New Upsurge?

Fusion

In a stimulating contribution in *New Labor Forum*, Katie Quan argues that the labor movement has had a difficult time dealing with issues of race, class, and gender. She outlines two models of how the labor movement might approach these issues; this book argues for a third model.

Quan's first model is *diversity*, "a term that implies inclusion of previously excluded groups of people, but within the existing institutional framework." In this view, the labor movement should incorporate women, people of color, sexual minorities, immigrants, and others into its membership, activities, staff, and leadership—but the labor movement as such does not need to make other fundamental alterations. The second model, which she favors, is a *united front* by various progressive movements, a position that "leads us to respect and ally with other social movements on an equal basis."

This book has argued for a third model, *fusion*. Rather than a united front of movements that remain separate and operate as partners, we need to abolish the distinctions between these movements. Labor must do more than build alliances; it must fuse with these movements such that it is no longer clear what is a "labor" issue and what is a "women's" issue or an "immigrant" issue.[1] When the Stamford Organizing Project helps organize and mobilize the (overwhelmingly black) union and nonunion residents of public housing to prevent the privatization of their complex, is this about labor, race, or housing? The answer, of course, is all three, and there's no easy way to make a separation between them.[2] When Yale clerical workers organize a union and go on strike for what is in effect comparable worth, is this about feminism or labor? When Wesleyan University students occupy a building to help Latino janitors win a union contract and a living wage, is this a student, labor, antipoverty, or antiracism struggle?

Let me immediately and emphatically state that my notion of "fusion" does not propose that all movements submerge themselves into labor. The only way progressive forces will deal with the needed issues is if groups organize autonomously around issues, identities, and concerns. We need a women's movement, as well as environmentalist, black, Latino, immigrant, gay, lesbian, and other movements—including movements not yet imagined. But the model should not be of separate movements forming alliances, but of movements that take up each other's concerns, incorporating them into their heart, soul, culture, and institutional structure. Not only the labor movement needs to change: the feminist movement needs to give greater priority to the needs of low-wage women workers, environmentalists need to be as concerned with pollution in the factory as in the wilderness, and so on.

Fusion, if and when it happens, will transform all of the movements involved. They will no longer deal with the same issues or involve the same participants; the process has the potential to lead to enormous expansion but will definitely lead to internal struggles. Historically, social movements mushroom when they break out of their past confines and tap into new constituencies and networks. This is what happened to the labor movement in the 1930s, as the craft base of earlier times gave way to industrial unions; to the student antiwar movement, when it moved outside elite institutions and expanded into the mass of public colleges and universities; and to the gay liberation movement, when it moved beyond respectable professionals and incorporated the bar scenes of San Francisco and New York. These past expansions have changed the character of movements, redefining the issues and introducing new cultural styles, with the initial core group often opposed to this transformation and uncomfortable with the new participants.[3] Today, a struggle understood to be narrowly about unions is unlikely to generate the same energy and enthusiasm as a campaign that unites labor and economic justice with race or gender or immigrant rights or the environment.

The failure of assorted social movements to connect with each other is one of the primary causes for the current weakness of the U.S. Left. It is difficult to imagine how progressive forces can win significant victories unless these separations are overcome. But these separations could be overcome in many different ways.

What Kind of Fusion?

The fusion of labor and new social movements might combine the best of both worlds—the energy, imagination, media savvy, and militant symbolic actions of the new social movements with the broad outreach, local chapters, face-to-face majoritarian mobilization, deep commitment, and staying power of the labor movement. Or it might combine the worst of both—the thin, direct-mail and phone solicitation based "membership" of some public interest movements with the social worker inside-the-box passivity of some bureaucratic unions. Which of these develops might help determine how likely it is that an upsurge emerges.

Many existing unions are weak and ineffective. The members are minimally involved, think "the union" is something separate from them, don't see the union as a way to mobilize to address the problems in their lives, figure that if anyone should address the problem it is the union staff who are paid to do so, but don't have much hope that will happen. Many union leaders and staff are overwhelmed, unable to solve most of the problems brought to them but also not knowing how to mobilize workers to develop their own power. Some union leaders and staff are no longer motivated by high ideals, and hold the job only because it provides more pay and rewards than the alternatives. A few union leaders are outright corrupt, stealing from the members.[4] But, unless it is outright corrupt, even a bad union is better than no union. It raises workers' wages, provides some grievance procedure, and creates an organizational vehicle that may be activated when faced with pressing problems.

Even run-of-the-mill unions include thousands of dedicated labor activists, and no force in our society has more democratic potential (or radical possibility) than the labor movement. Its base and focus is the large working-class majority underrepresented, or outright neglected, by many other social movements. Michael Zweig has argued that the existence of a working-class majority is "America's best kept secret"; within many movements the working class (majority) is almost invisible.[5] The labor movement's central premise is that workers have the right, the ability, and the power to at least participate in, and possibly to control, decisions about their work and their lives. It's not that some benevolent outside group should do this for workers, and it's not that it can only be done by some (especially talented or privileged) workers. Our society actively stifles most people's creativity. Every group of people has amazing capacities; unchaining that energy and vision leads to far better outcomes than does control by the experts and those with power. At its best the labor movement helps people discover their abilities and act on a level of commitment that inspires awe. It's not just that people mobilize more energy and power; they take up new ideas, developing alternatives the experts never considered.

The tension/contradiction between the radical democratic potential of the labor movement and the reality of actually existing unions is central to the possibility of a resurgence by labor. The Sweeney New Voice labor leadership, which came to power in 1995, understands and to some degree embraces the need to fuse with social movements. But the New Voice was not the result of a mass movement. Rather, labor's old guard recognized that labor might be entirely eliminated unless it changed. Because the new labor leadership was not brought to power by a social movement, when labor faces obstacles the leadership does not think in terms of social movements. It may not know what a movement would require, and may shrink from the (legal, financial, etc.) risks it would entail, instead seeking the solution in a better staff. In practice this often helps to perpetuate the structures that (may be needed to sustain what now exists but also) make a new upsurge improbable. Although the New Voice leadership has broken with the past and helped reorient labor in many ways, increased democracy has not been a priority, and does not seem likely to be in the future.

Because winning a union usually results from a battle where workers have to take risks and mobilize solidarity, newly organized unions almost always have at least a significant level of member support. But unless the union continues to mobilize workers, the initial support and involvement can quickly atrophy. Most union locals exist because they are long established, protected by custom and an institutional structure, relying on the passive support of members who may see the union as weak or irrelevant, but know they are better off with than without a union.[6] In many union locals, however, no one now working can remember the founding of the union, and quite possibly no one now working has been involved in a strike. The local may have held rallies or picket lines, but has never mobilized the breadth or depth of support that is required to win an organizing campaign or to carry through a successful strike.

Even the smartest, toughest, most capable staff can accomplish relatively little by themselves. The power and potential of the labor movement depend on the solidarity of millions of workers, no one of whom has much power on his or her own. Almost by definition, massive growth and a new paradigm require mass participation—and leadership—by rank-and-file workers. On the other hand, workers are taught, both in school and on the job, that they have neither the ability to understand what needs to be done nor the right to make key decisions.

Because of that, union staff can often play a crucial role in helping to build workers' self-confidence, abilities, power, and leadership. But they can do so only if they organize, not lead; help workers realize their full human potential, not become the person who does everything for workers. In the words of labor socialist Eugene Debs, "Too long have the workers of the world waited for some Moses to lead them out of bondage. He has not come; he never will come. I would not lead you out if I could; for if you could be led out, you could be led back again. I would have you make up your minds that there is nothing you cannot do for yourselves."[7]

That means labor needs not just to add to its numbers, but also to help workers make existing unions more effective. An internal organizing campaign for the members of an established union can mirror conventional organizing: reach out to all members of the workforce, develop internal leadership, identify and take up the issues that concern workers, build solidarity, and mobilize for action. Such a campaign can be as empowering as an initial organizing campaign, and can make as much difference in transforming workers' lives and working conditions. If half of the thirteen-million-plus members of the AFL-CIO, and half of the more than thirty thousand union locals, engaged in such internal organizing, labor power would increase dramatically. This in turn would make unions more appealing to unorganized workers. As John Sweeney said at the 1997 AFL-CIO convention, "You could make a million house calls and run a thousand television commercials and stage a hundred strawberry rallies, and still not come close to doing what the UPS strike did for organizing."[8]

The moral argument for democratizing unions and involving the membership is compelling, but there is also a practical argument. Democratic and participatory unions, especially those open to progressive politics and connections, are more effective. In studies of a wide range of 1930s and 1940s union locals, Judy Stepan-Norris and Maurice Zeitlin conclude that "contracts won by the locals of stable, highly democratic international unions were systematically more likely to be pro-labor," that unions with organized factions won more prolabor contracts, and that in general "union democracy makes a difference in the daily lives of workers."[9] The same holds true today. Employer arguments about the union as an "outside force" have some plausibility if existing unions are run by staff, not workers; if the staff differ significantly from the workers (in education, income, race, gender, neighborhoods where they live, whether they drink coffee or latte); and if the union organizer is someone new to the town, who will depart as soon as the organizing drive is over. If area unions are run by friends, neighbors, and fellow members of your congregation; if the organizing drive involves meetings with enthusiastic workers who are already members of the local undertaking the organizing drive; if the campaign started because nonunion workers kept comparing their situation to the wages, benefits, security, and sense of power of their union neighbors; then employer anti-union campaigns face serious obstacles.[10]

Labor is currently caught in a vicious circle; gains, both in new organizing and in internal transformation, might change that to a virtuous circle of self-reinforcing growth. Because such a small fraction of workers are unionized, it's difficult to win much at the bargaining table: if conditions for the union workers get too far out of line with those for nonunion workers, employers will try to break the union or move elsewhere. But because unions find it difficult to win major improvements, unorganized workers are reluctant to take risks when the benefits may be modest. Labor advances would reverse that equation: internal transformation would improve organizing, and organizing victories would make it more possible to develop union power.

The Meaning of Upsurge

Slow and incremental advances, sustained over many years, are unlikely, however, to lead to labor revival. Even if unions could recruit twice as many new members each year, it would still take more than thirty years to return labor to where it was in 1980 (never mind 1960); although labor increasingly emphasizes internal organizing, at present that too is a slow and incremental process. The most likely source of labor revival is some sort of upsurge, leading to a period where labor's numbers and power triple or quadruple in a short period. But is this a realistic possibility, or a magical incantation I invoke because it's hard to see what could change the situation? Am I vainly hoping that maybe *something* will come along?

In the language of academics we might ask whether an upsurge is exogenous or endogenous to labor; that is, will an upsurge come out of nowhere, appearing for reasons having nothing to do with labor itself, or will it be the result of the actions undertaken by the labor movement? If an upsurge could come only for reasons external to labor, this would be a statement that labor itself is so weak and conditions so inauspicious that no reasonable course of union action seems likely to reverse labor's decline. One interpretation might be that labor should sit back and wait for someone or something else to create an opportunity.

If we look at other social movements through history, some periods of explosive growth were caused by external events, and some were caused by the actions of the movement itself. Compare the labor upsurge of the 1930s, which was heavily dependent on external factors, to the civil rights movement, which created momentum through its own actions.

In 1929, the United States began an economic slide which went on for years and became the most severe in the nation's history. Each year the economy went further downhill; ultimately one out of three workers lost their jobs, and those who kept their jobs had wages cut by 25 percent. Unions were not quick to take advantage of these conditions: from 1929 to 1933 unions lost more than 20 percent of their membership. Most of the pre-1934 labor struggles were failures. External conditions—the year-by-year decline of the economy, not caused by labor unions—exercised a continuing influence. The downward spiral had no end in sight so people increasingly felt that desperate measures were necessary. Although unions were not the first option tried, eventually masses of people became willing to take huge risks to build unions and achieve a measure of control over their work lives.

The civil rights movement, on the other hand, created the conditions for its own upsurge. The Montgomery bus boycott, for example, was planned in advance. Rosa Parks was an officer of the local NAACP and a long-time activist; in order to create a test case she refused to move to the back of the bus. As soon as she was arrested, organizing began for a one-day boycott. Only because of the success of that first day did the movement's organizers decide to continue the boycott. The confrontation at Little Rock came from a long history of black activism around the schools. The sit-in wave of the spring of 1960 came because thousands of students and others took action, risking abuse and arrest. At later stages as well, the movement itself created crises, forcing the system to address its issues, rather than relying on external events.

A new upsurge might be the result either of external factors or of internal organizing. A war, an economic recession, a series of corporate scandals, an environmental or health disaster, a privatized Social Security meltdown, dramatic movement advances in other countries, a campaign finance scandal of epic proportions, or any of a variety of other "external" events might change the political-legal terrain and the climate of public opinion. Alternatively, like the civil rights movement, the labor movement itself might create the crises that would lead to an upsurge.

Even in current conditions of "weak" labor, hundreds of thousands of workers join unions each year, and some of those struggles involve the kinds of stories and actions that, in the right conditions, could catch the public imagination. A set of militant workers, with good organizers, building broad alliances, and targeting a high-visibility employer might create a confrontation and win a victory that would change the terrain and became a model inspiring others.

The exogenous-endogenous continuum is useful for some purposes, but this division is also problematic—nothing is entirely external, and the actions of the movement itself are always influenced by opportunities. The 1930s Great Depression was the external factor creating U.S. labor's explosive growth from 1933 to 1945—but in Germany the Depression led to Nazism. Although the civil rights movement created its own crises and momentum, its ability to do so depended in part on the increase in the black urban population, the mechanization of southern agriculture, and the fact that the northern power structure did not depend on the sort of racial caste etiquette system prevalent in the South. The problems of an exogenous-endogenous division are also evident in evaluating the women's movement or the gay and lesbian movements. They were created by participants' dedication, creativity, and commitment, but their task was far easier because the civil rights movement had created a public agenda focused on equality and freedom.

This book is about some of the ways the labor movement has positioned itself either to create an upsurge, or to take advantage of favorable external conditions. The New Deal labor regime was developed for a world that is (in many ways) long gone. Changes in the political economy—increased women's employment, growing numbers of immigrants and changes in the minority population, globalization, the expansion of higher education—constantly create new challenges and new opportunities. A vital movement adapts and responds to challenges; a weak movement gets overwhelmed. For too long, business was the stronger and often the more creative force, taking advantage of each new opportunity and preventing labor and other groups from making gains in areas where business should be vulnerable. Today, labor is increasingly taking the initiative.

Any labor regime is embodied in law, institutional structures, employer and union practices, and cultural expectations. The New Deal "gave" labor rights and protections on condition that unions operated within the rules and became a part of the system. A set of rewards and penalties coerced labor to accept certain routinized and limited ways of advancing its interests, and rewarded unions for doing so. These rules required unions to behave legalistically, while severely penalizing those practices that create the greatest solidarity and power (sit-down strikes, sympathy strikes, secondary boycotts, unconventional and unpredictable short strikes). Then, over time, in the face of a relentless employer assault, one which became more severe in the late 1970s, workers' and unions' rights were restricted, one step at a time.

The New Deal labor system, and all that sustains it, is weakened and ineffective, but still holding—just barely. In order for it to endure, it would need to be reformed enough to provide labor incentives to operate by the system's rules. Normally you'd expect the labor movement to be pushing for labor law reform, but it isn't doing so, and for good reason. A generation ago unions tried to reform the system, and despite a Democratic president and strong Democratic majorities in both houses of Congress, business defeated even that very mild reform proposal.[11] Today, given the extent of business and conservative dominance, the AFL-CIO is well aware that any purely legislative attempt at labor law reform would probably make the system worse. For example, in the summer of 2002 House Republicans began a move to outlaw card-check recognition, the approach used in many of labor's innovative campaigns. Richard Bensinger, formerly head of the AFL-CIO Organizing Department, argues that until people are aware of the extent of labor law violations, until a movement succeeds in changing the culture, it would be counterproductive to attempt reform. Violations of workers' rights to form unions may be the most systematic and pervasive violation of human rights in the United States today, but the media report them rarely if at all. Most people, including most members of progressive movements, are not aware of what happens when workers try to organize. Electoral politics (and even more so, lobbying) can't bring about significant social change unless a powerful and independent social movement has already put the issue on the agenda.[12]

The inability or unwillingness to reform the system means that most of the time workers and unions will lose, and often will be embittered by a system that blatantly violates expectations of fair play. Workers and unions therefore have less and less reason to play within the system. Within-the-system rules that stack the deck against workers de facto encourage workers and unions to adopt outside-the-rules innovative and militant tactics. If NLRB elections were swift, employers were prevented from coercing workers, and employer violations were quickly and severely punished, unions would have an incentive to work within the system. When the rules themselves permit massive coercion, employers routinely violate the laws that are supposed to protect workers, justice is delayed for two or three years, and the worst violations lead to a slap on the wrist, it's not surprising unions decide there is little reason to play by the rules. The logic of the current system coerces the labor movement, even those within it who are reluctant, to mobilize community struggles, to join forces with student allies, to take up the cause of immigrant workers, to take to the streets to protest the World Trade Organization. Not only the employer offensive but also the changing composition of the labor movement itself pushes labor to adopt new stances and approaches. Unions with high proportions of immigrant workers led the drive for labor to support undocumented workers and unions with high proportions of women workers led the push to get the AFL-CIO to oppose war with Iraq.

No one needs to be told that predicting the future is dangerous territory. By far the safest prediction, and the one that is usually right, is that things will continue much as they have been going. But *there are discontinuities in history*. Looking at past predictions of when mass movements would erupt makes it clear that some very smart people have made predictions that in hindsight make them look like fools. During the middle of World War I, Lenin, trained revolutionary and perennial optimist, said that he did not expect to see revolution in his lifetime. At the end of the 1950s Daniel Bell proclaimed the "end of ideology," declaring that "the old passions are spent" and there is a "rough consensus" on political issues; Seymour Martin Lipset concurred.[13] No sooner had they done so than the mass movements of the 1960s broke out and turned our world upside down, with some of the sharpest conflicts taking place inside the institutions Bell and Lipset should have known best, universities. Focusing more specifically on American labor unions, in his 1932 presidential address to the American Economic Association, Harold Barnett declared that "American trade unionism is slowly being limited in influence by changes which destroy the basis on which it is erected. . . . I see no reason to believe that American trade unionism will . . . become in the next decade a more potent social influence." George Meany, who should have known something about labor, declared in 1962 that "it is impossible to bargain collectively with the government"—and public-sector unions immediately took off.[14]

These past predictions make it evident, if anyone needed the reminder, that even well-positioned observers make embarrassing predictions. But *if* it turns out that in the next decade labor and other groups transform American politics and society, fifty years later historians will look back and say this should have been no surprise, the signs were evident: look at the student no-sweat movement, at the Seattle anti-WTO protests, at the Teamsters' UPS strike.

Today we dwell on the reasons why advances by labor seem unlikely. Business is overwhelmingly dominant, not only in politics but in universities, foundations, the media, and the culture more generally. But, just like the stock-market bubble, that won't necessarily last forever. By their nature, discontinuities are unpredictable. We don't know whether they will come, and we don't know what's required to bring them about. If an upsurge comes tomorrow, or the day after, I am convinced that labor will be one central element of the upsurge—not the only element, but a central one.

The post-1995 shift in labor leadership may not have mobilized a mass movement, but it has dramatically opened and improved the relationship of the labor movement to a wide range of causes and groups. The old labor movement was often insular and hostile to outsiders of any kind. A minor example of that, but one vividly etched in my own personal experience, was the beginning of a strike in western Massachusetts. A group of us had built what was in effect a precursor to Jobs with Justice, a network to support each other's struggles. At 6:30 one morning, I received a phone call from a worker saying, "We've just gone on strike and none of us know what to do. Can your group come down and help us?" By 8:00 A.M. we had a dozen people on their (large, militant) picket line, and were talking with them about the strike. The striking workers, 75 percent of whom were women (as were all the officers of the local), reported that their union "business agent" had told them they couldn't go on strike, they were just a bunch of girls and wouldn't know what to do. The business agent didn't arrive until 10:00 A.M., when he drove up in a long black car (in my memory a Cadillac, but I suspect that's apocryphal), and immediately went to talk to the *police*. After doing so, without any discussion with any of the elected leadership of the local, he told the picketers to let scabs through, and next approached me to ask "What the hell are you doing here? Who are you? Are you a member of the Communist Party? Why are these people here?" We referred him to the other union with which we'd been working; the business agent later reported that to his amazement officials of the first union had said we were a major asset.[15]

Today's labor movement, at least AFL-CIO headquarters and the headquarters level of many of the most vibrant unions, completely reverses that old pattern. I sometimes worry that today's labor movement gives more priority to alliances with other social movements than it does to mobilizing its own membership. There's still lots more old guard than new labor, but increasingly labor is eager for alliances and actively pursues them. It's not just that labor is willing to work with other groups.

Along with that willingness, and in significant part because of its increased involvement with assorted social movements, labor has changed its position on a range of crucial issues, perhaps most notably in its support for undocumented immigrants. Labor's links with other groups are denser and stronger than they have been for a half-century, and people on all sides are eager to further strengthen those links.

But social movements do not arise simply because groups have made links or intellectuals think they've identified a burning issue. Nor do oppressive conditions necessarily give rise to movements. Nor is it enough that a group is ready to lead. In order for a mass movement to arise, large numbers of people must be willing to devote time and energy, to invest their hopes in the movement, and to take risks despite their fears. But people do so only if the issues are deeply felt. Social movements are fundamentally democratic in a way that most of the rest of politics is not: nothing happens unless thousands of people act.

That's why this book has focused not on an abstract vision of what I think labor could or should do, but rather on what people have actually been doing. What are the issues that drive their concerns? In what circumstances have people been prepared to engage in struggle? What concerns have seized people's imaginations and in what circumstances have people been able to mobilize the solidarity and power needed to win? Almost by definition a new period of upsurge will redefine the terrain and create new possibilities, but the new ways will not come out of nothing. Understanding what is already moving people, why (in a few cases) people are able to win and why (in most cases) they get defeated, or achieve only very limited goals, is the best guide to what might happen in a period of upsurge.

Notes

Why Organize?

1. Data for 2001 full-time workers, from http://www.bls.gov/cps.

2. Why wasn't Steve fired? Probably because it was a small (70–80 worker) shop, and he was an excellent worker and had skills no one else had, serving as Mr. Fix-It for a range of problems.

3. An extended and insightful account of one of Richard Sanders's earlier organizing campaigns is presented in Rick Fantasia, *Cultures of Solidarity: Consciousness, Action, and Contemporary American Workers* (Berkeley: University of California Press, 1988). Rick and I are both friends of Richard's; we met him through our involvement in his first union organizing campaign, in Amherst, Massachusetts, near where we all live.

4. Compare this to the feelings of Steve Shraison's co-workers in the Christmas massacre.

5. "Quotations" from supervisors are comments offered by Richard Sanders or workers I interviewed; I did not attempt to speak to supervisors themselves and doubt they would have given me any usable information.

6. Most workers, of course, can't bring that off; it was a goal, not the routine practice.

7. Actually, a worst case would be even worse than the scenario I sketch. In the worst case a corrupt union leader affiliated with organized crime cut a deal with an employer that gave workers no choice about whether or not to join a union, and then negotiated a contract that provided little or no benefit to workers but (in one way or another) enriched the owner and union "boss" (and here the term is justified).

8. This is in contrast to the dominant approach in today's labor movement, which emphasizes "house calls," visits to a worker's home which involve meeting with people one at a time.

9. This means that if there is not a solid base of support the campaign can be called off or put on hold without exposing workers to massive employer attacks.

Chapter 1. Labor Revival: What Would It Take?

1. *Statistical Abstract of the United States 2000*, p. 410, table 636. *Time*, June 13, 1994.

2. AFL-CIO membership data for 2000–2001 versus 1992–93 provided by AFL-CIO.

Increase in labor force calculated from *Statistical Abstract 2001*, tables 568 and 638. Average number of new members per year is taken from the AFL-CIO's *Work in Progress* year-end reports for 1999 (474,140), 2000 (160,793), and 2001 (463,429). Note that these numbers include new members gained through affiliations of previously independent groups. If unions were able to triple the number of new members per year they would regain their 1983 position by 2014. The AFL-CIO's Organizing Department and its Media Relations Department each provided me with somewhat different figures from those reported in *Work in Progress* (with a 2000 figure more than double that reported in the weekly updates), but no matter which set of figures is used the basic conclusion is the same.

3. Calculated from Richard Freeman and Joel Rogers, *What Workers Want* (Ithaca, N.Y.: Cornell University Press, 1999).

4. Nelson Lichtenstein, "Can Unions Change?" *The Nation*, September 3/10, 2001, p. 29.

5. For U.S. figures see U.S. Bureau of the Census, *Historical Statistics of the United States* (Washington, D.C.: U.S. Government Printing Office, 1975), p. 177, which is also the source for the 1930s data presented below. See also Richard B. Freeman, "Spurts in Union Growth: Defining Moments and Social Processes," in *The Defining Moment: The Great Depression and the American Economy in the Twentieth Century*, ed. Michael D. Bordo, Claudia Goldin, and Eugene N. White (Chicago: University of Chicago Press, 1998), pp. 265–95. For 1904 comparisons see Howard Kimeldorf, *Battling for American Labor: Wobblies, Craft Workers, and the Making of the Union Movement* (Berkeley: University of California Press, 1999), p. 1.

6. Quoted in G. William Domhoff, *Who Rules America?* (Englewood Cliffs, N.J.: Prentice-Hall, 1967), p. 153.

7. Of course the old forms hang on, in some pockets almost completely unaltered, in many areas as a component subpart of the new arrangements, but the basic rules of the game are altered.

8. A large literature discusses what are variously called "Social Structures of Accumulation" or "regulatory regimes." Three of the best accounts are David M. Gordon, Richard Edwards, and Michael Reich, *Segmented Work, Divided Workers: The Historical Transformation of Labor in the United States* (New York: Cambridge University Press, 1982); David Harvey, *The Condition of Postmodernity: An Enquiry into the Origins of Cultural Change* (Cambridge, Mass.: Blackwell. 1989); and John O'Connor, "From Welfare Rights to Welfare Fights: Globalization, Class Struggle, and Welfare System Change" (Ph.D. diss., University of Massachusetts, Amherst, 2002). The latter two discuss how to characterize the current period.

9. Rosa Luxemburg argued that socialism was not inevitable, but we would have either socialism or barbarism, and the choice would depend on what we did (or did not do). A similar point applies here. Employer political dominance is achieved in significant part, though by no means exclusively, through big-money campaign contributions; see Dan Clawson, Alan Neustadtl, and Mark Weller, *Dollars and Votes: How Business Campaign Contributions Subvert Democracy* (Philadelphia: Temple University Press, 1998).

10. Charles Heckscher, "Participatory Unionism," *Labor Studies Journal* 25, no. 4 (2001): 3–18.

11. Bill Fletcher Jr. and Richard W. Hurd, "Beyond the Organizing Model: The Transformation Process in Local Unions," in *Organizing to Win: New Research on Union Strategies*, ed. Kate Bronfenbrenner et al. (Ithaca, N.Y.: ILR Press, 1998), pp. 37–53. Ruth Milkman, *Farewell to the Factory: Auto Workers in the Late Twentieth Century* (Berkeley: University of California Press, 1997), pp. 138, 174. Final quotation from Thomas Kochan, "Using the Dunlop Commission Report to Achieve Mutual Gains," *Industrial Relations* 34 (1995): 355. For representative examples of the procooperation labor regime discussed here, see Charles Heckscher, *The New Unionism: Employee Involvement in the Changing Cor-*

poration (Ithaca, N.Y.: ILR Press, 1996); Thomas Kochan, Harry C. Katz, and R. B. McKersie, *The Transformation of American Industrial Relations* (New York: Basic Books, 1986); Richard Freeman and Joel Rogers, *What Workers Want* (Ithaca, N.Y.: Cornell University Press, 1999); Richard Freeman and Joel Rogers, "A Proposal to American Labor" in *The Nation*, June 24, 2002. For deadly critiques of "teamwork" arguments see Mike Parker, *Inside the Circle: A Union Guide to QWL* (Boston: South End Press, 1985); and Mike Parker and Jane Slaughter, *Choosing Sides: Unions and the Team Concept* (Boston: South End Press, 1988).

12. The obvious: what follows are broad sweeping generalizations.

13. Thomas L. Gais, Mark A. Peterson, and Jack L. Walker, "Interest Groups, Iron Triangles, and Representative Institutions in American National Government," *British Journal of Political Science* 14 (1984): 169. See also David Vogel, "The Public Interest Movement and the American Reform Tradition," *Political Science Quarterly* 95 (1981): 607–27, and Robert D. Putnam, *Bowling Alone: The Collapse and Revival of American Community* (New York: Simon & Schuster, 2000) as well as Fred Rose, *Coalitions Across the Class Divide* (Ithaca, N.Y.: ILR Press, 2000).

14. Quoted in Linda M. Blum, *Between Feminism and Labor: The Significance of the Comparable Worth Movement* (Berkeley: University of California Press, 1991), p. 9; see also Paul Buhle, *Taking Care of Business* (New York: Monthly Review Press, 1999). For a damning critique of labor's record on race through the 1960s, see Herbert Hill, "Lichtenstein's Fictions: Meany, Reuther and the 1964 Civil Rights Act," *New Politics* 7 (1998): 82–107.

15. In sociology, resource mobilization theory argues that movements are created through the intervention of "social movement entrepreneurs," but in the full sense that applies only to media-driven, mailing-list, public interest movements. Organizations can play an important role in building mass movements, but those are rarely preexisting bureaucratic organizations; rather they are organizations like SNCC or SCLC or SDS created as part of the movement, after the movement itself is already underway.

16. See Stephen Lerner, "Three Steps to Reorganizing and Rebuilding the Labor Movement" (photocopy, n.d. [2002?]).

17. Eve Weinbaum, "Successful Failures: Toward a New Theory of Social Movements" (draft); see also her *With Economic Justice for None: Three Communities Challenge the Rules of the Global Economy* (New York: The New Press, 2003).

Chapter 2. The New Deal System: Employer Offensive, Labor Response

1. It is mandatory that the company bargain about discrimination against existing workers, but not about its hiring practices.

2. Income increases from Frank Levy, *The New Dollars and Dreams: American Incomes and Economic Change* (New York: Russell Sage Foundation, 1998), pp. 27, 50. Strike rates from Nelson Lichtenstein, *State of the Union: A Century of American Labor* (Princeton, N.J.: Princeton University Press, 2002), p. 136. Jack Metzgar, *Striking Steel: Solidarity Remembered* (Philadelphia: Temple University Press, 2000), pp. 37, 39, 40. This wonderful book is highly recommended as an excellent way to capture a feel for the meaning and consequences of unions in the 1940s through the 1960s.

3. Milkman, *Farewell to the Factory: Auto Workers in the Late Twentieth Century* (Berkeley: University of California Press, 1997), pp. 55–57. This terrific book is highly recommended. See also Charles Spencer, *Blue Collar: An Internal Examination of the Workplace* (Chicago: Lakeside Charter Books, 1977).

4. Michael Burawoy, *Manufacturing Consent: Changes in the Labor Process Under Monopoly Capitalism* (Chicago: University of Chicago Press, 1979), p. 110. Other statements of this perspective are to be found in Stanley Aronowitz, *False Promises* (New York: Mc-

Graw-Hill, 1973) and Rick Fantasia, *Cultures of Solidarity: Consciousness, Action, and Contemporary American Workers* (Berkeley: University of California Press, 1988).

5. Bert Cochran, *Labor and Communism: The Conflict That Shaped American Unions* (Princeton, N.J.: Princeton University Press, 1977), p. 322.

6. Burawoy, op. cit., p. 114.

7. Lichtenstein, op. cit., pp. 142–44.

8. Kim Moody, *An Injury to All: The Decline of American Unionism* (London: Verso, 1988), p. 64.

9. Lichtenstein, op. cit., p. 144.

10. The most impressive such movement has been Teamsters for a Democratic Union, which of course confronted the most spectacularly corrupt union; see Dan La Botz, *Rank and File Rebellion: Teamsters for a Democratic Union* (New York: Verso, 1990). See also Ray M. Tillman and Michael S. Cummings, *The Transformation of U.S. Unions: Voices, Visions, and Strategies from the Grassroots* (Boulder, Colo.: Lynne Riener, 1999).

11. See William Forbath, "Down by Law? History and Prophecy about Organizing in Hard Times and a Hostile Legal Order," in *Audacious Democracy: Labor, Intellectuals, and the Social Reconstruction of America*, ed. Steve Fraser and Joshua Freeman (New York: Houghton Mifflin, 1997). James A. Gross, *Broken Promise: The Subversion of U.S. Labor Relations Policy, 1947–1994* (Philadelphia: Temple University Press, 1995), p. 12.

12. Gross, op. cit., p. 107.

13. Ibid., pp. 104–6.

14. Tom Geoghegan, *Which Side Are You On? Trying to Be for Labor When It's Flat on Its Back* (New York: Farrar, Strauss & Giroux, 1991), p. 259.

15. A fired worker is required to make a good faith effort to find another job—if he or she does not do so the back pay judgment is reduced. On departures of returned workers, see Paul Weiler, "Promises to Keep: Securing Workers' Rights to Self-Organization Under the NLRA," *Harvard Law Review* 96 (1983): 1792. On media noncoverage, see Josh Carreiro, "The Labor Movement and Media Discourse: The NLRB and Anti-union Firings" (photocopy, Department of Sociology, University of Massachusetts, Amherst, 2002).

16. Kate Bronfenbrenner and Tom Juravich, "It Takes More than House Calls," in *Organizing to Win: New Research on Union Strategies*, ed. Kate Bronfenbrenner et al. (Ithaca, N.Y.: ILR/Cornell University Press, 1998), pp. 19–36. In addition, 64 percent of employers used five or more captive audience meetings and 76 percent used one-on-one meetings with supervisors.

17. For discussion of the political economy of this period see Samuel Bowles, David Gordon, and Thomas Weiskopf, *Beyond the Wasteland* (New York: Doubleday, 1983) and John O'Connor, "From Welfare Rights to Welfare Fights: Neo-liberalism and the Retrenchment of Social Provision," (Ph.D. diss., University of Massachusetts, Amherst, 2002).

18. Rockefeller cited in Nancy MacLean, "The Hidden History of Affirmative Action: Working Women's Struggles in the 1970s and the Gender of Class," *Feminist Studies* 25 (1999): 43. For 1973 meetings see Leonard Silk and David Vogel, *Ethics and Profits* (New York: Simon & Schuster, 1976), pp. 44, 45, 72. Silk (a *New York Times* reporter) and Vogel (a graduate student) were the only outsiders permitted to attend, and were required not to identify any of the business executives.

19. Dan Clawson, Alan Neustadtl, and Mark Weller, *Dollars and Votes: How Business Campaign Contributions Subvert Democracy* (Philadelphia: Temple University Press, 1998), pp. 7–8.

20. Quoted in Dan Clawson, Alan Neustadtl, and Denise Scott, *Money Talks: Corporate PACs and Political Influence* (New York: Basic Books, 1992), p. 142.

21. Milkman, op. cit., p. 55; R. Prosten, "The Rise in NLRB Election Delays: Measuring Business' New Resistance," *Management Labor Review* 102 (1979): 38–40; R. L. Seeber and W. N. Cooke, "The Decline in Union Success in NLRB Elections," *Industrial Relations* 22 (1983): 43.

22. Quoted in Thomas A. Kochan, H. C. Katz, and R. B. McKersie, *The Transformation of American Industrial Relations* (New York: Basic Books, 1986), p. 263. Janice A. Klein and E. David Wanger, "The Legal Setting for the Emergence of the Union Avoidance Strategy," in *Challenges and Choices Facing American Labor*, ed. Thomas A. Kochan (Cambridge, Mass.: The MIT Press, 1985), pp. 75–88. Cited in Bruce Nissen, "A Post–World War II 'Social Accord?' " in *U.S. Labor Relations, 1945–1989: Accommodation and Conflict*, ed. Bruce Nissen (New York: Garland, 1990), pp. 173–207.

23. See above all the many works of G. William Domhoff. See also Lawrence Shoup and William Minter, *Imperial Brain Trust*, (New York: Monthly Review Press, 1977) and Robert M. Collins, *The Business Response to Keynes* (New York: Columbia University Press, 1981). For the 1970s CED see G. William Domhoff, *Who Rules America? Power and Politics in the Year 2000*, 3d ed. (Mountain View, Calif.: Mayfield, 1998), pp. 150–54.

24. For the Trilateral Commission see Holly Sklar, ed., *Trilateralism: The Trilateral Commission and Elite Planning for World Management* (Boston: South End Press, 1980). See also Samuel P. Huntington, "The United States," in *The Crisis of Democracy: Report on the Governability of Democracies to the Trilateral Commission*, ed. Michel Crozier, Samuel P. Huntington, and Joji Watanuki (New York: New York University Press, 1975), pp. 59–118. Most of the Carter administration were members of the Trilateral Commission, including Carter himself (who, when picked for membership on the Commission, was the undistinguished governor of a backwater state), Vice President Mondale, and most key Cabinet officials.

25. The best overview of think tanks in the 1970s is Joseph Peschek, *Policy Planning Organizations: Elite Agendas and America's Rightward Turn* (Philadelphia: Temple University Press, 1987). For a discussion of how the conservative think tank and policy apparatus operates, see Louis Prisock, "How Conservatives Created Their Network" (photocopy, 1999). For the funding shift see Dan Clawson and Mary Ann Clawson, "Foundations of the New Conservatism," in *The Structure of Power in America: The Corporate Elite as a Ruling Class*, ed. Michael Schwartz (New York: Holmes & Meier, 1987), p. 207.

26. Clawson and Clawson, op. cit., p. 208.

27. See Clawson, Neustadtl, and Weller, op. cit., pp. 149–50; and Thomas Byrne Edsall, *The New Politics of Inequality* (New York: Norton, 1984).

28. My entire account of this employer mobilization relies on Gross, op. cit., esp. pp. 200–216. This section—and the book as a whole—contains wonderful archival research and explosive material, although the book is not the most engaging read. Both this and the following quotation are from p. 203.

29. Ibid., pp. 207–8.

30. Ibid., p. 209.

31. Ibid., p. 213.

32. Communication Workers of America, Service Employees International Union, Hotel Employees and Restaurant Employees, and Union of Needletrades, Industrial, and Textile Employees.

33. Nelson Lichtenstein made this point to me, but is not responsible for this formulation. Note that in the 1960s students were becoming workers for a summer, but in the 1990s students became union staff for a (few weeks in the) summer.

34. In cutbacks following 9/11, the department was abolished, but the director became an assistant to the president charged with carrying on the same work.

35. Steve Early and Larry Cohen, "Jobs With Justice: Mobilizing Labor-Community Coalitions," *WorkingUSA* (November–December 1997): 55.

36. Steve Early, "Membership-Based Organizing," in *A New Labor Movement for the New Century*, ed. Greg Mantsios (New York: Monthly Review Press, 1998), pp. 82–103. See also Steve Lopez, *Reorganizing the Rustbelt* (Berkeley: University of California Press, 2003), for an example of staff stumbling in dealing with attempts to empower rank-and-file workers. On the other hand, a ranking AFL-CIO staff member argued to me that the

real issue is good versus bad organizing; in practice, this person said, most member organizers are ineffective, and may have been recruited for political loyalty. For a related article see Eve Weinbaum and Gordon Lafer, "Outside Agitators and Other Red Herrings: Getting Past the `Top-Down/Bottom-Up' Debate," *New Labor Forum* no. 10 (spring/summer 2002): 26–35.

37. October 12, 1974, p. 120. See Tom Franks, *One Market under God* (New York: Doubleday, 2000), for discussion of some of the elements involved in accomplishing this transformation.

Chapter 3. Gender Styles and Union Issues

1. Barbara Reskin and Irene Padavic, *Women and Men at Work* (Thousand Oaks, Calif.: Pine Forge Press, 1994), p. 143; *Historical Statistics of the United States*, p. 133. *Statistical Abstract of the United States 2001*, p. 373, table 578.

2. See Kate Wiegand, *Red Feminism: American Communism and the Making of Women's Liberation* (Baltimore: Johns Hopkins University Press, 2001).

3. It's a mistake to believe that the most promise lies in what is most widely accepted. An earlier book I edited focused on the most influential books in sociology. In preparing that I learned that books that are universally praised are typically not the books that become most influential. The ultimately influential books are controversial when they appear, precisely because they are challenging conventional wisdom. Similarly, the most promising union initiatives may be those that are most controversial within the labor movement. See Dan Clawson, ed., *Required Reading: Sociology's Most Influential Books* (Amherst: University of Massachusetts Press, 1998).

4. Richard Sullivan, "Exploring the Contours of the New Labor Movement: Mapping the California Frontier" (paper presented at American Sociological Association Meetings, Chicago, August 18, 2002).

5. *Historical Statistics of the United States*, p. 380. Only 10.3 percent of men had completed one or more years of college.

6. Reskin and Padavic, op. cit., pp. 144–45, 149, the latter citing Diane Crispell, *Wall Street Journal*, September 13, 1993; Richard B. Freeman, "The Feminization of Work in the U.S.A.: A New Era for (Man)kind?," in *Gender and the Labor Market: Econometric Evidence of Obstacles to Achieving Gender Equality*, ed. Siv. S. Gustafsson and Danièle E. Meulders (New York: St. Martin's Press, 2000), pp. 3–22. Thirty percent of black women earn more than their husbands, as do 28 percent of white women with college degrees (table 4).

7. See Caroline Bird, "Ladies' Day in the House," in *Born Female: The High Cost of Keeping Women Down* (New York: McKay, 1974).

8. *Historical Statistics of the United States*, p. 139 for 1940, *Statistical Abstract of the United States 1999*, p. 445, table 702, for 1998 and today.

9. Ruth Milkman, "Union Responses to Workforce Feminization in the United States," in *The Challenge of Restructuring: North American Labor Movements Respond*, ed. Jane Jenson and Rianne Mahon (Philadelphia: Temple University Press, 1993).

10. *Statistical Abstract of the United States 1998*, p. 444; Ruth Milkman, op. cit. n. 9; See Kate Bronfenbrenner, "Organizing Women Workers in the Global Economy: Findings from NLRB Certification Election Campaigns—1998–1999" (presentation to the Los Angeles AFL-CIO March 8, 2001). The lead organizer data at the end of the paragraph come from this same source.

11. *Statistical Abstract of the United States 1998*, p. 420.

12. Cobble, "Recapturing Working-Class Feminism: Union Women in the Postwar Era," in *Not June Cleaver: Women and Gender in Postwar America, 1945–1960*, ed. Joanne Meyerowitz (Philadelphia: Temple University Press, 1994), pp. 61–63, 74. This wonderful

article is highly recommended, and I rely on it heavily. Dennis Deslippe, "Organized Labor, National Politics, and Second-Wave Feminism in the United States, 1965–1975," *International Labor and Working-Class History* 49 (1996): 143–65.

13. Cobble, op. cit., pp. 69–71; Deslippe, op. cit., pp. 155–57.

14. Cobble op. cit., p. 75.

15. See Daniel Horowitz, *Betty Friedan and the Making of The Feminine Mystique: The American Left, the Cold War, and Modern Feminism* (Amherst: University of Massachusetts Press, 1998); Nancy MacLean, "The Hidden History of Affirmative Action: Working Women's Struggles in the 1970s and the Gender of Class," *Feminist Studies* 25 (1999): 50. I rely heavily on this highly recommended article.

16. Susan Davis, "Organizing from Within," *Ms.* 1 (1972): 92–99.

17. MacLean, op. cit., p. 45; Davis, op. cit., p. 96 (emphasis in original).

18. MacLean, op. cit., p. 53.

19. MacLean, op. cit., p. 56; Nussbaum quoted in Ruth Milkman, ed., *Women, Work, and Protest: A Century of U.S. Women's Labor History* (Boston: Routledge & Kegan Paul, 1985), p. 315.

20. Lawrence Mishel, Jared Bernstein, and John Schmitt, *The State of Working America 2000/2001* (Ithaca, N.Y.: ILR/Cornell University Press, 1999), p. 133. For the period 1979–97, wages fell 16.0 percent for the lowest decile of women workers, 7.6 percent for the second decile, and 0.8 percent for the third decile. Wages increased 24.0 percent for the top 10 percent, 19.5 percent for women in the 80th–89th percentiles, and 14.0 percent for women in the 70th–79th percentiles. It should be noted that for men as well, lower-wage workers have done worse than higher-wage workers, although the differences are not as great as for women.

21. Reskin and Padavic, op. cit., pp. 103, 104. The 1965 figure was 59.9 percent and that for 1975 was 58.8 percent, the worst figure of the previous half-century. The 1999 figure is from Mishel et al., op. cit., p. 128.

22. My account of San Jose relies heavily on Linda M. Blum's excellent 1991 study, *Between Feminism and Labor: The Significance of the Comparable Worth Movement* (Berkeley: University of California Press). All information not explicitly attributed to another source comes from Blum, especially chap. 3, pp. 54–91. The "feminist capital" quote is from p. 56.

23. Blum, op. cit., p. 63.

24. Ibid., p. 73.

25. In this case workers drove the study process and themselves became experts, seemingly against the wishes and without the support of the certified experts. We could also imagine a set of experts with left politics who would want to demystify and democratize expertise, and who would actively assist the workers in developing the needed skills. For a discussion of this and related points see Barbara Ehrenreich and John Ehrenreich, "The Professional-Managerial Class," in *Between Labor and Capital*, ed. Pat Walker (Boston: South End Press, 1979).

26. John Wilhelm, in *Will Teach for Food: Academic Labor in Crisis*, ed. Cary Nelson (Minneapolis: University of Minnesota Press, 1997), pp. 36–37. The UAW also attempted to begin a campaign, but after a time withdrew. As discussed in the next section, Kris Rondeau of the Harvard union was (temporarily) fired because she recommended the UAW leave Yale organizing to HERE since it had the support of the workers.

27. Molly Ladd-Taylor, "Women Workers and the Yale Strike," *Feminist Studies* 11 (1985), p. 469.

28. Yale worker Aldo Cupo, in "Beep, Beep, Yale's Cheap," *Radical America* 18, no. 5 (1984): p. 16.

29. Aldo Cupo, ibid., pp. 16–17.

30. Ladd-Taylor ibid., p. 13.

31. Ladd-Taylor, op. cit. n. 27, p. 478.

32. Milkman, op. cit. n. 9. Given the extent of occupational segregation, it would be easy to conclude that unions rarely face gender-integrated bargaining units. Easy, but mistaken: who gets included in the bargaining unit is decided by the NLRB (National Labor Relations Board), with the employer and union each pushing that the unit be defined in the fashion most favorable to their interests. A nursing home's (all-male) maintenance workers are placed in the same unit as the (all-female) direct care workers; a university's truck drivers and electricians in the same unit as food service workers. In Milkman's study, for example, more than 40 percent of the bargaining units contained at least 25 percent men and 25 percent women. The data did not make it possible for Milkman to analyze differences based on race.

33. *Radical America*, p. 15.

34. This took place before the passage of the federal Family and Medical Leave Act.

35. Bill Fletcher, at the time assistant to the president of the AFL-CIO, notes that there are problems with the phrase "working families": many aren't working, and many aren't living in "families" in any conventional sense. He argues that the phrase indicates the labor movement's reluctance to talk about the working class. Opening remarks, Scholars, Artists, and Writers for Social Justice National Conference on Child Care and the Labor Movement, Washington, D.C., November 13, 2000. Quotation from Bureau of National Affairs, *Work and Family and Unions: Labor's Agenda for the 1990s*, Special Report no. 20 (Washington, D.C.: Bureau of National Affairs, 1989), p. 4. The next section draws on my joint work with Gerstel; by now I can no longer tell which ideas are mine and which Naomi's. Although she's not responsible for these formulations, many of the best interviews and best ideas came from her, and she should be considered an unnamed co-author. See our joint paper, "Unions' Responses to Family Concerns," *Social Problems* 48 (2001): 277–98. See also Naomi Gerstel, Dan Clawson, and Robert Zussman, eds., *Families at Work: Expanding the Bounds* (Nashville: Vanderbilt University Press, 2002).

36. See Kitty Krupat and Patrick McCreery, *Out at Work: Building a Gay-Labor Alliance* (Minneapolis: University of Minnesota Press, 2001).

37. Center for the Child Care Workforce, "Current Data on Child Care Salaries and Benefits in the United States" (pamphlet, Center for the Child Care Workforce, March 2000), presenting data for 1998. Fewer than 1 percent of professional occupations earn an average wage of less than $8.50 an hour. In Europe, where child care is universal and publicly provided, child care workers are paid wages equivalent to those for grade-school teachers. See Wolfgang Tietz and Debbie Cryer, "Current Trends in European Early Child Care and Education," *Annals of the American Academy of Political and Social Science* 563 (1999): 47–56.

38. Ewing Marion Kauffman Foundation and Pew Charitable Trusts, "Financing Child Care in the United States: An Illustrative Catalog of Current Strategies" (pamphlet, Kauffman Foundation and Pew Charitable Trusts, n.d.). Median income families spent "only" 8 percent of their income to send a child to a public college or university.

39. Dan Clawson and Naomi Gerstel, "Caring for Our Young: Child Care in Europe and the United States," *Contexts* 1, no. 4 (2002): pp. 28–35.

40. The informal care subsidy is the most popular with members, even though it provides less money.

41. Long ago Marx noted the materialist argument that people "are products of circumstances and upbringing, and that, therefore, changed [people] are products of other circumstances and upbringing." Marx took the point a step further: he presented the crude materialist position (in the third of the *Theses on Feuerbach*) precisely to argue against its simplicity. This theory, Marx noted, "forgets that it is [people] that change circumstances." Marx's *Theses on Feuerbach* are included in most collections of his writings. See, for example, pp. 28–30 in Karl Marx and Friedrich Engels, *Selected Works* (New York: International Publishers, 1968). See also Rick Fantasia, *Cultures of Solidarity: Con-*

sciousness, Action, and Contemporary American Workers (Berkeley: University of California Press, 1988) for a discussion of how workers' views change during the process of struggle.

42. For a more member-driven campaign, see Ruth Milkman, "Organizing Immigrant Women in New York's Chinatown: An Interview with Katie Quan," in *Women and Unions: Forging a Partnership*, ed. Dorothy Sue Cobble (Ithaca, N.Y.: ILR Press, 1993), pp. 281–98.

43. Workers can choose to put in additional overtime, but cannot be required to do so.

44. Talk by Sandy Ellis at Labor Notes conference, Detroit, April 2001, and *Worcester Telegram & Gazette*, May 19, 2000.

45. Harvard apparently pushed for this to make it impossible (as the university saw it) for the union to win; the union had been gaining ground in the medical school, but was weak or nonexistent elsewhere. The long-term consequence, of course, was that Harvard's action led the union to organize many more workers.

46. Wages and benefits obviously changed over fifteen years, but in 1981 Harvard paid only 40 percent of health care premiums, did not offer dental coverage, and although it had child care facilities the cost was more than clerical workers could afford. John Hoerr, *We Can't Eat Prestige: The Women Who Organized Harvard* (Philadelphia: Temple University Press, 1997), p. 125.

47. Except as noted, this and all following quotations from Kris Rondeau are from an interview I conducted with her on September 18, 1996.

48. John Hoerr, "Solidaritas at Harvard: Organizing in a Different Voice," *The American Prospect* (summer 1993), p. 75, for these two quotes and the subsequent one from Anne Taylor. See also Hoerr, op. cit. n. 46 for background information about the Harvard organizing campaigns and union.

49. Quoted in David Brody, *In Labor's Cause* (New York: Oxford University Press, 1993), p. 245. For a similar statement for the nineteenth century, see David Montgomery, "Workers' Control of Machine Production in the Nineteenth Century," in *Workers' Control in America* (Cambridge: Cambridge University Press, 1979), pp. 13–14. In an interesting gender twist, in speeches today Linda Chavez-Thompson, executive vice president of the AFL-CIO, tells a story of how, as a child, she saw her father, a Chicano farmworker, humiliated by a supervisor, and explains that we need unions today so that no child will need to see her father humiliated in this fashion.

50. See Mary Ann Clawson, *Constructing Brotherhood: Class, Gender, and Fraternalism* (Princeton, N.J.: Princeton University Press, 1989).

51. Daisy Rooks, "Sticking it Out or Packing it In?: Organizer Retention in the New Labor Movement" (paper presented at the Institute for Labor and Employment Conference on Organizing, Los Angeles, May 17, 2002), pp. 19–20.

52. Roslyn L. Feldberg, "Women and Trade Unions: Are We Asking the Right Questions?" In *Hidden Aspects of Women's Work*, Christine Bose, et al., eds. (New York: Praeger, 1987), p. 300.

53. Karen Brodkin Sacks, "Gender and Grassroots Leadership," in *Women and the Politics of Empowerment*, ed. Ann Bookman and Sandra Morgen (Philadelphia: Temple University Press, 1988), p. 77. Most but by no means all of the workers in the union organizing drive were African American women.

54. Ibid., p. 79; see also Sacks, *Caring by the Hour: Women, Work, and Organizing at Duke Medical Center* (Urbana: University of Illinois Press, 1988).

55. And for numerous other drives, including the University of Minnesota, University of Illinois, University of Massachusetts Worcester Medical Center, and the Connecticut Local 1199 nurses.

56. Richard Sanders, the Rhode Island Hospital organizer (see chapter 1), makes a different but related argument: often men who are angry and see themselves as fighters are the people who abandon the union when things get tough; often women who are

much less assertive become stronger and more militant as the drive develops (personal interview); also see Fantasia, op. cit.

57. Harvard, however, was never as viciously anti-union as Yale. It's doubtful the Harvard approach could have worked at Yale.

58. Hoerr, op. cit. n. 48, pp. 68, 77.

59. Kris Rondeau, presentation at Roundtable on Unions, Gender, and Worktime, May 10, 2002, at the Institute for Research on Women, Rutgers University. It may be that one of the reasons HUCTW won such a contract, one that is both innovative and consistent with the organizing team's approach, is that the organizing staff remained in place after the organizing win, continuing to work with the members. Often one person specializes in organizing, leaving a union shortly after the victory, with an entirely different staff taking over to negotiate the contract. This invites miscommunication and problems.

60. Patricia A. Gwartney-Gibbs and Denise H. Lach, "Gender Differences in Grievance Processing the Implications for Rethinking Shopfloor Practices," in *Women and Unions: Forging a Partnership* (Ithaca, N.Y.: ILR Press, 1993), p. 311.

61. Larry Cohen and Richard W. Hurd, "Fear, Conflict, and Union Organizing," in *Organizing to Win: New Research on Union Strategies*, ed. Kate Bronfenbrenner et al. (Ithaca, N.Y.: ILR Press, 1998), pp. 182, 193.

62. See Dan Clawson, Karen Johnson, and John Schall, "Fighting Union Busting in the 1980s," *Radical America* 16 (1982): 45–62.

Chapter 4. New Tactics, Community, and Color

1. For a theoretical elaboration of this position, see Ian Robinson, "Does Neoliberal Restructuring Promote Social Movement Unionism? U.S. Developments in Comparative Perspective," in *Unions in a Globalized Environment: Changing Borders, Organizational Boundaries, and Social Roles*, ed. Bruce Nissen (Armonk, N.Y.: M. E. Sharpe, 2002), pp. 189–235.

2. See Steve Lerner, "Taking the Offensive, Turning the Tide," in *A New Labor Movement for the New Century*, ed. Greg Mantsios (New York: Monthly Review Press, 1998), pp. 69–81.

3. See Kate Bronfenbrenner and Tom Juravich, "It Takes More Than Housecalls: Organizing to Win with a Comprehensive Union-Building Strategy," in *Organizing to Win: New Research on Union Strategies*, ed. Kate Bronfenbrenner et al. (Ithaca, N.Y.: ILR/Cornell University Press, 1998), pp. 19–36.

4. See Staughton Lynd, ed., *"We are All Leaders": The Alternative Unionism of the Early 1930s* (Urbana: University of Illinois Press, 1996).

5. Robin Kelley, *Yo' Mama's DisFUNKtional! Fighting the Culture Wars in Urban America* (Boston: Beacon Press, 1997), pp. 125–26.

6. Bill Fletcher Jr. and Richard Hurd, "Is Organizing Enough? Race, Gender, and Union Culture," *New Labor Forum* (spring/summer 2000): 59–69. Related to this, I did not find an experienced organizer of color, who had won the resources, independence, and space to develop and theorize an approach specifically adapted to organizing workforces with large majorities of people of color as Kris Rondeau has done for gender. (Obviously, my not finding such a person does not mean they do not exist.) For one article that addresses these issues, see Marshall Ganz, "Resources and Resourcefulness: Strategic Capacity in the Unionization of California Agriculture, 1959–1966," *American Journal of Sociology* 105 (2000): 1003–62.

7. Dorothy Sue Cobble, "Lost Ways of Organizing: Reviving the AFL's Direct Affiliate Strategy," *Industrial Relations* 36 (1997): 290, and Cobble, "Lost Ways of Unionism: Historical Perspectives on Reinventing the Labor Movement," in *Rekindling the Labor Movement:*

Labor's Quest for Relevance in the 21ˢᵗ Century, ed. Lowell Turner, Harry C. Katz, and Richard W. Hurd (Ithaca, NY: ILR Press, 2001), pp. 82–96. For CLCs see Immanuel Ness and Stuart Eimer (eds.), *Central Labor Councils and the Revival of American Unionism: Organizing for Justice in Our Communities* (Armonk, NY: M. E. Sharpe, 2001).

8. Quoted in David Bensman, *The Practice of Solidarity: American Hat Finishers in the Nineteenth Century* (Urbana: University of Illinois Press, 1985), p. 119.

9. See Dan Clawson, *Bureaucracy and the Labor Process: The Transformation of American Industry 1860–1920* (New York: Monthly Review Press, 1980), p. 155; original is Frederick W. Taylor, "The Principles of Scientific Management," reprinted in *Scientific Management* (1947): 52.

10. For some compelling examples see Herbert Hill, "Race and the Steelworkers Union: White Privilege and Black Struggle," *New Politics* 8 (2002): 1–58, and Bruce Nelson, *Divided We Stand: American Workers and the Struggle for Black Equality* (Princeton, N.J.: Princeton University Press, 2001).

11. Paul B. Worthman, "Black Workers And Labor Unions in Birmingham, Alabama, 1897–1904," *Labor History* 10 (1969): 381, 385, 384. This is a wonderful article, rich in historical detail about remarkable struggles, and serves as my only source. The national AFL thinking is discussed on p. 383 and the UMW concern about strikebreakers on p. 388.

12. Ibid., pp. 390–91.

13. Ibid., pp. 401–2. See also Roger Horowitz, *Negro and White, Unite and Fight! A Social History of Industrial Unionism in Meatpacking 1930–1990* (Urbana: University of Illinois Press, 1997); Kim Scipes, "Theorizing Ideological Forms of Economic Trade Unionism in America: Unions in Chicago's Steel and Meatpacking Industries and their Respective Approaches to Racial Oppression" (photocopy, 2001).

14. See Bernstein, *The Turbulent Years*; Bert Cochran, *Labor and Communism*; Sidney Fine, *Sit Down*; Sol and Genora Dollinger, *Not Automatic: Women and the Left in the Forging of the Auto Workers' Union* (New York: Monthly Review Press, 2000). I believe the reason we have the 1935 Wagner Act is the Flint sit-down strike of 1936–37. Am I trying to run history backward? How can a 1937 strike be responsible for a 1935 law? Because laws in the United States aren't final until approved by the Supreme Court. The Supreme Court at that time was conservative and had struck down previous legislation that attempted to guarantee worker and union rights. The Wagner Act preamble explicitly says the act is to promote labor peace (translation: to prevent more militant strikes like the general strikes in Toledo, Minneapolis, and San Francisco). I believe the Supreme Court would have struck down the Wagner Act, but the Flint sit-down strike broke out as the Supreme Court was considering the Act's constitutionality. Mr. Dooley's conclusion was that the Supreme Court follows the election returns; in this case, the Supreme Court followed social movement militance, and concluded the Wagner Act was preferable to the outbreak of sit-down strikes by desperate workers.

15. For examples of the strength of these connections in the immediate post-World War II period see George Lipsitz, *A Rainbow at Midnight*, and Joshua Freeman, *Working Class New York: Life and Labor Since World War II* (New York: New Press 2000).

16. See *Historical Statistics of the United States*, pp. 22–23. In the South, 64.0 percent of the black population was rural. In 1940, data were reported for "non-whites."

17. Ibid. for 1940 data. *Statistical Abstract of the United States 1997*, p. 34, table 34. For a fascinating discussion about organizing among undocumented immigrants, see Hector L. Delgado, *New Immigrants, Old Unions: Organizing Undocumented Workers in Los Angeles* (Philadelphia: Temple University Press, 1993). Delgado expected that the key obstacle would be workers' undocumented status; he found that to be a less significant factor than the employer's willingness (and ability) to fire pro-union workers. Since most of the workforce were undocumented, the employer could not easily call the INS for fear it would lose many skilled and difficult-to-replace employees. See also Ruth Milkman, ed., *Organizing Immigrants: The Challenge for Unions in Contemporary California* (Ithaca, N.Y.: ILR

Press, 2000); and Hector Figueroa, "Back to the Forefront: Union Organizing of Immigrant Workers in the Nineties," in *Not Your Father's Union Movement: Inside the AFL-CIO*, ed. Jo-Ann Mort (New York: Verso, 1998), pp. 87–98. For change in immigrants see Donald J. Hernandez, "The Past and Future of America's Families: Economic and Demographic Revolutions" (paper delivered at the conference "Work and Family: Expanding the Horizons," San Francisco, March 2000). See especially figs. 13, 14, and 15.

18. See for example Kathleen Barker and Kathleen Christensen, *Contingent Work: American Employment Relations in Transition* (Ithaca, N.Y.: ILR Press, 1998); Lawrence Mishel, Jared Bernstein, and John Schmitt, *The State of Working America 2000/2001* (Ithaca, NY: ILR/ Press, 2001), pp. 241–55.

19. See Leon Fink and Brian Greenberg, *Upheaval in the Quiet Zone: A History of Hospital Workers' Union, Local 1199* (Urbana: University of Illinois Press, 1989).

20. This section relies primarily on Roger Waldinger, Chris Erickson, Ruth Milkman, Daniel J. B. Mitchell, Abel Valenzuela, Kent Wong, and Maurice Zeitlin, "Helots No More: A Case Study of the Justice for Janitors Campaign in Los Angeles," in *Organizing to Win*, ed. Kate Bronfenbrenner et al. (Ithaca, N.Y.: ILR Press, 1998), pp. 102–19. This information is from pp. 104–5. Additional information for this section comes from Catherine L. Fisk, Daniel J. B. Mitchell, and Christopher L. Erickson, "Union Representation of Immigrant Janitors in Southern California: Economic and Legal Challenges," in Milkman, op. cit. n. 17, pp. 199–224, as well as a presentation by Steve Lerner, a conversation (unfortunately not taped) with him, and assorted conference presentations. Also recommended is the Ken Loach film *Bread and Roses*, a fictionalized account of a Justice for Janitors Los Angeles organizing drive.

21. However, in practice, as opposed to abstract possibility, there was significant stability among the cleaning contracts at least for big downtown office buildings. Janitors receive the keys for offices and work alone at night; tenants need to trust them. Building owners want to contract with large companies that can be held accountable; two such large companies were responsible for more than one-quarter of all employment, and were central targets for the drive. See Fisk, Mitchell, and Erickson, op. cit. The architect of the campaign has written a highly stimulating article theorizing this approach. See Lerner, op. cit.

22. Waldinger et al., op. cit., pp. 111, 102.

23. Fisk et al., op. cit.

24. Richard Sullivan, "Exploring the Contours of the New Labor Movement: Mapping the California Frontier" (paper presented at American Sociological Association Annual Meeting, Chicago, August 18, 2002).

25. My account relies heavily, almost exclusively, on the outstanding article by Ruth Milkman and Kent Wong, "Organizing the Wicked City: The 1992 Southern California Drywall Strike," in Milkman, op. cit. n. 17, pp. 169–98.

26. Ibid., p. 181.

27. Ibid., p. 189. For a discussion of the rights of labor versus other groups see William E. Forbath, "Down by Law? History and Prophecy about Organizing in Hard Times and a Hostile Legal Order," in *Audacious Democracy: Labor, Intellectuals, and the Social Reconstruction of America*, ed. Steven Fraser and Joshua B. Freeman (Boston: Houghton Mifflin, 1997), pp. 132–51.

28. However, even in late July, twenty strikers remained in jail, and by October a total of six hundred strikers had been arrested.

29. Tom Juravich and Jeff Hilgert, "UNITE's Victory at Richmark: Community-Based Union Organizing in Communities of Color," *Labor Studies Journal* 24 (1999): 31–32. Almost my entire account of these events is drawn from this highly recommended article, supplemented by discussions with Russ Davis of Jobs with Justice. The film *Norma Rae* has its problems, but is well worth seeing for the remarkable scene where workers stop production.

30. Milkman and Wong, op. cit., p. 189.

31. Juravich and Hilgert, op. cit., p. 36; remark originally appeared in the *Boston Globe*.

32. Employers presumably wanted to take wages out of competition, so that the largest employers did not end up as the only ones unionized.

33. Milkman and Wong, op. cit., p. 196. In San Diego, no settlement was reached; the area was less heavily unionized, and the general contractors were a smaller and more cohesive group that fought the union relentlessly. San Diego industry forces filed a RICO suit against the Carpenters, and the union reached an out-of-court settlement in September 1994, reportedly paying a substantial amount to do so.

34. Juravich and Hilgert, op. cit., p. 39

35. Jennifer Gordon, "We Make the Road by Walking: Immigrant Workers, The Workplace Project, and the Struggle for Social Change," *Harvard Civil Rights–Civil Liberties Law Review* 30 (1995): 132–51, n. 110. Membership data from "Organizing Low-Wage Immigrants—The Workplace Project," interview with Jennifer Gordon, *WorkingUSA* 5 (2001): 88, 94. Salvadoran immigrant militance may be due to their experience with social movements and guerrilla struggles in El Salvador.

36. Jennifer Gordon, "Immigrants Fight the Power: Workers Centers are One Path to Labor Organizing and Political Participation," *The Nation*, January 3, 2000, p. 16. In another case a worker went to a different agency to complain about discrimination, only to be told that she would have to bring her own translator—but the translator was forbidden to provide simultaneous translation. Gordon, "We Make the Road by Walking," pp. 420–22.

37. Gordon, op. cit. n. 36; interview with Ingrid Semaan; Jeff Hermanson, "Organizing for Justice: ILGWU Returns to Social Unionism to Organize Immigrant Workers," *Labor Research Review* 20 (1993): especially p. 57.

38. Gordon, *WorkingUSA* interview, p. 97. Gordon, "We Make the Road by Walking," pp. 435–36.

39. Gordon, *WorkingUSA* interview, pp. 95–96.

40. Gordon, "We Make the Road by Walking," p. 429.

41. Gordon, *WorkingUSA* interview, pp. 88–89. "Organize not unionize" quotation from Abby Scher, "Immigrants Fight Back: Workers Centers Lead Where Others Don't," *Dollars and Sense* September–October 1996, p. 35.

42. Gordon, *WorkingUSA* interview, pp. 88–89.

43. Hermanson, op. cit., p. 54.

44. This section is based on two trips to Stamford, interviews with several organizers there, participation in events for two days, a host of newspaper articles and other materials compiled by the Stamford Organizing Project, and various follow-up activities. My work follows the lead of Hector Delgado, who took the initiative in arranging the initial visit, stayed much longer, did many more interviews, and has a far greater knowledge of Stamford events. Hector and I are working together on an article, and Hector has shared materials with me. None of this account would be possible without Hector's leadership and the cooperation of Stamford organizers, workers, and community members.

45. In 2000 this local merged into SEIU 32B-32J.

46. Wage figure assumes that 30 percent of income goes for rent and the person works forty hours a week. *The Stamford Advocate*, September 10, 1999, p. A1.

47. The quotations and information in this paragraph come from the *Stamford Advocate*, May 27, 1999, p. A3, and June 4, 1999, p. A4.

48. Ibid., May 25, 1999, pp. A1, A6. The following quotation also comes from this article.

49. Ibid., July 30, 1999, p. A1, and August 2, 1999, pp. A3, A7.

50. Ibid., September 27, 1999, p. A6.

51. It seems reasonable to wonder whether the authority wanted the project to run down, both to make it less appealing to residents and to build a case that the buildings needed overhaul. The alternative explanation—massive incompetence—is also plausible.

52. For example, see Eric Mann, "'A Race Struggle, a Class Struggle, a Women's Struggle All at Once': Organizing on the Buses of L.A.," in *Working Classes, Global Realities: Socialist Register 2001*, ed. Leo Panitch and Colin Leys (New York: Monthly Review Press, 2001), pp. 259–74.

53. Interview with Shannon Jacovino, director of the Stamford Organizing Project (replacing Jane McAlevey), August 29, 2002.

54. The AFL-CIO pledge was covered in numerous press articles, including the *Stamford Advocate*, March 20, 2000, p. A3; the *Hartford Courant*, March 20, 2000, pp. A3–4; the *Waterbury Republican-American*, March 21, 2000; the *New London Day*, March 21, 2000; the *Connecticut Post*, March 21, 2000, pp. A1, 13; *The Herald*, March 21, 2000; the *New Haven Register*, March 21, 2000, pp. A3, 5. The AFL-CIO is not offering to give the money away, but rather to invest it.

55. Note that this does not mean multi-union organizing campaigns are common or easy to create; Stamford's strong working relationships are an accomplishment. A similar but more ambitious project in Los Angeles (LA-MAP) never got off the ground. See Hector L. Delgado, "The Los Angeles Manufacturing Action Project: An Opportunity Squandered?" in Milkman, op. cit. n. 17, pp. 225–38.

56. See Steve Hart, *Cultural Dilemmas of Progressive Politics: Styles of Engagement among Grassroots Activists* (Chicago: University of Chicago Press, 2001), for a discussion of the role of churches in today's progressive political movements. See also Mark Warren, *Dry Bones Rattling: Community Building to Revitalize American Democracy* (Princeton, N.J.: Princeton University Press, 2001).

57. See Steve Early, "Membership-Based Organizing," in Mantsios, op. cit., pp. 82–103, for a discussion of this approach, which Early explicitly contrasts with that of the AFL-CIO Organizing Institute.

58. Or their sense of community might undercut rather than reinforce their workplace consciousness. Two important books argue that for the predominantly white populations they studied, class consciousness was much sharper at work, whereas in the community people focused primarily on a notion of citizenship as unifying people and transcending divisions. See Robert Zussman, *Mechanics of the Middle Class: Work and Politics among American Engineers* (Berkeley: University of California Press, 1985) and David Halle, *America's Working Man* (Chicago: University of Chicago Press, 1984).

59. Phone interview, August 23, 2002.

60. Janice Fine, "Building Community Unions," *The Nation*, January 1, 2001.

61. John J. Sweeney, *America Needs a Raise: Fighting for Economic Security and Social Justice* (Boston: Houghton Mifflin, 1996), p. 8.

62. Even when labor should be at the heart of an environmental or race-gender issue, it is amazing the extent to which union issues get neglected.

63. In Canada and other countries, card check is a recognized way of achieving union status. In the United States it once was, but the Taft-Hartley Act includes a provision that card check can be used only if the employer agrees to do so.

64. Steve Early and Larry Cohen, "Jobs With Justice: Mobilizing Labor-Community Coalitions," *WorkingUSA* 1 no. 4 (November–December 1997): pp. 49–57.

65. See Mike Parker and Martha Gruelle, *Democracy Is Power: Rebuilding Unions from the Bottom Up* (Detroit: Labor Notes, 1999), pp. 13–14. The book as a whole is highly recommended. See also Michael Eisenscher, "Critical Juncture: Unionism at the Crossroads," in *Which Direction for Organized Labor?* ed. Bruce Nissen (Detroit: Wayne State University Press, 1999), pp. 217–45.

66. For published accounts see Waldinger et al., op. cit., p. 118 and Fisk, Mitchell, and Erickson, op. cit., p. 207. The national union ultimately divided the local in half, separating the health care and janitorial components.

67. Linda Delp and Katie Quan, "Homecare Worker Organizing in California: An Analysis of a Successful Strategy" (paper presented at the University and Labor Educators Association Annual Conference, Boston, April 27, 2001).

68. Frances Fox Piven and Richard A. Cloward, *Poor People's Movements: Why they Succeed, How they Fail* (New York: Vintage, 1979), pp. xxi–xxii.

69. Moreover, if Union A has a nursing home, a grocery store, and some busdrivers, Union B will also represent a couple of nursing homes, and Union C will have some bus drivers. This doubly fragmented structure (within the union, within the occupational grouping) makes it difficult to develop either solidarity or leverage.

70. See Kim Voss and Rachel Sherman, "Breaking the Iron Law of Oligarchy: Union Revitalization in American Movement," *American Journal of Sociology* 106 (2000): 303ff. It's worth noting that in the Stamford Organizing Project all the organizers had worked for nonlabor social movements at some point in their careers, and indeed most of their past experience was outside labor.

71. For the Montgomery bus boycott see Aldon Morris, *The Origins of the Civil Rights Movement* (New York: Free Press, 1984). For resource mobilization theory, see John D. McCarthy and Mayer N. Zald, "Resource Mobilization and Social Movements: A Partial Theory," *American Journal of Sociology* 82 (1976): 1212–41.

72. For an argument that the top-down versus bottom-up debate is misplaced, see Eve Weinbaum and Gordon Lafer, "Outside Agitators and Other Red Herrings: Getting Past the `Top-Down/Bottom-Up' Debate," *New Labor Forum* (spring/summer 2002): 26–35.

Chapter 5. Neoliberal Globalization

1. Jonathan Perraton, David Goldblatt, David Held, and Anthony McGrew, "The Globalisation of Economic Activity," *New Political Economy* 2 (1997): 261, 262. This is an excellent overview packed with useful data. Their book version contains much more complete information; see David Held, Anthony McGrew, David Goldblatt, and Jonathan Perraton, *Global Transformations: Politics, Economics, and Culture* (Stanford, CA: Stanford University Press, 1999). Air transport costs also fell, although not nearly as rapidly. Data for today's imports are 1999 data from *Statistical Abstract of the United States 2001*, tables 641 and 1306.

2. Thomas L. Friedman, *The Lexus and the Olive Tree: Understanding Globalization*, rev. ed. (New York: Anchor Books, 2000), pp. xxi–xxii.

3. "Original condition" quotation from Hugo Radice, "Taking Globalisation Seriously," in *Socialist Register 1999: Global Capitalism versus Democracy*, ed. Leo Panitch and Colin Leys (New York: Monthly Review Press, 1999), p. 3. For previous work on the general topic see, for example, the voluminous literatures on multinational corporations, on "modernization" and "development," on imperialism, colonialism, international relations, etc. Constraints to autonomy quotation from Jonathan Perraton, David Goldblatt, David Held, and Anthony McGrew, "The Globalisation of Economic Activity," *New Political Economy* 2 (1997): 259.

4. Piven, "Globalization, American Politics, and Welfare Policy," *Annals of the American Academy of Political and Social Science* 577 (2001): 26–37; Piven and Richard A. Cloward, "Power Repertoires and Globalization," *Politics and Society* 28 (2000): 413–30; Leo Panitch, "The New Imperial State," *New Left Review* 2 (2000): 5–20; and Panitch, "Reflections on Strategy for Labour," in *Working Classes: Global Realities: Socialist Register 2001*, ed. Leo Panitch and Colin Leys (New York: Monthly Review Press, 2000), pp. 367–92. *Economist*, October 7, 1995, p. 16, quoted in James Crotty and Gerald Epstein, "In Defence of Capital Controls," in *Socialist Register 1996: Are There Alternatives?* ed. Leo Panitch (New York: Monthly Review Press, 1996), p. 144; emphasis theirs.

5. Crotty and Epstein, op. cit., pp. 126–27.

6. Naomi Klein, "Reclaiming the Commons," *New Left Review*, May–June 2001, pp. 87–88. The Multilateral Agreement on Investment (MAI) was intended to be a further step in quietly building the neoliberal version of globalization. Originally to be com-

pleted by 1997, it had to be repeatedly postponed because of difficulties securing its passage; that is, it was part of a political struggle, by no means an inevitability. Its passage would have drastically restricted the ability to regulate business, and would have required that many existing regulations be repealed. See the excellent article by Elissa Braunstein and Gerald Epstein, "Creating International Credit Rules and the Multilateral Agreement on Investment: What are the Alternatives?" in *Global Instability: The Political Economy of World Economic Governance*, ed. Jonathan Michie and John Grieve Smith (New York: Routledge, 1999), pp. 113–33.

7. Friedman, op. cit., p. 442.

8. See Fred Block's wonderful *The Origins of International Economic Disorder* (Berkeley: University of California Press, 1977).

9. The costs (to business) of a strong welfare system increase because to compete globally firms "need" workers to be as desperate and low-wage as possible; the benefits decrease since the funds transferred to the less affluent may be spent on imports. See John O'Connor, "From Welfare Rights to Welfare Fights" (Ph.D. diss., University of Massachusetts, Amherst, 2002).

10. John Eatwell, "The International Origins of Unemployment," in *Managing the Global Economy*, ed. Jonathan Michie and John Grieve Smith (New York: Oxford University Press, 1995), p. 277. See also Crotty and Epstein, op. cit., p. 132.

11. Eatwell, op. cit., p. 279.

12. Probably the best data on and discussion of this are in Frank Levy, *The New Dollars and Dreams: American Incomes and Economic Change* (New York: Russell Sage Foundation, 1998), from which these figures are taken. Levy provides data for 1949 (p. 27), and 1973 and 1996 (p. 50); pp. 40–41 provide data on the equality of distribution over this period. I calculated the 1999 hypothetical using data from table 669 of the *Statistical Abstract of the United States: 2001*. Growth rates and increases in income were still higher in Europe and Japan. From 1973 to 1996, incomes for the bottom 40 percent of the population declined, but for the top 20 percent incomes increased by $20,900 or 37.4 percent, raising the Gini Coefficient from .356 to .425. Similar changes took place in Thatcher's Britain. All "average" comparisons are made using median family incomes.

13. Karl Marx and Frederick Engels, *The Communist Manifesto* (1848), in *Selected Works* (Moscow: Progress Publishers, 1970), pp. 38–40.

14. Ajit Singh and Ann Zammit, "Employment and Unemployment, North and South," in Michie and Grieve, op. cit., p. 102, the source of much of the following information; more generally, the article is highly recommended.

15. David Denslow Jr. and William G. Tyler, *Perspectives on Poverty and Income Inequality in Brazil: An Analysis of the Changes during the 1970s*, World Bank Staff Working Papers No. 601 (Washington, D.C.: The World Bank, 1983), table A-1. These figures conceal huge urban-rural differences; in rural areas, only 15 percent had a television and 13 percent a refrigerator, but these were increases from 1.6 percent and 3.2 percent in 1970, not to mention 1950. Quotation from Singh and Zammit, op. cit., p. 102.

16. Eric Toussaint, *Your Money or Your Life! The Tyranny of Global Finance*, trans. Raghu Krishnan (London: Pluto Press, 1999), p. 125. Toussaint cites Robert S. McNamara, *One Hundred Countries, Two Billion People* (New York: Praeger, 1973).

17. Singh and Zammit, op. cit., p. 93.

18. *Statistical Abstract of the United States 1999*, p. 427, table 676; again the classification by degree of vulnerability to globalization is my own.

19. This and the following data on threats of closure come from Kate Bronfenbrenner, "Organizing in the NAFTA Environment: How Companies Use 'Free Trade' to Stop Unions," *New Labor Forum* 1 (1997): 51–60. The quotation is from page 56.

20. Data from *Directory of U.S. Labor Organizations*, ed. Court Gifford (Washington, D.C.: Bureau of National Affairs, 2000), pp. 250–51.

21. See Don Stillman, "The Devastating Impact of Plant Relocations," *Working Papers for a New Society*, July–August 1978, pp. 42–53.

22. Manfred Bienefeld, "Capitalism and the Nation State in the Dog Days of the Twentieth Century," *The Socialist Register* (1994) p. 122; quoted in Crotty and Epstein, op. cit., p. 135.

23. See Crotty and Epstein, op. cit., pp. 137–38; David Felix and Ranjit Sau, "On the Revenue Potential and Phasing in of the Tobin Tax," in *The Tobin Tax: Coping With Financial Volatility*, ed. M. Ul Haq, I. Kaul, and I. Grunberg (New York: Oxford University Press, 1996). Felix reports that "over four-fifths of global forex round trips have been for a week or less." Felix, "Asia and the Crisis of Financial Globalization," in *Globalization and Progressive Economic Policy*, ed. Dean Baker, Gerald Epstein, and Robert Pollin (New York: Cambridge University Press, 1998), p. 191 n. 23.

24. This presentation of the standards comes from Robert Castle, D. P. Chaudhri, and Chris Nyland, "Integration of Market Economies and the Rights of Labour: International Regulation of Labour Standards," in *Handbook on the Globalization of the World Economy*, ed. Ammon Levy-Livermore (Cheltenham, U.K.: Edward Elgar, 1998), p. 598. For "universal standards" quotation see Werner Sengenberger and Frank Wilkinson, "Globalization and Labour Standards," in *Managing the Global Economy*, ed. Jonathan Michie and John Grieve Smith (New York: Oxford University Press, 1995), p. 116. Mark Brenner has analyzed the issues involved in attempting to specify a global living wage: "Defining and Measuring a Global Living Wage: Theoretical and Conceptual Issues" (paper presented at the Global Labor Standards and Living Wages Conference, University of Massachusetts, Amherst, April 19, 2002).

25. See Human Rights Watch, *Unfair Advantage: Workers' Freedom of Association in the United States under International Human Rights Standards* (New York: Human Rights Watch, August 2000; available at www.hrw.org, pp. 44–47, 10, 9, 16. Françoise Carré, Virginia duRivage, and Chris Tilly, "Representing the Part-time and Contingent Workforce: Challenges for Unions and Public Policy," in *Restoring the Promise of American Labor Law*, ed. Sheldon Friedman et al. (Ithaca, N.Y.: ILR Press, 1994), pp. 314–23.

26. Human Rights Watch, op. cit., p. 7.

27. See, for quote, Steve HughesRorden Wilkinson, "International Labour Standards and World Trade: No Role for the World Trade Organization?" *New Political Economy* 3 (1998): 375ff. See also Jerome Levinson, "International Labor Standards: The Missing Clause in Trade and Investment Agreements," in *Reclaiming Prosperity*, ed. Todd Schafer and Jeff Faux (Armonk, N.Y.: M. E. Sharpe, 1996), p. 267, and other sources.

28. Ankie Hoogvelt, "Debate: International Labour Standards and Human Rights," quoted by Christopher Candland, "Reviewing the Options and Issues," *New Political Economy* 1 (1996): 263. Also see Mark Anner's paper presented at the 2001 American Political Science Association meetings for a more complete review of the issue.

29. Castle et al., op. cit., p. 615; the next quote comes from the same source, p. 597.

30. Elaine Bernard, "The Battle in Seattle: What Was That All About?" *Washington Post*, December 5, 1999, page B1.

31. Levinson, op. cit., p. 271.

32. For an account of nationalist trade restriction efforts, and labor's role in them, see Dana Frank, *Buy American: The Untold Story of Economic Nationalism* (Boston: Beacon Press, 1999). For NAFTA debate see Michael Dreiling, *Solidarity and Contention: The Politics of Security and Sustainability in the NAFTA Conflict* (New York: Garland, 2001), esp. p. 70. *Seattle Post-Intelligencer* December 1, 1999, p. A14; cited in an Internet posting by Jeremy Brecher, with Tim Costello and Brendan Smith. Zapatista report from Jeff Crosby Internet posting, "The Kids Are Alright," also printed in *New Labor Forum* (spring/summer 2000): 35–40. Sweeney quoted in Internet posting by Jeremy Brecher, early December 1999.

33. Crosby, op. cit.

34. Kim Moody, *Workers in a Lean World: Unions in the International Economy* (New York: Verso, 1997), pp. 227–48.

35. Tom Juravich and Kate Bronfenbrenner, *Ravenswood: The Steelworkers' Victory and the Revival of American Labor* (Ithaca, N.Y.: ILR Press, 1999).

36. Henry Frundt, "Cross-Border Organizing in the Apparel Industry: Lessons from Central America and the Caribbean," *Labor Studies Journal* 24 no. 1 (spring 1999): 90–91, 96; Henry Frundt, *Trade Conditions and Labor Rights* (Gainesville: University Press of Florida, 1998); David Moberg, "Lessons from the Victory at Phillips Van Heusen," *WorkingUSA*, May/June 1998, p. 40.

37. Moberg, op. cit., p. 40. Frundt, "Cross-Border Organizing," p. 98.

38. Moberg, op cit., pp. 44, 39.

39. Ibid., p. 45.

40. Frundt, "Cross-Border Organizing," p. 99.

41. The high levels of public support are probably one of the key reasons that President Clinton did not intervene in the strike, an intervention that inevitably would have aided management.

42. My account relies (almost) exclusively on John Russo and Andy Banks, "How Teamsters Took the UPS Strike Overseas," *WorkingUSA*, January–February 1999, pp. 75–87. For German employment and the relative weight of U.S. Teamsters, see pp. 84, 77.

43. Ibid., p. 77.

44. Ibid., p. 79.

45. Ibid., p. 82.

46. Ibid., p. 85.

47. See Ellen Starbird, "The Saga of the *Neptune Jade*: Free Speech at Laney College," posted at www.louisville.edu/journal/workplace/starbird.html. Ellen was the instructor of the course and a leader in all elements of the community struggle, both the picketing and the free speech defense. Another important case of an employer SLAPP suit (Strategic Lawsuits Against Public Participation) against an academic is Beverley Enterprises' attempt to intimidate Kate Bronfenbrenner, perhaps our nation's leading labor scholar, for her invited testimony before a Congressional town meeting.

48. Larry Cohen and Steve Early, "Globalization and De-Unionization in Telecommunications: Three Case Studies in Resistance," in *Transnational Cooperation among Labor Unions*, ed. Michael E. Gordon and Lowell Turner (Ithaca, N.Y.: ILR Press, 2000), pp. 202–22. See also Larry Cohen and Steve Early, "Defending Workers' Rights in the Global Economy: The CWA Experience," in *Which Direction for Organized Labor?* ed. Bruce Nissen (Detroit: Wayne State University Press, 1999), pp. 143–64. Information on garment workers from talk by Ron Blackwell at Columbia University teach-in, October 1996.

49. See, for example, Gay Seidman, "Deflated Citizenship: Labor Rights in a Global Era," and Joe Bandy and Jennifer Bickham Mendez, "A Place of Their Own?—Women Organizers Negotiating National and Transnational Civil Society in the Maquilas of Nicaragua and Mexico" (both presented at the American Sociological Association Meetings, Chicago, August 18, 2002); Peter Waterman and Jane Wills, eds., *Place, Space, and the New Labour Internationalisms* (Malden, Mass.: Blackwell, 2001), especially Rohini Hensman, "World Trade and Workers' Rights: In Search of an Internationalist Position," pp. 123–46.

Chapter 6. Code of Conduct and Living Wage Campaigns

1. See Irving Bernstein, *Turbulent Years: A History of the American Worker 1933–1941* (Boston: Houghton Mifflin, 1970), esp. pp. 184–85, 372–79.

2. See Mike Parker and Martha Gruelle, *Democracy Is Power* (Detroit: Labor Notes Books, 1999).

3. *Boston Globe*, June 24, 2001, p. D8.

4. There is no universal agreement on how to calculate this figure. Some use the Census Bureau's poverty threshold, some the Health and Human Services poverty guidelines; some divide the poverty line income by 2,000 hours of work, some by 2,080, and so on. All the figures are reasonably close to each other, but they do differ somewhat. The average living wage won in 2001 was $8.94 with health benefits, or $10.44 without.

5. Robert Pollin and Stephanie Luce, *The Living Wage* (New York: The New Press, 1998), p. 40. This is the best and most complete source of information about the concept, economics, and politics of the living wage. The figures here have been updated from an article by Holly Sklar, August 29, 2001, distributed by Knight Ridder/Tribune News Service, and posted on the Internet. CEO pay from Internet posting by Greg LeRoy, August 28, 2001, based on "Executive Excess," annual survey of CEO pay released by the Institute for Policy Studies and United for a Fair Economy; the full report is available at www.ips-dc.org/projects/execexcess2001.html.

6. The current formulation/conceptualization is new, but the term has a long history. It was used extensively in early twentieth-century battles for a minimum wage, and by Martin Luther King and the Memphis Sanitation Workers in 1968. See Lawrence Glickman, *A Living Wage* (Ithaca, N.Y.: Cornell University Press, 1997).

7. Jen Kern and Stephanie Luce, "Living Wage Movement Greets the Recession with New Victories," *Labor Notes*, March 2002. The *Boston Globe* estimates that 100,000 workers are now covered by such ordinances; June 24, 2001, p. D8.

8. See Pollin and Luce, op. cit., esp. pp. 88–98. It's also worth noting that few if any of the beneficiaries of a living wage ordinance are unionized workers. Unions typically raise wages above the level of a living wage; widespread unionization would be an alternative way to win a living wage, and the need for these campaigns is an indication of the limited reach of unions.

9. Nelson Lichtenstein, phone conversation, November 1999.

10. The introduction of a living wage may reduce turnover, and a more stable workforce may increase the chances of winning a union.

11. See David Reynolds's excellent article, "The Living Wage Movement Sweeps the Nation," *WorkingUSA*, September/October 1999, p. 67.

12. See Pat McDonnell Twair, "In the Lap of Luxury: From City Council to Rodeo Drive: Campaigning for a Living Wage in Los Angeles," *Sojourners*, September–October 1998, pp. 34–37. Other material on CLUE also comes from this article.

13. Stephanie Luce, "Building Political Power and Community Coalitions: The Role of Central Labor Councils in the Living Wage Movement," in *Central Labor Councils and the Revival of American Unionism: Organizing for Justice in Our Communities*, ed. Immanuel Ness and Stuart Eimer (Armonk, N.Y.: M. E. Sharpe, 2001), p. 145 (also next quotation). Her work, and conversations with her, have fundamentally shaped my thinking.

14. "Politically" should be understood broadly to include, for example, a university faced with pressure from alumni contributors, or the threat of losing promising student recruits.

15. The most extensive treatment of this case is found in Randy Shaw, *Reclaiming America: Nike, Clean Air, and the New National Activism* (Berkeley: University of California Press, 1999), pp. 99–113; Shaw's book is also the main source for the following account of Nike. See also Ruth Needleman, "Building Relationships for the Long Haul: Unions and Community-Based Groups Working Together to Organize Low-Wage Workers," in *Organizing to Win: New Research on Union Strategies*, ed. Kate Bronfenbrenner et al. (Ithaca, N.Y.: ILR Press, 1998), pp. 71–86.

16. Quoted in Kitty Krupat, "From War Zone to Free Trade Zone: A History of the National Labor Committee," in *No Sweat: Fashion, Free Trade, and the Rights of Garment Workers*, ed. Andrew Ross (New York: Verso, 1997), p. 60.

17. Bob Herbert, *New York Times*, July 12, 1996; see Shaw, op. cit., pp. 38–39. Indonesia: ibid., p. 63.

18. Shaw, op. cit., p. 91.

19. Or, at the University of Wisconsin Madison, Reebok.

20. United Students Against Sweatshops web site, narrative history: www.usasnet.org.

21. The total "apparel retail market reached $180 billion in 1997" according to Edna Bonacich and Richard P. Appelbaum, *Behind the Label: Inequality in the Los Angeles Apparel Industry* (Berkeley: University of California Press, 2000), p. 322, n. 13.

22. Ibid., p. 3.

23. For El Monte see Richard Appelbaum and Peter Dreier, "The Campus Anti-Sweatshop Movement," *American Prospect*, September 1, 1999, pp. 71ff. See also Bonacich and Appelbaum, op. cit., p. 165. For monitoring see Jill Esbenshade, "The Social Accountability Contract: Private Monitoring from Los Angeles to the Global Apparel Industry," *Labor Studies Journal* 26 (2001): 98–120; El Monte is discussed on p. 104.

24. Note that this act had been rediscovered earlier during the southern California drywall tapers' strike discussed in chapter 4.

25. Bonacich and Appelbaum, op. cit., p. 233.

26. Esbenshade, op. cit., p. 103.

27. Ibid., p. 106.

28. Ibid., pp. 108, 114.

29. See WRC web site, www.workersrights.org. Unger quoted in Martin Van Der Werf, "The Worker Rights Consortium Makes Strides Toward Legitimacy," *Chronicle of Higher Education*, April 21, 2000. Larry Carr, the director of the bookstore at Brown University, insisted, "Sooner or later, there needs to be some corporate presence. It is going to take a while for it to sink in with the students how necessary that is." Another student said that definitely would not happen, that it is "basically a nonnegotiable issue."

30. USAS web site, www.usasnet.org.

31. WRC web site, www.workersrights.org.

32. Esbenshade, op. cit., p. 100.

33. For the best analysis of campus-based living wage movements, see Jess Walsh, "Living Wage Campaigns Storm the Ivory Tower: Low Wage Workers on Campus," *New Labor Forum* 6 (2000): 80–89. See also www.acorn.org/acorn10/livingwage/campus/current_campaigns.html.

34. I focus on Wesleyan University not only because I consider it a particularly important model, but also because I have access to unusual sources of information: my wife, Mary Ann Clawson, has taught there for twenty years, and our daughter Laura attended both Wesleyan and Union Summer and was an active participant in USLAC, graduating prior to the events discussed here. In the aftermath of the building occupation described below, when it came time to negotiate a Code of Conduct, by agreement the president chose one faculty member to assist him, and the students chose one faculty member to assist them; the students chose Mary Ann, who thus participated in the twenty-some hours of negotiations over the Code of Conduct.

35. Brian Edwards-Tiekert, "Justice for Janitors: Fighting Wesleyan's Service-Sector Sweatshop," *Hermes* (spring 2000); also posted at USLAC web site www.wesleyan.edu/uslac. Although written before the occupation, this is the best overview of the campaign.

36. Author's interview with Olivia Debree, May 7, 2001. I interviewed five of the student participants in the campaign. Except as otherwise indicated, quotations from students are from Olivia Debree. Another valuable source of information is the SLAC's web site: www.wesleyan.edu/uslac. (Although most campus-based student labor groups call themselves "SLACs," Wesleyan's calls itself "USLAC.") Kevin Brown says that "Olivia was the key. If she wasn't an engine that didn't stop it wouldn't have happened." Phone interview, July 30, 2002.

37. Edwards-Tiekert, op. cit.

38. Gay Seidman, "Deflated Citizenship: Labor Rights in a Global Era" (paper delivered at the meetings of the American Sociological Association, August 18, 2002, Chicago).

39. Imagine a man who had been caught not once or twice, but repeatedly, engaging in large scale theft (and failure to pay workers minimum wage and overtime is exactly that). Would that man be permitted to hire his own monitors with the promise that if those monitors caught him violating the law, he would correct the problem and report it to the government?

40. Kevin Brown, phone interview, July 30, 2002.

Chapter 7. A New Upsurge?

1. Katie Quan's two models are presented in "The End of Whiteness? Reflections on a Demographic Landmark," ed. David Roediger, *New Labor Forum* no. 8 (spring/summer 2001): 61. Her second model is in some ways close to my fusion model; she argues that the united front model "allows us to consider that organizing around race and gender might sometimes be more of a motivation to action than traditional labor issues."

2. Preventing the condo-ization of Stamford's most attractive public housing development is also a women's issue, a children's issue, a community issue.

3. See Irving Bernstein, *The Turbulent Years: A History of the American Worker* (Boston: Houghton Mifflin, 1970); John D'Emilio, *Sexual Politics, Sexual Communities: The Making of a Homosexual Minority in the United States, 1940–1970* (Chicago: University of Chicago Press, 1983); Todd Gitlin, *The Whole World is Watching: Mass Media in the Making and Unmaking of the New Left* (Berkeley: University of California Press, 1980).

4. For an outstanding ethnographic account that explains the reality of worker attitudes about their relation to the union, and the difficulties a progressive union had when it began to try to mobilize workers in what had been a staff-run union, see Steve Lopez, *Reorganizing the Rustbelt: Social Movement Unionism and the SEIU in Pennsylvania* (Berkeley: University of California Press, 2003). Union leaders and staff typically receive salaries that are significantly more than those received by workers in the union and significantly less than those paid to people exercising similar skills and authority in other settings. If a member of Congress loses an election, he or she will typically earn more money in their next position (as a lobbyist or corporate lawyer). If a local union leader on full-time union salary loses an election and returns to the shop or office floor, he or she will typically earn significantly less money and may well face working conditions that the member of Congress could never imagine. It's easy to understand why union leaders are reluctant to rotate out of their jobs. Union leaders who see their positions as well-paid jobs are unlikely to wish to make alliances with other social movements, and other social movements would be unlikely to welcome their participation.

5. Michael Zweig, *The Working Class Majority: America's Best Kept Secret* (Ithaca, N.Y.: ILR Press, 2000).

6. Even if member support is mostly passive, in many locals it requires considerable energy, and often small-scale heroism, to keep the union going, fighting grievances and winning contracts and fending off political (or other) challenges.

7. Cited in Hal Draper, *The Two Souls of Socialism* (Highland Park, Mich.: International Socialists, 1970).

8. Quoted in Kenneth C. Crowe, "Organizing is Focus, AFL-CIO Leader Says," *Newsday*, September 23, 1997, p. A49.

9. Judith Stepan-Norris and Maurice Zeitlin, *Left Out: Reds and America's Industrial Unions* (New York: Cambridge University Press, 2002). They also found that unions with Communist leaderships won more pro-labor contracts and were more likely to be democratic.

10. See Steve Early, "Membership-Based Organizing," in *A New Labor Movement for the New Century*, ed. Gregory Mantsios (New York: Monthly Review Press, 1998) pp. 82–103.

11. See Dan Clawson, Alan Neustadtl, and Denise Scott, *Money Talks: Corporate PACs and Political Influence* (New York: Basic Books, 1992), chap. 5, and Thomas Byrne Edsall, *The New Inequality* (New York: W.W. Norton, 1984).

12. Progressive movements thus bear a (partial) collective responsibility for the inadequate electoral choices offered voters. A common pseudo-left analysis, offered after each election, is that the candidate (Gore, or whoever) ran a terrible campaign and lost because he (more rarely, she) failed to tap into progressive issues. The implicit message is that the Left has already created a widespread understanding of these issues and they have broad popular appeal such that if candidates would just mention the issues they'd be sure to win. In reality, both labor and the Left remain weak; a presidential candidate can't/won't change that. Unless and until we build a movement and change popular consciousness, candidates won't embrace our issues, and even if they did (absent a movement) the issues would not carry the candidate to victory.

13. See Daniel Bell, *The End of Ideology* (Glencoe, Ill.: Free Press, 1960), and Seymour Martin Lipset, *Political Man* (London: Heinemann, 1960). See also Russell Jacoby, *The End of Utopia: Politics and Culture in an Age of Apathy* (New York: Basic Books, 1999).

14. The Barnett and Meany quotations are from Richard Freeman, "What Does the Future Hold for U.S. Unionism?" in *The Challenge of Restructuring: North American Labor Movements Respond*, ed. Jane Jenson and Rianne Mahon (Philadelphia: Temple University Press, 1993), p. 361.

15. The business agent was never willing to trust us, but the strike was settled in less than a week, and the local's officers reported that management had said that they didn't want to get into the kind of situation that had developed at another shop in the area, where we had helped mobilize militant actions.

Index